The Psychology of Mathematics Education

NEW DIRECTIONS IN MATHEMATICS AND SCIENCE EDUCATION
Volume 13

Series Editors
Wolff-Michael Roth
University of Victoria, Canada
Lieven Verschaffel
University of Leuven, Belgium

Editorial Board
Angie Calabrese-Barton, *Teachers College, New York, USA*
Pauline Chinn, *University of Hawaii, USA*
Brian Greer, *Portland State University, USA*
Lyn English, *Queensland University of Technology*
Terezinha Nunes, *University of Oxford, UK*
Peter Taylor, *Curtin University, Perth, Australia*
Dina Tirosh, *Tel Aviv University, Israel*
Manuela Welzel, *University of Education, Heidelberg, Germany*

Scope

Mathematics and science education are in a state of change. Received models of teaching, curriculum, and researching in the two fields are adopting and developing new ways of thinking about how people of all ages know, learn, and develop. The recent literature in both fields includes contributions focusing on issues and using theoretical frames that were unthinkable a decade ago. For example, we see an increase in the use of conceptual and methodological tools from anthropology and semiotics to understand how different forms of knowledge are interconnected, how students learn, how textbooks are written, etcetera. Science and mathematics educators also have turned to issues such as identity and emotion as salient to the way in which people of all ages display and develop knowledge and skills. And they use dialectical or phenomenological approaches to answer ever arising questions about learning and development in science and mathematics.

The purpose of this series is to encourage the publication of books that are close to the cutting edge of both fields. The series aims at becoming a leader in providing refreshing and bold new work—rather than out-of-date reproductions of past states of the art—shaping both fields more than reproducing them, thereby closing the traditional gap that exists between journal articles and books in terms of their salience about what is new. The series is intended not only to foster books concerned with knowing, learning, and teaching in school but also with doing and learning mathematics and science across the whole lifespan (e.g., science in kindergarten; mathematics at work); and it is to be a vehicle for publishing books that fall between the two domains—such as when scientists learn about graphs and graphing as part of their work.

The Psychology of Mathematics Education
A Psychoanalytic Displacement

Edited by
Tony Brown
Manchester Metropolitan University

SENSE PUBLISHERS
ROTTERDAM / TAIPEI

A C.I.P. record for this book is available from the Library of Congress.

ISBN 978-90-8790-556-9 (paperback)
ISBN 978-90-8790-557-6 (hardback)
ISBN 978-90-8790-558-3 (e-book)

Published by: Sense Publishers,
P.O. Box 21858, 3001 AW
Rotterdam, The Netherlands
http://www.sensepublishers.com

Printed on acid-free paper

All Rights Reserved © 2008 Sense Publishers

No part of this work may be reproduced, stored in a retrieval system, or transmitted in any
form or by any means, electronic, mechanical, photocopying, microfilming, recording or
otherwise, without written permission from the Publisher, with the exception of any material
supplied specifically for the purpose of being entered and executed on a computer system,
for exclusive use by the purchaser of the work.

Dedicated to Dick Tahta, with love.

CONTENTS

Introduction 1

PART 1. WHAT COUNTS AS A PSYCHOANALYTIC THEORY OF EDUCATION?

Chapter 1   What Counts as a Psychoanalytic Theory of Education?
Tony Brown (Bristol) 21

PART 2. RELATIONALITY AND ANXIETY FOR STUDENTS OF MATHEMATICS

Chapter 2   The Experience of Learning in Classrooms: Moving Beyond Vygotsky.
Tamara Bibby 37

Chapter 3   I Love Maths Anxiety.
Roberto Ribeiro Baldino and Tânia Cristina Baptista Cabral 61

PART 3. BECOMING A TEACHER

Chapter 4   Becoming a Teacher.
Tony Brown (Bristol) 95

Chapter 5   Developing Theory to Explain Learning to Teach.
Margaret Walshaw 119

Chapter 6   Enacting Identity Through Narrative: Interrupting the Procedural Discourse in Mathematics Classrooms.
Elizabeth De Freitas 139

PART 4. THE RESEARCH FILTER

Chapter 7   Imagine There's no Haven: Exploring the Desires and Dilemmas of a Mathematics Education Researcher.
Kathleen Nolan 159

Chapter 8   'What is it Really Like?' Developing the Use of Participant Voice in Mathematics Education Research.
Tony Cotton 183

PART 5. EVER PRESENT AFFECTIVITY

Chapter 9   The Transference Relation in Teaching.
Dave Wilson 201

Chapter 10 Ever Present Affectivity.
Dick Tahta 211

Chapter 11 Tugging at Psychological Threads in Mathematics Education.
Chris Breen 219

About the Authors 231

vii

TONY BROWN (MANCHESTER)

INTRODUCTION

Mathematics education emerged as a research field perhaps some forty years ago, centred on a marriage of mathematics with psychology. Figures such as Skemp (1971) in the UK, for example, constructed a discipline built around a conception of individual cognitions confronting mathematical phenomena. This form of psychology drawing on Piaget's work had congruency with the work of a group of émigré European psychologists relocating in the USA shortly after the Second World War. Ego psychology, as the movement had been called, had grand ambitions in terms of making lives better. These ambitions were noted and embraced by the US government who took up the ideas within their mode of governance as, meanwhile, private enterprise drew on psychoanalysis in the field of public relations, in which Freud's son in law Edward Bernays was a prominent figure. The individualistic conception of psychology based on notions of the normal human being became enshrined in public life, and maintains a lucrative lifestyle in mainstream American ideology.

The marriage became stronger with the *International Group on the Psychology of Mathematics Education* (PME) forming in the seventies to become a leading international annual meeting for mathematics educators. However, throughout the nineties various other associations emerged such as with constructivist, sociological, anthropological and cognitive science perspectives. Whilst a symbolic attachment privileging psychology had been maintained in PME, divorce proceedings reached a climax at the 2005 meeting in Melbourne of that group. An overwhelming vote proposed by one of the authors in this book removed from the group's constitution the need to consult psychologists in preference to other thinkers. A group of older members had sought to retain earlier traditions but whilst the name of the organisation was preserved in the name of continuity, the stirrings of new blood had ensured that more polygamous arrangements with intellectual disciplines were to be envisaged and acted upon. The recalcitrant child had retained its name despite not living up to its parents' hopes and aspirations, upon which they had conceived that name.

At a rather smaller meeting at the same conference two authors each with a chapter in this book presented a joint paper on the psychoanalyst Jacques Lacan (e.g. Lacan, 2006). It concerned the emotional fall out resulting from a mathematical learning experience. It spoke about psychology, but a psychology understood more through relations between people. It was a form of resistance to the conceptions of psychology that had prevailed within mathematics education research. The conception of the human was also rather different to that envisaged

T. Brown (ed.), The Psychology of Mathematics Education: A Psychoanalytic Displacement, 1–17.
© 2008 Sense Publishers. All rights reserved.

in the politically centred orientation of the *Mathematics Education and Society* conference, which had met up the coast the week before, a group whose co-founder is an author in this book. The paper proposed a plan to rethink psychology through a psychoanalytic frame. The emphasis on psychoanalysis as an extension of psychology was in fact a return to Sigmund Freud's wider theories prior to ego psychology's reductionism in the name of tempered societal reform. And the paper's emphasis on Lacan marked a new choice with regard to the alternative trajectories implied by Freud's aspirations. For Lacan had set himself in opposition to the ego psychology school from the outset. The paper itself was generally well received. There was, however, some disquiet in relation to its depiction of the notion of the *unconscious* central to the work of both Freud and Lacan. The unconscious was an ever-present phenomenon in such work but, according to Freud, this was like an iceberg making only a small part of itself visible. Two responses from the audience questioned the ontological status of the unconscious. Firstly, there was direct enquiry as to whether we could assume the existence of the unconscious. Secondly, the authors were quizzed as to whether the notion would stand up to empirical enquiry. How might one respond to such questions? If the unconscious does indeed exist, how does it? But it became clear that this line of enquiry presupposed a mode of existence that was also contingent on certain assumptions. Empiricism, as commonly understood within research enquiry, defines a particular way of looking associated with specific processes of validation. In an assessment of the task of psychoanalysis the Marxist philosopher Althusser (1971) suggested that for a science to be a legitimate science, it needs to have an object. For Freudian and Lacanian psychoanalysis the object is the unconscious, where for Lacan the unconscious is to the human subject what the mind is to brain. Yet this throws in to the ring some difficulties as regards whether we believe in the unconscious or not. To believe the work of these two thinkers, that assumption is necessary. But even within those modes of enquiry we might similarly ask questions as to psychology's status as a science given that that too rests on the assumption of an object, namely the mind. The mind is a notion assumed by the apparatus of psychology and held in place by that very apparatus. Yet, the notion of the mind is a cultural construction derived from the 'brute facts about how the stuff between our ears is related to what we think and feel' (Brian Greer, in conversation) and so historically situated (Foucault, 1989; Hacking, 2002). Mind is less prominent as a notion in some cultures and not a tangible entity in any clear way. It can be approached from many directions. And this resistance to immediate encapsulation puts it in a similar boat to the unconscious as regards its ontological status. The two aspirant sciences then, cognitive psychology and psychoanalysis, each require ontological assumptions relating to their objects. That is, there is a need to *believe* in them one way or another.

In short, the logic of the psyche does not need to be understood in cognitive terms. This positively conceived world would be *imaginary* in Lacan's terms, a construct within a specific reality frame. Psychology has been subject to much recent criticism emanating from within its own ranks as a result of its perceived restrictions that understand humans against specific conceptions of what it is to be human (e.g. Parker, 2007). By surveying some contemporary work in social theory and philosophy we would encounter what might at first seem a surprising re-conception of psychology impacting on how we understand social relations. Such work (e.g. Badiou, 2002; Žižek, 2006, 2008a, 2008b) draws on contemporary psychoanalysis in providing an account of how humans aggregate within their social functioning. Humans are seen as relational beings that cannot be seen as being otherwise. Moving from a focus on psychology to one on subjectivity, where the psychological is redistributed, goes with an assumption that individuals are defined differentially by their relations to other people, rather than as entities in themselves.

At root psychoanalytical thinking is predicated on a reality centred on two people talking in a doctor-client relation for the benefit of the client. This benefit however can be understood in various ways. Freud's work passed through many phases and his influence is diverse, spanning conflicting interpretations. Whilst originally motivated by activating neurological shifts in his patients his legacy might be better understood in retrospect in terms of enabling patients to reassess their pasts with view to opening up and making visible alternative paths for the future. For Freud, a central concept was that of *ego*. Nevertheless, Freud's work developed over some fifty years and the way in which Freud deployed such key terms evolved through successive meanings. The notion of ego has been the basis of some especially contentious debate. Without doubt Freud was ambivalent on this issue and some of his later work left it unresolved. In his earlier work (e.g. Freud, 1923) Freud understood the ego as a biological entity and his paper established a cartographic representation of the human mind comprising *ego, id* and *super ego*. In this conception of the ego, psychoanalytical treatment was understood in terms of developing the ego to increasingly occupy the territory governed by the id. This was announced by the slogan: *Where the id was the ego shall be.* It was this version of the ego that was embraced by the ego psychology school and has gained an image of seeing psychoanalytic therapy in terms of calming the ego to be more conformist. In this school the ego was understood as a biological entity to be strengthened in line with a supposed model of good citizenship. Freud often saw psychoanalytic consultancies as being about achieving a cure, by helping the subject to overcome distortions in her understanding of life. The psychologist purported to know what to do to achieve this result. At various other points, including some of Freud's very latest work, the ego was understood very differently. It was understood as a relational entity produced through the subject's identification with other people and the world around. It was this version of the ego that has been developed by Lacan.

Lacan was without doubt the most famous of those who followed in Freud's path and promoted the shift from bio-scientific to narrative emphases in interpreting Freud's work. The task for Lacan was not to remove supposed distortions in speech in the style of the Freuds and later Habermas but rather to learn from speech to see what it revealed. Specifically, such speech was scanned for symptoms of what Lacan called 'the truth of desire'. Lacan (1990) famously declared that 'I always speak the truth' meaning that whatever I say works towards revealing or presenting myself, including aspects of self of which I may not be aware. For Lacan the ego is both formative and informative but not something that you would want to strengthen. This was a point of contention between Lacan and the American ego psychology school that saw psychoanalysis in terms of strengthening the ego to placate disruptive tendencies, that is, tendencies that disrupt smooth running according to the governing ideology. The insistence on any image brings with it a violence to ensure conformity. For Lacan the ego is an inauthentic agency derived from a delusional stance in which the human subject has an image of his or her self. Here the psychoanalyst does not purport to know the best outcome. As such the ego (or in Lacan's terms 'Imaginary identification') is something to be challenged. Lacanian therapy is targeted instead at locating the truth of the patient's desire. That is, treatment is seen in terms of understanding how the unconscious functions in conditioning the patient's expressed demands. Lacan suggests that when the analysand says 'I', the analyst should be mistrustful. That is, the image of self that is portrayed needs to be inspected to discover how it is a distortion of the desires being activated.

The psychological basis of so much mathematics education research in the tradition of the *Psychology of Mathematics Education* organisation is centred on individual teachers interacting with individual classes or individual pupils. Lacan's alternative is not sociological in that we work from a holistic conception of society that shapes individuals within it. Lacan's relational ego (sometimes called the narcissistic ego) is a result of fantasy. This understanding of fantasy however does not have negative connotations. Rather, our understanding of reality is seen as being structured through such fantasies. Fantasies might be seen as the filters through which we inspect reality; a reality that in a sense cannot be perceived directly, and in some other senses is not there at all except through its manifestation in the fantasies of individuals. In this cartography we would not have a standalone biological human confronting an independent object. For analytical purposes the space would be carved up differently. There would be no overarching perspective from an independent arbiter. The analysis would be centred on the human subject's supposed relation to the object and the world he or she crafts around it. Rather than a self-contained ego 'that is a biological result of the interaction of psychical and social relations' that can be objectively described, the ego envisaged 'depends on the subject's relations with others' and 'is governed by fantasy, and modes of identification, and introjection'. (Grosz, 1990, p. 31) Just as Badiou (2002) has argued that ethics and the rights accorded to Man are very much a function of how we understand 'Man' and, more particularly, whom we include in 'Man', Lacan resists the countenance of specific images to which we should aspire.

THE RESEARCH TASK

This book explores mathematics education from the point of view of how the learner, teacher and researcher are understood. It seeks to better understand how the boundaries of this domain are shifting. Yet, the formation of this domain, of course, depends on how authors in that domain understand their field and their audience. Their writing is shaped as a result of their own jockeying for acceptance within that domain. That is, those who feel a need to be part of that domain, shape the domain, partly in their own image. Their writings might be seen as requests to be included. Laclau (2005, p. 53) insists that group formations derive from libidinal motivations; they result from excitements for individuals to do with feelings of being a part of or apart from current trends, fashions, innovations, transgressions or taboos. Individuals find themselves identifying or not with a range of alternative modes of life, according to the particular social needs that they feel, the form of alignment or non-alignment they wish to pursue, or the particular ambitions that they set themselves. In a field like mathematics education research there are tightly stratified arrangements for contributions to be received and disseminated. Research orthodoxy in mathematics education is discussed in Valero & Zevenbergen (2004). Through peer review processes, a few major journals exert significant influence on the themes to be explored within the domain, what counts as important, what is seen as interesting and what needs to be cited for effective positioning to have been achieved. Meanwhile, local professional circumstances, funding provision and personal preferences all have an impact on the types of research carried out. And it is against these parameters that individual authors offer their contributions and become who they are with respect to the domain. Yet research preferences create the analytical frames we use, which in turn create the objects we research; objects that evolve whether we acknowledge this evolution or not. And as such classroom activities observed within research enterprises and notions like 'learners', 'teachers' and 'mathematics' cannot escape such filtering especially those selected for specific analytical purposes. The activities cannot be seen independently of the analytical lens brought to them by the researchers. And such lenses are predicated on the matrix of ideologies underpinning our actions, governed by trends of which they are not always aware.

In the book that follows all of the authors are teachers of mathematics as are all of the teachers they describe. Yet there has been no editorial insistence that the specifically mathematical elements of their stories be presented. The attempt is to portray the life around mathematics teaching, in many cases well beyond the content of that teaching. This policy is deliberate in that the book sees itself as resisting models of teaching mathematics that presuppose the centrality of certain facets, whether those facets be the centrality of interactions or specific understandings of mathematical knowledge. As one of the chapters declares, with mathematics we occupy a realm that severely restricts the language that we are able to use, yet that very restriction produces specific forms of life that provide the central theme of this book.

Psychoanalysis is not entirely new to the field of education. Britzman (1998, 2003) has used the work of Anna Freud and Melanie Klein to investigate problematical and ambivalent aspects of teaching. Meanwhile, Pitt and Britzman (2003, p. 756) have argued that a growing body of psychoanalytic educational research, through its emphasis on concepts such as the unconscious, phantasy, affect and sexuality, has worked 'to unseat the authorial capabilities of expression to account exhaustively for qualities of experience, to view history as a causal process, and to separate reality from phantasy'. Henriques, Hollway, Urwin, Venn & Walkerdine (1984), Felman (1987) and others have taken the work of Lacan to explore issues of pedagogy and learning. The authors in a book edited by Todd

(1997) have discussed the place of desire and fantasy in teaching and learning. Other authors broaching this territory include: Appel (1996), Jagodzinski (1996, 2001), Pitt (1998), England & Brown (2001), Atkinson (2002, 2004), Brown & England (2004; 2005), Bradford & Brown (2005) and Brown, Atkinson & England (2006), Brown, 2008a. In mathematics education a special issue of *For the Learning of Mathematics* did much to initiate interest in this area, featuring work by authors in this book (e.g. Breen, 1993; Brown, Hardy & Wilson, 1993; Tahta, 1993a/b). In my own work on two UK government funded studies I used a psychoanalytical filter to consider how primary teachers learn to include mathematics and its teaching within their professional work (Brown & McNamara, 2005). More recently I have published two papers in *Educational Studies in Mathematics* (ESM), one explicitly considering Lacan in relation to mathematics education (Brown 2008b) and another considering how some papers in mathematics education research produce conceptions of psychology (Brown, 2008c).

Significantly, however, within mathematics education research more generally, it is Piaget and Vygotsky that continue to have considerable influence on how we understand the psychology of learning. There has been much discussion about whether we should privilege the individual cognitive psychology of Piaget or more socially oriented models such as Vygotsky's. That is, do we conceptualise the task of mathematics teaching to activate and transform the minds of children, which are assumed to be responsive to such external agitation, or do we suppose that individuals can only be understood as integral and amenable to more collective conceptions of who humans are and how they develop? I have argued more fully in one of the ESM papers how the psychoanalytic theory of Lacan provides a radical contemporary alternative to these two thinkers in the context of mathematics education (Brown, 2008b). That paper also provides an introduction to Lacan's thinking that may assist readers of this book, where other authors draw on Lacan's work. (See also Brown, 2008a, which provides a Lacanian account of teacher reflective research, whilst Homer, 2005 provides a more general introduction to Lacan. Meanwhile, Baldino & Cabral (2005) provides a rare example of a Lacanian analysis of mathematical learning). To briefly summarise some relevant aspects of the ESM paper: Lacan objected to Piaget's separation of the individual and the social and his assertion of an individual child passing through successive stages, which, he suggests, neglects the cultural dependency of the child's constructions. For Lacan, any attempt to synthesise a supposed individual's activity in a multitude of discursive networks seemed flawed. Piaget's emphasis on ego-centred analysis of learning underplayed the child's responsiveness to external demands. Lacan believed that the child is always responding to what the child perceives to be a demand to fit in. Walkerdine (1988) argued that the concrete mathematical objects of Piaget's analysis were necessarily implicated in the child's conception of social relations. Whilst Piaget (e.g. 1965) centred his approach on a conception of individual cognition, Walkerdine contrarily posited both 'student' and 'mathematics' as being constructed in discourse. That is 'students', 'mathematics' and 'teachers' are understood through specific constructions of the world. They are not things in themselves. I have discussed this point in detail in relation to mathematics education reports (Brown, 2008c). Vygotsky (1986, pp. 12-57), meanwhile, shared some of Lacan's objections to Piaget, such as, how minds are social from the outset, on how children are differentiated from adults. Yet Vygotsky's (e.g. 1978, p. 36) encapsulation of the child posits an intentional being with essentialist characteristics. His work has had a longer-term influence on some major thinkers promoting a more culturally oriented conception of psychology, where mind is co-constructed and distributed, an agenda compatible with Lacan's. Such thought has extended its hand to the cultural psychology/ activity theory of Cole (e.g. Roth & Lee, 2004) and into situated cognition (e.g. Lave & Wenger, 1991; Cobb & Bowers, 1999; Graven, 2004). Cole (1996. p. 108), a student of Vygotsky's colleague Luria, argues that the structure and development of human psychological processes emerge through culturally mediated, historically developing, practical activity. The objects created in this structure reflect and define the human's sense of self and her relation to the world. As an example from a mathematics classroom, Radford (2006, p. 7) argues how a wooden ruler, a number line and mathematical signs on a piece of paper can all be seen as artefacts, which *'mediate and materialise* thinking'. Blanton, Westbrook & Carter, 2005 and Goos, 2005 also analyse mathematics classrooms through such apparatus. Lacan and Vygotsky would agree on much of this but differ in their understanding of how humans relate to this symbolic mediation. Lacan claims that humans feed off the linguistic apparatus that surrounds them but at the same time they are alienated from this apparatus, it never quite fits their sense of reality, and sits ill with their sense of self. Such apparatus regulates humans and produces emotional responses (*jouissance*) around this regulation. Whilst Vygotsky's (1986, pp. 174-208) psychological notion of *Zone of Proximal Development* attends to the localised case of children trying to learn from adults, Lacan's assertion of humans being alienated from language is built into their very constitution as subjects. Emerson (1983, p. 256) suggests that for Vygotsky, 'the child's realization of his separateness from society is not a crisis; after all, his environment provides both the form and content of his personality. From the start, dialogue reinforces the child's grasp on reality, as evidenced by the predominantly social and extraverted nature of his earliest egocentric speech. For Lacan, on the contrary, dialogue seems to function as *the* alienating experience'. Lacan's model of child development pivots on the notional point at which the child identifies with an image outside of herself (such as a mirror image) and says 'That's me'. And the opposition this creates between the 'me' and the 'I' results in a 'permanent hunger' (ibid) to close this gap. As Emerson continues (ibid): 'The child is released from this alienating image only through discovering himself as subject, which occurs with language', a language steeped in cultural traditions. That is, the only way out of the restrictive caricature of self is to accept the turbulence of participation in discursive activity. Meanwhile Bibby (in this volume) argues that the 'seductive imagery conjured by Vygotsky's metaphor of the 'zone of proximal development' leaves hanging the nature of the zone and obscures the space it occupies, it allows us to ignore the difficulties and resistances which the learner will encounter and develop'. In summary: Piaget supposes progression through a sequence of predetermined stages, neglecting the social dimension; Neo-Vygotskian theory psychological

TONY BROWN (MANCHESTER)

supposes unproblematised engagement with the tools of society. My ESM papers also sought to engage with a group of mathematics education authors (e.g. Ongstad, 2006, Morgan, 2006; Radford, 2006) contemplating subjectivity and signification from a semiotic perspective in an ESM Special Issue (Saenz Ludlow & Presmeg, 2006).

The traditional realm of mathematics education researchers has been anchored theoretically by such educational psychology and also the philosophy of mathematics (e.g. Ernest, 1991), with work targeted on improving teaching techniques at a local interactive level rather than seeing the task so much in terms of socio-economic factors or policy setting. As such the field is not especially experienced in responding to alternative social paradigms. A survey by Lerman, Xu and Tsatsaroni (2002) of articles in ESM since 1990, featuring other theoretical fields, depicts a situation in which few alternative theories have sustained interest. The chief exception would be constructivism in its many guises but in forms primarily exclusive to mathematics education (e.g. von Glasersfeld, 1991, 1995; Ernest, 1998). There have also been some studies building on the sociology of Bourdieu and Bernstein, including some specifically examining school mathematics texts as cultural products (e.g. Dowling, 1998; Cooper & Dunne, 1999; Morgan, 2002). Such moves have characterised the major challenges to cognitive perspectives. There has, meanwhile, been a light sprinkling of reference to other contemporary theory such as post-structuralism and hermeneutics (e.g. Walkerdine, 1988; Brown, 2001; Walshaw, 2004) and feminism (e.g. Burton, 1995). Yet the influence of such alternative models is less evident than in the broader field of education. Bartolino Bussi & Bazzini (2003) provide a rare recent discussion of how mathematics education research might reach out to other social scientific fields. More recently Radford (in press) has sought to build a substantial conception of culture around school mathematical activity.

In mathematics education research we are dealing with both individuals and social groups and consequently we require a variety of apparatus that enable us to span variously conceived domains. The choice of apparatus depends on the task being addressed, whether that is about trying to support individual teachers or pupils, or perhaps alternatively trying to design and implement a policy. Mathematics education researchers can define their audience in a variety of ways, and so understand the dissemination of their work according to this definition of audience. For example, the policy level task of improving particular mathematical capabilities for specific populations of students requires way of thinking to an individual teacher assessing her own personal capabilities for work with particular individual children.

Self and subjectivity are often seen in much the same way but a key shift in contemporary social theory has been towards seeing the individual caught up in more or less committed participation in a multitude of discursive activity. That is, individuals partake in social languages that more or less fit what they are trying to say but the individual is obliged to use these languages if they are to be included in social exchanges. Self has often been understood as a biological entity held together by a cognitive unity. Lemke (1995, p. 82), however, argues that 'Even within the natural sciences there is no guarantee that physical, chemical and biological definitions of an organism coincide for all purposes'. Subjectivity is constituted discursively, defined by participations in a multitude of discursive practices. As such subjects identify with something outside of their selves. They identify with and partake in social discourses and through these identifications craft their subjectivity. Subjectivity as understood within mathematics education research discourses is often defined narrowly. For example, the individual pupil is reduced in formulations predicated on getting the mathematical learning structure straight. Yet the positioning of subjects more generally can assume somewhat restrictive possibilities within such work, perhaps characterised by suppositions that all subjects would witness equivalent events in given circumstances. This applies to all people implicated in research processes, whether they are the teachers and children being researched or the researchers themselves, as well as the audience predicated within the research design. There typically appears to be little scope for contestation of places assigned to such participants within mathematics education research discourses, reduced as they are to 'types', responsive in predictable ways according to prevailing discursive frames (Brown, 2008c). The tendency to create 'types' within mathematics education research appears to be in the name of promoting some sort of instrumental rationality whereby assessments of mathematics education phenomena are associated with the identification of a control technology to bring about tangible change. In this respect mathematics education research seems to be in the business of influencing populations rather than being about promoting differences in groups of children, and focussing on the institutionally defined beings rather than on individuals. As Varenne & McDermott (1998, p. 11) suggest: 'The fibers do not make the rope. A mass of fibers is not a rope. An aggregate of persons in a crowd do not make a cultural institution. But once fibers are made into a rope, or a crowd into an institution, something new has happened for all those who encounter it and cannot ignore it or escape from it'. Yet this shaping of research around societal-defined types seems to contrast with so many individual mathematics education research reports that are predicated on small-scale research understood from the perspective of an individual teacher, teacher educator or researcher, changing their immediate practice. Such perspectives are then communicated as if to individual teachers, teacher educators or researchers rather than policy makers or curriculum writers who are more able to influence a broader domain of activity. Authors in this book argue that the relational dimension of psychology is crucially important to mathematics education research in that we need to attend to the alternative and diverse needs of learners, their teachers and the communities with which they associate, and the alternative forms of research that support them. Mathematics is a function of the community that embraces it and evolves in relation to the needs expressed and tasks performed. For this reason it is necessary to resist moves in which mathematical achievement in schools is read against a register of *commodified* procedures, in a 'one size fits all' model, spanning diverse nations and communities. Such moves seem symptomatic of the twentieth century that has left a legacy of techno-scientific control governed by the ideology of 'real' social forces (Lather, 2003). The field of mathematics education spans science and social science and there is much contestation about the boundaries of each of those domains. Yet consensus is neither possible nor desirable. Whereas mathematics often continues to be conceptualized as a discipline resistant to social discourses, education resists conceptual immersion in the broader social sciences. As we begin to experience a new century during which such rationalistic aspirations have been re-routed in so many areas of social theory mathematics education research needs to move away from earlier instrumentalist tendencies concerned with understanding and 'improving' mathematical performance against unproblematised social registers.

BOOK OUTLINE

Sigmund Freud maintained that education is one of the three 'impossible professions', in which one can be sure beforehand of achieving unsatisfying results, the other two being government and psychoanalysis. In Freud's writing education is synonymous with 'upbringing'; a broad enterprise that necessarily includes but goes beyond schooling. Part One commences with a chapter by one of the two Tony Browns represented in this book. Tony Brown (Bristol) argues that in England it would be distorting the meaning of education to suggest that it is currently being pursued in schools and universities. In response to the question 'What do you think about education in Britain?' Gandhi is reputed to have replied, 'It would be a good idea.' A psychoanalytic theory of education and learning offers more than a language of relational and group learning, important though this is. Since resistance is at the heart of psychoanalytic theory, its use in the education context allows for critiques of the whole education business, from government policy through to institutional organisation, provision and the dynamics of teaching spaces. A psychoanalytical theory of education and learning must include teachers as well as students, privileging neither group in its study of the education process. The selective and unhelpful focus on cognitive aspects of the students' learning is avoided and the limits of constructivist theories of individual psychological development transcended. All those engaged in the education enterprise stand in relation to others and all are the subjects of psychoanalytic enquiry.

Part Two, which comprises two chapters, addresses the relationality and anxiety of learning mathematics. Chapter Two is written by Tamara Bibby. She extends theoretical apparatus introduced in the first chapter to include Vygotsky, Bion and Foukes, and Benjamin and relates this to a project concerned with children's learner-identities in mathematics in the later primary years. The chapter commences with a critique of Vygotsky's influence on mathematics education. Bibby argues that Vygotsky's account paints the developing child as overly amenable to the social structures she encounters. The chapter later focuses on some research following a class of children through the later primary years. This research examined the concerns and voices of the children themselves. It revealed how the separation of mathematics education research from other concerns can be problematic, prompting a decision to resituate analysis of mathematical learning back into broader school and classroom processes and experiences. Levels of emotion, for example, widely reported amongst mathematics learners of all ages were clearly evident in the later primary years. Yet such fear and anxiety often supposed to be exclusive to mathematics were found to be more widely felt and were seemingly related to the children's more general desire to be seen and heard. Observations and interviews, and research by the children themselves, led the team to conclude that children and teachers make very different assumptions about the purpose of learning. It appeared that teachers and children were often talking at cross purposes and focussing on different aspects of the learning environment that often led to misunderstandings of which the teachers seemed unaware. This left some children feeling angry, hurt and bewildered.

The next chapter by Tânia Cabral and Roberto Baldino is centred on students learning mathematics at a university. Yet it seeks to dig beneath the surface of the visible activity in which students work on algebra task while the teacher circulates to offer assistance to groups where needed. Here the teachers offer their perspectives on the rather surprising sorts of difficulties students encounter with elementary mathematics. They speculate on how mathematical difficulties and the anguish that can go with these difficulties presents itself in the students' overt classroom behaviour. They seek to explore these through the lens of psychoanalytic theory. In particular they invoke the work of Lacan who sees our self-conceptions as being linked to our sense of how we appear to the eyes of others. They describe their way of dealing with emerging anguish through actual examples of classroom situations. Paradoxically, instead of trying to relieve the student's anxiety, they seek to guide the student through to the very mathematics situations that generated anguish. They argue that what produces anguish is not failure itself, but the perspective of failure, that is, the possibility of consummating failure in the eyes of the others.

Part Three addresses some of the processes of becoming a teacher of mathematics. Tony Brown (Bristol) returns with Chapter Four, which surveys the lives surrounding several students deciding to become a teacher, extending frames for mathematics to include the kitchen sink, as emblematic of the domestic lives compromised as a result of joining the social enterprise of teaching mathematics. The chapter explores the psychodynamic forces that shape identity and which can lead to identificatory confusion. It challenges the current performativity culture with its emphasis on skills and training arguing that students and staff need to engage imaginatively with the transformative nature of becoming a teacher.

Margaret Walshaw's chapter is about learning to teach. Central to the discussion is the development of teacher identity during teaching practice experience within secondary school mathematics classrooms. She adds to recent discussions on identity by offering a theoretical grounding and empirical evidence base of how teaching identity develops. The approach to identity offered in this chapter engages the identity of one pre-service teacher in a way that attempts to address the shortcomings of familiar approaches that have tended to equate identity with the teacher's role and function. Using data drawn from an interview with one pre-service teacher she draws on the psychoanalytic development of subjectivity, and the way in which language is implicated in this, as a conceptual apparatus for understanding how pre-service teachers working in schools are constituted, and how they constitute themselves, as teachers. Using conceptual tools borrowed from both Foucault and Lacan she endeavours to capture the fluidity and complexity of identity construction. Foucault's ideas are used to theorise how identity is produced and regulated in discourses involving relations of power. Lacan, on the other hand, provides the grounding for understanding how power insinuates itself to make a pre-service teacher *want* to be a specific kind of teacher. Both approaches are helpful to the analysis, but, as a complement, the two together give us the tools and the language to get to the core of what learning to teach is all about. The approach alerts us to some of the tensions involved in creating a teaching identity. It allows us to grapple with the complex interplay between settings in which the pre-service teacher finds herself, and the constructions of the self that are at work in becoming a mathematics teacher.

Chapter Six, written by Elizabeth de Freitas, further theorises the process of becoming a teacher. It examines when, how and why mathematics teachers shift between the procedural and the personal narrative registers. It suggests that the shift between procedural and personal narrative register is almost always awkward because of the radically different subject positions constituted through the two discourses. Indeed, the two discourses are so radically displaced from each other, it is difficult to imagine the bridging or blending that might create a cohesive discourse that includes them both. This apparent incomprehensibility provides the focus of this chapter. The aim is to show how the personal narratives are actually used to enforce the legitimacy of procedural discourse. This chapter examines the relationship between these two registers, focusing on the way that teachers blend or join the registers. The chapter adds Judith Butler to Walshaw's heady mix of Foucault and Lacan, in theorising teacher identity. Butler offers a theory of partial agency by pointing to the ways in which resistance and transformation are possible through the construction of 'critical capacities' that allow identities to re-define their position within particular discursive practices. She is careful to insist that these moments of resistance or agency are not simply a matter of freely determined choice, but rather 'performative' in the sense of being discursive enactments of contingent cultural norms. Each enactment involves some form of modification of the cultural norm, but is simultaneously constrained by the rules of the discourse.

Part Four hones in more closely on the mediating filter of the researcher and provides two contrasting perspectives: of the teacher-trainer-researcher examining her practice, and of school children being encouraged to explore a research voice. Chapter Seven is written by Kathleen Nolan and considers her role as a researcher focussing on work with her own students who are training to be secondary school teachers. She argues that schools like to produce teachers in their own image, or so it appears in some recent instances of pre-service teacher education in secondary mathematics. Such instances, this chapter contends, perpetuate and further exasperate the existing chasm between theory and practice in the education of mathematics teachers and provide a haven for 'teaching as we were taught'. What hope is there then for non-traditional teaching practices knocking at the door of this haven, especially when this haven is so reminiscent of the teachers' own largely successful experiences as learners in mathematics classrooms? By resisting the status quo held in place by the mantra of 'if it ain't broke, don't fix it', might it be possible for these becoming teachers to transcend the *habitual* to think the *possible* in mathematics classrooms. This chapter is written from the perspective of a mathematics teacher educator and researcher, as she grapples with her desire to dismantle the haven of secondary mathematics teaching and learning through non-traditional pedagogies and assessments. This reflexive piece highlights the researcher's efforts to support pre-service teachers' professional growth while, at the same time, propose counter-narratives to dominant school traditions and images of mathematics knowledge. In desiring to go beyond just *imagining* and talking about more reflective, inclusive, creative, and critical mathematical practices, the researcher, along with her research agenda, are met with resistance and potential ethical dilemmas.

Tony Cotton argues in Chapter Eight that research in mathematics education needs to be conducted for the benefit of teachers and the children they work with (cf. Valero & Zevenbergen, 2004). Yet so often the voices of these key beneficiaries are marginalised within research to play the roles of clipped commentators allowed in only so long as they offer sound bites that sit neatly in the researcher's preferred story. He develops issues raised earlier by Bibby as to how children excluded from the education mainstream feel about their plight and how they respond to having being labelled as 'outside'. Cotton focuses on the images the children have of themselves as mathematicians, as learners and how this results in dissonance with regard to how the children understand and seek to meet or resist the expectations placed on them. The children seemed to have an emerging sense of identifying success in mathematics as external to their self-image. Cotton argues: If we are to find ways of making research more democratic we need to find ways of stepping out of this mould. Research is framed in its own culture of regulative practices. Claims that it might proffer to a wider truth can be problematic. Indeed such claims to truth may in themselves become oppressive leaving the researchers to sulk about their own complicity. The purpose of research might be viewed alternatively, however, as being about opening spaces that allow us all to think about how our worlds may be changed. This chapter examines ways in which researchers can work with pupils and teachers to develop an authentic 'voice' that speaks to researchers, academics, administrators, and those who have responsibility in policy formation. By privileging experience over theory as a basis for understanding, space is made for marginalised or 'silenced' groups to be heard. Using texts from of video and audio recordings from work with pupils and teachers in schools in crisis, a methodology is developed which both reflects 'what it is like' in these schools from pupil and teachers perspectives and offers some insights into broader educational issues. In particular he shows the varying ways in which school children see themselves identifying with mathematics and perhaps seeing it as part of their identity.

Part Five comprises a suite of articles inspired by Dick Tahta's pioneering work in the area of psychoanalysis and mathematics education. Dick had agreed to write a chapter for this book but sadly passed away after submitting his abstract but before he had begun to write the piece itself. A life long mathematics educator, Dick had many accolades, such as being the favourite teacher of physicist Stephen Hawking and, I am sure, of many others. He can probably also be attributed with having first combined psychoanalytic thinking with the practices of teaching mathematics, editing a special issue on the theme for the journal *For the Learning of Mathematics* in 1993. Chris Breen, Dave Wilson and I, who feature in this book, had material included in that special issue. Meanwhile, adding further to the

TONY BROWN (MANCHESTER)

similarities in our signified identities both Tony Browns had Dick as a supervisor.

This part of the book can at least include some material from Dick that he had agreed to include before his passing. This comprises his contribution to a written dialogue he had with Dave Wilson, a former colleague of mine in Manchester, which first appeared in 1995 in *Chreods,* a journal that I edited. The part begins with a chapter by Dave Wilson entitled 'The transference relation in teaching'. Dave described the piece at the time: 'During much of last year I attempted to reflect upon my teaching in a particular way. At the end of each day, or week, I sat quietly and allowed an incident from my teaching to enter my mind. Whatever that was, I tried to recapture the detail of that incident and to set it down in writing as objectively as I could. I then worked upon that fragment. My conjecture was that whatever entered my mind swiftly and easily would have some significance. The fact that they were significant I took for granted. Why otherwise, would I have remembered them? My task was to clarify and to articulate their significance and to draw from this some implications for my practice as a teacher. I tried to examine myself within these situations, to look at my feelings and actions. I tried to read and to reread my stories offering a variety of interpretations of the significance of them for me. As I proceeded in this way I produced generalities based upon the particularities of my (reflected upon) experience. When my reflection evoked a fragment from my reading I attempted to discuss those readings and to reflect upon their relevance for myself. I found that modern psychoanalysis was a particularly rich source of readings. It has been suggested that Jacques Lacan shifted from discussing psychoanalytic practice to using psychoanalysis to analyse discourse itself during the twenty-five year course of his seminars. At some stage as the year proceeded I began to consciously use this possibility to in my reflection'.

Dick Tahta's response comprises Chapter Ten where he suggests that there are lots of useful observations in the educational literature about learners learning but not so many about teachers teaching. This must be partly because it is so difficult to give an honest account of what it is actually like to teach –most attempts to do this slide into idealised intention or pious hope. In reflecting on some incidents in his own classroom, Dave Wilson exposed himself. He showed courage in revealing his feelings and the sensitivity with which he discussed the various interpretations open to him. The very delicacy of his self-awareness, Tahta claims, left the other participants and their effects on the situation somewhat ignored. This short piece re-opens the reflective possibility with a few remarks on Tahta's thoughts about the lesson. He suggests that if psychodynamic notions are to be invoked in classroom accounts then standard reflective procedures common to most therapists and counsellors might also have to be considered. People who wish to address the emotions which are stirred in classrooms need to have the courage to expose their own feelings, but they will also need to be able to sift through various interpretations of them and produce specific reasons why they come to the conclusions they do. The chapter includes a dialogue between Dave Wilson and Dick Tahta written between the productions of their two articles.

The book concludes with a chapter by Chris Breen. The chapter, which provides a present day response to the Wilson/ Tahta exchange, explores the contribution that an awareness of psychoanalytic and psychotherapeutic techniques and insights

INTRODUCTION

might add to the teaching of mathematics made with reference to Tahta's lasting influence.

Before concluding this introduction I would also like to acknowledge behind the scenes activity by Brian Greer who was supportive throughout and offered helpful comments on an earlier draft.

REFERENCES

Althusser, L. (1971). *Lenin and philosophy and other essays*. London: New Left Books.

Appel, S. (1996). *Positioning subjects: psychoanalysis and critical educational studies*. Westport, CT: Bergin & Garvey.

Atkinson, D. (2002). *Art in education: identity and practice*. Dordrecht: Kluwer.

Atkinson, D. (2004). Theorising how student teachers form their identities in Initial Teacher Education, *British Education Research Journal, 30*(3), 379–394.

Badiou, A. (2002). *Ethics*. London: Verso.

Baldino, R., & Cabral T. (2006). Inclusion and diversity from Hegel-Lacan point of view: Do we desire our desire for change? *International Journal of Science and Mathematics Education, 4*, 19–43.

Bartolini Bussi, M., & Bazzini, L. (2003). Research, practice and theory in didactics of mathematics: Towards dialogue between different fields', *Educational Studies in Mathematics, 54*(2–3), 203–223.

Blanton, M., Westbrook, S., & Carter, G. (2005). Using Valsiner's zone theory to interpret teaching practices in mathematics and science classrooms. *Journal of Mathematics Teacher Education, 8*(1), 5–33.

Bradford, K. & Brown, T. (2005) Ceci n'est pas un "circle", *For the Learning of Mathematics, 25*(1), 16-19.

Breen, C. (1993). Holding the tension of opposites. *For the Learning of Mathematics, 13*(1), 6–10.

Britzman, D. (1998). *Lost subjects, contested objects*. Albany, NY: State University of New York Press.

Britzman, D. (2003). *After education*. Albany, NY: State University of New York Press.

Brown, T. (2001). *Mathematics education and language, interpreting hermeneutics and post-structuralism*. Revised second edition. Dordrecht: Kluwer.

Brown, T. (2008a). Desire and drive in researcher subjectivity: The broken mirror of Lacan. *Qualitative Inquiry, 14*(4).

Brown, T. (2008b). Lacan, subjectivity and the task of mathematics education research. *Educational Studies in Mathematics*.

Brown, T. (2008c). Signifying 'learners', 'teachers' and 'mathematics': A response to a special issue. *Educational Studies in Mathematics*.

Brown, T., Atkinson, D., & England, J. (2006). *Regulative discourses in education: A Lacanian perspective*. Bern Switzerland: Peter Lang.

Brown, T., & England, J. (2005). Identity, narrative and practitioner research. *Discourse: Studies in the Cultural Politics of Education, 26*(4), 443–458.

Brown, T., & England, J. (2004). Revisiting emancipatory teacher research: A psychoanalytic perspective. *British Journal of Sociology of Education, 25*(1), 67–80.

Brown, T., Hardy, T., & Wilson, D. (1993). Mathematics on Lacan's couch. *For the Learning of Mathematics, 13*(1), 11–14.

Brown, T., & McNamara, O. (2005). *New teacher identity and regulative government: The discursive formation of primary mathematics teacher education*. New York: Springer.

Burton, L. (1995). Moving towards a feminist epistemology of mathematics. *Educational Studies in Mathematics, 28*, 275–291.

Cobb, P., & Bowers, J. S. (1999). Cognitive and situated learning perspectives in theory and practice. *Educational Researcher, 28*(2), 4–15.

Cole, M. (1996). *Cultural psychology: A once and future discipline*. Cambridge, MA: Belknap Press.

15

TONY BROWN (MANCHESTER)

Cooper, B., & Dunne, M. (1999). *Assessing children's mathematical ability*. Buckingham Open University Press.

Dean, J. (2006). *Zizek's politics*. London: Routledge.

Dowling, P. (1998). *The sociology of mathematics education*. London: Falmer.

Emerson, C. (1983). The outer world and inner speech: Bakhtin, Vygotsky, and the internalization of language. *Critical Inquiry, 10*(2), 245–264.

England, J., & Brown, T. (2001). Inclusion, exclusion and marginalisation. *Educational Action Research, 9*(3), 335–371.

Ernest, P. (1991). *The philosophy of mathematics education*. Basingstoke: Falmer.

Ernest, P. (1998). *Social constructivism as a philosophy of mathematics*. Albany, NY: SUNY.

Felman, S. (1987). *Jacques Lacan and the adventure of insight: Psychoanalysis in contemporary culture*. Cambridge, MA: University of Harvard Press.

Foucault, M. (1989). *The archaeology of knowledge*. London: Routledge.

Freud, S. (1991/1923). The ego and the id. In S. Freud (Ed.), *The essentials of psychoanalysis*. London: Penguin.

Glasersfeld, E. von (Ed.). (1991). *Radical constructivism in mathematics education*. Dordrecht: Kluwer.

Glasersfeld, E. von (1995). *Radical constructivism: a way of knowing and learning*. London: Falmer.

Goos, M. (2005). A sociocultural analysis of the development of pre-service and beginning teachers' pedagogical identities as users of technology. *Journal of Mathematics Teacher Education, 8*(1), 35–59.

Graven, M. (2004). Investigating mathematics teacher learning within an in-service community of practice. *Educational Studies in Mathematics, 57*(2), 177–211.

Grosz, E. (1989). *Jacques Lacan: A feminist introduction*. London: Routledge.

Hacking, I. (2002). *Historical ontology*. Cambridge: Harvard University Press.

Henriques, J., Hollway, W., Urwin, C., Venn, C., and Walkerdine, V. (1984). *Changing the subject*. London: Methuen.

Jagodzinski, J. (1996). The unsaid of educational narratology: Power and seduction of pedagogical authority. *Journal of Curriculum Theorizing, 12*(3), 26–35.

Jagodzinski, J. (2001). *Pedagogical desire*. Westport, CT: Bergin and Garvey.

Lacan, J. (1990). *Television*. New York: Norton.

Lacan, J. (2006). *Ecrits*. New York: Norton.

Laclau, E. (2005). *On populist reason*. London: Verso.

Lather, P. (2003). Applied Derrida: (Mis)reading the work of mourning in educational research. *Educational Philosophy and Theory, 35*(3), 257–270.

Lave, J., & Wenger, E. (1991). *Situated learning: Legitimate peripheral participation*. Cambridge: Cambridge University Press.

Lemke, J. (1995). *Textual politics*. London: Taylor and Francis.

Lerman, S., Xu, G., & Tsatsaroni, A. (2002). Developing theories of mathematics education research. *Educational Studies in Mathematics, 51*(1–2), 23–40.

Morgan, C. (2002). *Writing mathematically*. London: Taylor and Francis.

Morgan, C. (2006). What does social semiotics have to offer mathematics education research? *Educational Studies in Mathematics*, 61(1–2), 219–245.

Ongstad, S. (2006). Mathematics and mathematics education as triadic communication? A semiotic framework exemplified. *Educational Studies in Mathematics*, 61(1–2), 247–277.

Parker, I. (2007). *Revolution in psychology*. London: Pluto Press.

Piaget, J. (1965). *The child's conception of number*. London: Routledge.

Pitt, A. (1998). Qualifying resistance: Some comments on methodological dilemmas. *International Journal of Qualitative Studies in Education, 11*(4), 535–554.

Pitt, A., & Britzman, D. (2003). Speculations on qualities of difficult knowledge in teaching and learning; an experiment in psychoanalytic research. *International Journal of Qualitative Studies in Education, 16*(6), 755–776.

Radford, L. (2006). The anthropology of meaning. *Educational Studies in Mathematics*, 61(1–2), 39–65.

Radford, L. (in press). The ethics of being and knowing: Towards a cultural theory of learning. In L. Radford, G. Schubring, & F. Seeger (Eds.), *Semiotics in mathematics education: Epistemology, history, classroom, and culture*. Rotterdam: Sense Publishers.

Roth, W.-M., & Lee, Y. (2004). Interpreting unfamiliar graphs: A generative, activity theoretic model. *Educational Studies in Mathematics, 57*(2), 265–290.

Saenz-Ludlow, A., & Presmeg, N. (2006). Guest editorial. 'Semiotic perspectives on learning mathematics and communicating mathematically'. *Educational Studies in Mathematics, 61*(1–2), 1–10.

Skemp, R. (1971). *The psychology of learning mathematics*. London: Pelican.

Tahta, D. (1993a). Editorial. *For the Learning of Mathematics, 13*(1), 2–3.

Tahta, D. (1993b). Victoire sur les maths. *For the Learning of Mathematics, 13*(1), 47–48.

Todd, S. (Ed.). (1997). *Learning desire*. London and New York: Routledge.

Valero, P., & Zevenbergen, R. (Eds.). (2004). *Researching the socio-political dimensions of mathematics education*. Dordrecht: Kluwer Academic Publishers.

Varenne, H., & McDermott, R. (1998). *Successful failure*. Boulder, CO: Westview Press.

Vygotsky, L. (1978). *Mind in society*. London: Harvard University Press.

Vygotsky, L. (1986). *Thought and language*. London; The MIT Press.

Walkerdine, V. (1988). *The mastery of reason*. London: Routledge.

Walshaw, M. (2004). *Mathematics education within the postmodern*. Greenwich, CT: Information Age.

Žižek, S. (2006). *The parallax view*. Cambridge MA: MIT Press.

Žižek, S. (2008a). *Violence*. London: Profile.

Žižek, S. (2008b). *In defense of lost causes*. London: Verso.

Tony Brown
Institute of Education
Manchester Metropolitan University

PART ONE

WHAT COUNTS AS A PSYCHOANALYTIC THEORY OF EDUCATION?

TONY BROWN (BRISTOL)

1. WHAT COUNTS AS A PSYCHOANALYTIC THEORY OF EDUCATION?

INTRODUCTION

Education is a troubling experience. Contemporary debate about education often seeks to avoid drawing attention to the disturbance that education creates in learners and teachers. Instead, education does its best to ignore and explain away the trouble it causes us. There is strong resistance in many quarters to Freud's observation that education has consequences for psychical health and development, so why should the writers of this book choose to pursue a path that will be resisted? One reason is that ideologies can be blind to particular circumstances. Psychoanalytical perspectives are particularly sensitive to denial, procrastination and other forms of avoidance. We are concerned about the current state of health of education generally and the teaching and learning of mathematics in particular. Using a psychoanalytic lens offers a fresh perspective and an alternative discourse, which can help to illuminate blind spots in contemporary thinking.

In this chapter we start by asking what a psychoanalytically informed debate about education would sound like. We work on several different explorations of the discourse that is needed if we are to explore pedagogy from a psychoanalytical perspective. We explore the notion of a psychical life. This shift of attention takes us away from more familiar discourses that dissociate the individual and the group from discussions of curriculum design, syllabus content and assessment. Instead we explore what it means to place the relational experience of education – the self in relation to other – at the centre of our discourse.

Current debate on education tends to marginalise psychosocial processes and their impact on our development. A psychoanalytic theory of education brings relational dynamics within the debate about pedagogy and acknowledges our ambivalence to learning as a central facet of our educational endeavour. Why do some students and teachers promote mathematics as the only really important thing to do? Why do some resist all opportunities to explore it, whilst others 'fault themselves for their inability to navigate the educational system'? (Spindler & Spindler, 2000, p. 368)

A theory of education that draws on psychoanalysis needs to embrace both the results of historical explorations by Freud and his contemporaries and theoretical insights developed by more recent writers.

T. Brown (ed.), The Psychology of Mathematics Education: A Psychoanalytic Displacement, 21–33.
© 2008 Sense Publishers. All rights reserved.

TONY BROWN (BRISTOL)

EDUCATION AS A DISTURBANCE

'Something about education makes us nervous' (Britzman, 2003, p. 1) and education, both in terms of schooling and in the wider sense that Freud used it – education as upbringing – is inherently disturbing. Freud's view that education is about upbringing chimes with a contemporary anxiety that education in schools since the introduction of a national curriculum has become a mechanistic training process aimed at producing the next generation of workers – trained and skilled but not necessarily educated.

Appel (1999) revisits Freud's contentious observation that 'one's education inevitably produces discontents that can themselves later be changed in some way'. (p. xvi) Freud's observation was that:

> It almost looks as if analysis were the third of those 'impossible' professions in which one can be sure beforehand of achieving unsatisfying results. The other two, which have been known much longer, are education and government. (Freud, 1933, p. 248)

Education – the impossible profession – seen from this perspective is, according to Britzman a constant flow between present and past, which includes presence and absence and uncanny self-reference which Sigmund Freud (1914) describes as deferred – education is achieved only after the intended educational experience is reinterpreted, worked through and internalised. Education is recognised and modified by the processes of remembering, repeating and working through.

Our education continuously unfolds and is reworked in our present life – a turbulence of unanticipated conjunctions of affect, re-workings of old learning, and unexpected responses to our present life experiences. Every education is therefore borne out of a confluence of experiences never intended as education and those that emerge from intended study, though often with unintended consequences.

Working within a psychoanalytic paradigm means working within this flux of past and present, where current sensitivities to self and others emerge in ways that provoke the reworking of previous experience into what Freud calls after-education. In Freud's (1914) view the role of the psychoanalyst is to offer an after-education that reworks the damage that education inflicts. Freud's view goes beyond the argument that 'damage' can be caused by the introduction of simple mathematical ideas – Fischbein's (1987) 'pedagogical dilemma' – where teachers may use simple mathematical ideas that subsequently need to be modified or given up if further elaboration is to be possible. Freud's after-education is achieved in a space-time quite different from contemporary discussions about schooling. The challenge faced by a psychoanalytically informed pedagogy is to bring relational dynamics to the forefront of subject study, to make the necessary transformation from analyst to teacher and from therapy to education. In this way the focus of pedagogical study is the development of the self in relation: to other, to the discipline and to the relational associations to which mathematical symbols and processes can be applied.

EDUCATION AND AFTER-EDUCATION

According to Freud education is derived from a reconnecting process that reworks previous experiences of formal schooling and more general upbringing in ways that make learning from earlier disturbance. Working through the disturbance of earlier education leads us to a later 'coming to know' – a more profound connection between self-other and our place in the (educational) world. Thus it follows that every education is necessarily a difficult education, one that produces consequentially an after-education or *Nacherziehung.*

Melanie Klein took up Freud's theoretical ideas and applied them in therapeutic interventions, particularly in her work with children. Following Klein's theoretical work, our engagement with education cannot be separated from our phantasies - our unconscious desires and fears. Klein's world is one of love, passion, hatred and anger, feelings whose strength threatens to overwhelm us. Our affective responses emerge out of the need to preserve the core self as it is buffeted by the ebb and flow of our passions.

Education and schooling in particular take place within group settings. We feel the consequences of the relational dynamics of groups in powerful ways and we seek to protect ourselves from the potentially threatening forces created in groups by employing a number of different psychological defences. Klein's contribution was to identify and describe these forces and the defences we employ to preserve ourselves and influence others.

A seemingly more benign perspective developed by Winnicott, a child psychoanalyst and contemporary of Klein, theorised the dyadic relationship of mother and infant in ways that can be applied to the nurturing relationship of teachers in their caring role for students. A psychoanalytic paradigm posits that we construct relations with teachers and significant others based on – but not necessarily duplicating, our earliest experiences of being parented. Lakoff (2002) draws attention to the role of metaphors of the nurturing and the authoritarian parent in discussions of political ideologies. A psychoanalytical paradigm anticipates strong resonance between the way we relate to others – especially those in authority and power (teachers, police, politicians) and our earliest experiences of being parented.

Psychoanalytic theory is the only theoretical perspective that engages directly with the affective-cognitive dynamic of learning, recognising that it is shaped by our passions and the ways in which we defend against the disturbances we experience in our relations with other individuals and groups. It is the only theoretical perspective that sees disturbance is an inevitable part of learning and classroom interaction. Far from pretending that learning can be or should be smooth and untroubled, psychoanalytic theory addresses the turbulent process of learning which is immediately recognisable to students and teachers alike, but which is often denied in public discussions about the process and experience of being educated.

In the UK education is frequently described in terms that transform it into normative statements of teacher effectiveness and student disability.

> When a child who may find it difficult to do certain things at certain times enters those settings where [learning disability] is going to show up, it is not so much that the child changes as it is that those around the child change the way they respond, and thereby (temporarily) construct the child as a particular ['learning disabled'] kind of person. (McDermott & Varenne, 1998, p.13)

The problem of education then becomes the regulation of the problem people; the ineffective teacher, the dyslexic student, the failing school, the pregnant teenager, the single parent: if only everyone were normal, the dominant ideologies imply, then education could return to being that benign, tranquil, untroubled process that is often associated with metaphors of seeds and flowers and growth. We fully recognise the *desire* for our education to be like that, but we seek here to challenge the daydream and this denial of reality. We also suggest that from a psychoanalytic perspective our responses to students – those with 'learning disabilities' included – are seen as shaped by defences that we create to avoid the truth about the danger, risk, loneliness, exposure and the exploration that education demands. Resistance to employing a psychoanalytical perspective is stimulated at least in part by a desire to avoid engaging with what this exploration will bring to our attention.

A BRIEF HISTORY OF PSYCHOPEDAGOGY

The history of psychoanalytic pedagogy is worth exploring, if only to learn why it is inevitably problematic. In 1929-30 at the same time as Anna Freud (1930) was delivering her lectures for teachers and parents on ways in which psychoanalysis could offer educational insights, another short-lived education project attempted to achieve the same goals. The project is worthy of review. Now, as in the 1930s there is a growing interest in psychoanalytic pedagogy. Also (in what is an uncanny echo) there is a growing dread of the unknown other. In 1930s Austria the fear was projected onto gypsies, Jews and other non-Aryans. Today we are being encouraged to fear the unidentifiable fanatical Muslim: a politics of fear that seeks to exercise control over us and our thinking.

The *Movement for Psychoanalytic Pedagogy* is a little-known aspect of both educational history and Viennese psychoanalysis. It existed briefly during the interwar years and its history is recounted in Ascher[1] (2005) who traces her father's involvement in the movement as a teacher who sought further training as a psychoanalytic pedagogue in Austria. She begins with his application to the *Vienna Psychoanalytic Society* for training in 1926 and explores the ambitions of the movement, which supported both the development of educational ideas and the drive towards democratic socialism in Austria. Members of the movement sought to share psychoanalytic understanding of the processes and consequences of education within the group and to bring their ideas to a wider audience.

It foundered not only because of the political events in Germany, the invasion of Austria and the forced closure of all psychoanalytic establishments, but also because there was a failure to articulate the special characteristics of the schools involved in the project. Partly reflecting the prevailing cultural and social forces of the period, those involved focused on ways of avoiding excessive control of children, rather than developing a theoretical framework for education. The opportunity for developing a psychoanalytic pedagogy passed.

Anna Freud was more interested in applying psychoanalytic theory to education and schools than was her father. She engaged with several education projects and gave a series of lectures for teachers and parents that suggested ways in which education and psychoanalysis could benefit from collaboration. Following her father's theme that education is essentially problematic Anna Freud wrote, 'As a method of therapy, the analysis of children endeavours to repair the injuries which have been inflicted upon the child during the process of education'. (1930, p. 129)

What she offered in her lectures were her findings of how psychoanalysis could inform education by shedding light on:
- The possible consequences of excessive control and of too little direction on children and their development
- The complex relationships between adults and children, through an understanding of the unconscious and libido
- Analysis as a therapeutic process, which could address the needs that emerge in an after-education following the child's earlier educational experience

So, a psychoanalytical theory of education challenges conventional wisdom that education is essentially a force for liberation, self-development and a smooth path to an adult role in society. It offers a bleaker view that educators and others may wish to resist and defend against. In Anna Freud's view education is the source of injury. In Sigmund Freud's it is an impossible profession. If education is inherently problematic then it becomes education to study itself as a problem, rather than remain uninformed.

EDUCATION AS RELATIONAL DYNAMICS

To learn who I am becoming is the personal project of all teachers and students. This project has become sidelined in today's education where the focus is more utilitarian – more often focused on the development of skills for employment acquired through the study of a subject-dominated curriculum. A psycho-analytically informed pedagogy needs to take up the project of who I am and how I relate to others as a central rather than peripheral theme. This includes recognition of the role our desires and destructive phantasies play in our engagement with education.

What we eventually come to learn from our personal educational project - if we learn anything - is that our desires and destructive phantasies belong to us and have to be borne by us along with the externalised destructiveness that is projected onto us by others.

Understanding the dynamics of our own internal aggression and recognising their origin within us, is the cornerstone of our education. The denial of our darker side and pursuit of our desire to be other than we are inhibits the process and progress of our education. 'When we need to find the things we disapprove of

TONY BROWN (BRISTOL)

outside of ourselves [it is] at a price'. (Winnicott, 1986, p. 82) We pay the price at least twice. Once, when as babies the hated and loved mother who alternately cares for and abandons us is finally recognised as one and the same, we learn to use the feelings of guilt about having harboured destructive feelings for our immediate carers by creating a conscience. We pay the price again as adolescents when the same lesson needs to be re-learned, this time when our desire is to abandon the parent. We dress, behave and talk in ways that we believe support our claim to be increasingly independent but which in fact bind us, often to transient affiliations whose main purpose is to protect us from a fear of abandonment as we negotiate the parental separation. Winnicott's view is that we have to own our passionate loves and hatreds rather than blame others for creating them within us. Only by tolerating the discomfort of knowing that our phantasies are ours, can we begin to live with the inner being that is truly us. Winnicott's observation is that when we defend ourselves by expelling destructive thoughts and only recognise them in others, we gain some temporary relief but become madder as a consequence. Unable to tolerate the rich complexity of our inner self, we fragment it, splitting off and expelling the intolerable bits, often associating them with other people. The resulting fragmented and depleted self consequentially moves away from what Klein referred to as the *depressive position* and towards what she called the *paranoid-schizoid position*: a journey that, according to Klein, is as inevitable as it is essential. The return to the depressive position wherein we are able to recognise self and others as complex, part good part bad, is essential if we are to see our self as 'good enough' for life's project. Our particular location along the continuum between the paranoid-schizoid and depressive positions depends on our ability to recognise, accept, reclaim and internalise the previously intolerable parts of our self that we expelled into others. The process of after-education becomes the process of reclaiming the denied and projected destructive elements of our self and then learning to live with our own bad objects. Reabsorbing these destructive elements and tolerating them without recourse to projection is a significant part of stable adulthood. According to Winnicott and Klein, the self is strengthened as a consequence of the reclaiming process; we become less fractured, more rounded and complex, less stereotypical and uni-dimensional.

A psychoanalytic pedagogy will recognise the tendency of individuals to take up Klein's paranoid-schizoid position with its reactive defence to threats and the consequent portrayal of self and others as useless or perfect, weirdoes or cool, outsiders or groupies, leaders or followers, puppets or puppeteers, evil or godlike. A psychoanalytically informed pedagogy can suggest ways in which students and teachers alike can work towards a more rounded view of self and other that tolerates imperfection by managing destructive desires. Thus such a pedagogy promotes agendas and times for both students and teachers to recognise and create opportunities for working on the after effects of education in order to make an after-education that is beneficial to personal growth and development.

WHAT COUNTS AS A PSYCHOANALYTIC THEORY OF EDUCATION?

LEARNING TO LIVE WITH THE PAST IN THE PRESENT

For us like any other fugitive,
Like the numberless flowers that cannot number
And all the beasts that need not remember,
It is to-day in which we live.
W. H. Auden *Another Time*

When we work as students and teachers in formal education settings the narratives of our unconscious world reach back into our individual histories of learning, bringing our history into the present moment, often in dramatic and unexpected ways: algebra becomes incomprehensible in the presence of a teacher we come to hate, who reminds us vaguely of someone else; we find ourselves perpetually anxious that we will never satisfy the needs of a particular student who in fact makes no demands on us, but whom we fear could do so at any moment. Anxieties disturb us; we dream of being made to enter a classroom naked or of being required to write about a topic the details of which are kept secret from us.

The full educational experience includes the affective charge of current pleasures and anxieties, our relationship to the contents of study, our immediate experience of the relational dynamics within the group, and our attempts to defend ourselves from inner anxieties and to take inside ourselves the good parts that we recognise in others. We are constantly challenged by our need to succeed or fail, and our fears and hopes of being recognised or ignored.

What we can make of education at any time is not necessarily what is intended by us or by others *to be* an education – but that which leaves an impression, or has previously left an impression that now strikes us as important. Our after-education begins and continues when the possibility exists for us to work through previous educational experiences and settle them within a new us.

The complexity of the educational experience together with this potential for re-membering and re-working earlier experiences renders impossible the smooth transformation of the subject curriculum into learning. A temporally constructed, theoretically or didactically coherent curriculum will not necessarily transform into coherent learning. This is not to suggest we should give up the notion of syllabus, but it does mean that teaching a subject discipline does not equate to education. This is in direct contradiction to many contemporary curriculum models where effective memorisation of curriculum content is equated with effectiveness of teaching, which in turn conflates learning and education.

Wherever there is education there is always disturbance – experienced by teachers and students. Resistance and desire are at the heart of the education project. It includes rejection brought about by fears of being overwhelmed or changed by the subject material, the teaching process or the teacher. It also includes the desire to be invaded, rescued or taken over, for example by a libidinal 'crush' on a teacher or student,[2] or the feeling of omnipotence that mastery of mathematics can offer.

TONY BROWN (BRISTOL)

RESISTANCE AND COMPLIANCE IN EDUCATION

Education is a complex theatre of conflicting hopes, demands and expectations. Teachers have been trained to deflect students' desires and to resist students' demands. Spindler & Spindler (2000) draw attention to schooling as training in delayed gratification. Where students have learned to tolerate the associated frustrations, they may do well in school.

Some teachers need to collude with their students in order to maintain harmony in the classroom. Young teachers may wish that students perceive them as 'part of the group' rather than as part of the establishment. Teachers may resist or comply with collegial pressures and government requirements. In their turn, students and teachers inevitably disturb the teaching, the learning, each other and themselves. The source of this disturbance is generally dismissed as part of the trauma of adolescence. Teachers are careful to displace their libidinal feelings relating to their teaching, their subject and their students on to others – difficult colleagues, adolescence or 'problem learners'. All this has the effect of normalising learning as an inherently unproblematic process with those who present difficulties becoming pathologised. Resistance is displaced, removed from education and into a pathology of individual behaviour which re-presents behaviour as separate from learning.

This chapter asks what we might have to learn if resistance is acknowledged as central to education rather than being defended against. What space does a psychoanalytic theory of education need to occupy if it is to offer insights into teaching and learning? It must provide some understanding of the intrapersonal and interpersonal relational dynamics of learners and teachers. It needs to elaborate on the intellectual, physical and psychological spaces offered and needed for learning. Freud's (1930) recommendation in *Civilisation and its discontents* is for teachers to prepare students for the difficulties and struggles in life and to avoid idealisations. According to Freud in *Three essays on the theory of sexuality* (1905), the psychic imperative of adolescence is 'detachment from parental authority'. Not separation from the immediate parent or carer so much as a separation from the internalised parent that has become built up as a result of the experience of childhood. This requires challenging the values and beliefs that were imposed or received and then internalised as ideals.

Teachers and others often complain of secondary education that the curious child of five may show little of that same curiosity at fourteen. A psychoanalytic pedagogy would not be surprised at this apparent lack of motivation. Education itself of course occupies a parental role as part of the idealised parent of earlier learning and has to be challenged at least in part by adolescents. Where education's parental demand for uniformity, for obedience and coherence to the rules resonates with the biological parents' or carers' demands, the adolescent may well respond with strategies of anxious defence: avoidance, inhibition and resistance to education's coerciveness. Separation from the parent of education may well appear in adolescence as a denial of curiosity.

For psychoanalysis, phantasy[3] is central to an after-education. For formal education as envisaged by the prevalent pedagogies of today, engagement with phantasy is to be resisted. To attend to the strangeness of classroom encounters rather than resist their implications demands an educational paradigm that tolerates greater complexity than is currently acceptable; one which does not automatically invoke defences nor seek to satisfy the desire for control and authority of the other. This raises enormous challenges for teachers and pedagogues, but also offers a way of re-engaging with the problems that education currently faces.

Psychoanalysis offers to education 'an informing lens and a source of 'pedagogical rhetoric'. (Felman, 1994, p. 404) Psychoanalytic pedagogy requires the teacher to be a student of the student's self-knowledge. Additionally teachers have to become students of their own ways of 'coming to know' themselves and others.

The often-heard defence, *I teach my subject* ceases to be compatible with the education project. Becoming a teacher of students is to see one's chosen discipline or curriculum subject as a context for teaching students about what the discipline evokes in self and others. It is to engage - through the discipline – in teaching students what they already know of themselves but which may be disconnected, unavailable and inaccessible. It also means recognising how that whole scene plays for *us* as individuals who choose to teach, and how reconnection with the inaccessible and disconnected parts of the self can be made possible by and through skilful means.

For Freud (1911, p. 224) education is 'an incitement of the pleasure principle and … its replacement by the reality principle'. Education 'makes use of an offer of love as reward from educators'. In today's world where anxiety over relationships between school students and teachers is the stuff of TV soaps and crime dramas, the space between teacher and student is highly regulated and charged. All too frequently it is over-simplified, trivialised and sexualised in public renditions such as TV soaps and tabloid headlines. Education as an offer of love does not translate easily in today's anxious society, where physical contact between teachers and even young children disturbs us because we no longer know who we can trust (cf. Piper & Stronach, 2008). We may be more comfortable translating education as love in Kosovo, Afghanistan, Gaza or Darfur where we can project it safely into others and avoid the anxieties it provokes in our own teaching and learning.

Additionally, the observation that education inevitably creates feelings of helplessness and dependency, which both students and teachers must experience and work through, is problematic for our contemporary culture which celebrates individuality and personal strength above all else: vulnerability is framed in terms of deficiency rather than development. 'Working with vulnerable others' has been elevated to a specialist professional role, where vulnerability is equated not with growth but with a failure to thrive.

A psychoanalytic paradigm introduces an uncomfortable tension: teachers are caught between a requirement to provide unconditional respect and love for their students as people, whilst being challenged by the sceptical student to demonstrate this commitment at every turn. The adolescent's experience that the violent realities of life are a contradiction to what society claims education offers, means that the teacher's offer of love has to be rejected, but must never be withdrawn. And of course the adolescent is right - education's potential is not only for love, but also for authority, power and coercion. The offer of love is often contingent on many other factors. Thus a psychoanalytically informed education makes huge demands on insightfulness for both student and teacher.

Education and phantasy are inseparable yet contemporary pedagogies work to banish phantasy, forced as education is into claiming a spurious distinction between a so-called 'reality' of schooling and the unconscious desires of the individual. A psychoanalytically informed mathematics education is an education of self-other relations and an exploration of authority and power but from a central position within and through the subject discipline. It involves the acknowledgement of loneliness and learning to be alone with others, of recognising difference and maintaining respect for the otherness of the other, even as our phantasies and the coercive social and political forces in and around us make it easier to deny complexity and through anxiety of what education might become, to wish for the replacing of authority with control.

EXAMPLES FROM THE FIELD OF MATHEMATICS

Mathematics has a unique role to play as a vehicle for exploration of many of the theses touched on in this chapter. It allows examination of specific instances of general laws and various ways making representations. It is not surprising then that several writers, (Weyl-Kailey, 1985; Pimm, 1994; Blanchard-Laville, 2000) illustrate the powerful use made by primary and secondary school students to represent troublesome aspects of their lives, for example through the unconscious use of set theory or algebra to represent aspects of their anxieties and mental trauma. [4]

In a chapter entitled *Les Porteurs de Fantasmes,* Weyl- Kailey (1985)[5] first draws attention to the child's view of the apparent absurdity of mathematics and then to the difficulties faced by specific children and adolescents. In her work with students referred to the Claude-Bernard clinic[6] Lusiane Weyl-Kailey became interested in why some students are particularly dysfunctional in mathematics. From her therapeutic work she is able to show how affectivity infiltrates the cognitive processes that relate to mathematical thinking.[7] She reminds us of the fact that the concept of number is acquired in early childhood at the time when the infant is becoming aware of its relations with significant others, and she shows that certain numbers, especially 2 and 3 can be carriers of infantile phantasies. The number 2 can represent the relation with the other: the child with the mother, the father or another principal carer. Two is also the parental couple or the rivalry with a sibling. The number 3 can represent the triangulation of mother, father and child and also the loss of that triangulation through death or divorce or the arrival of a sibling[8]. Subtraction is often synonymous with removal:

a father who has left, a sister who has died, it represents absence. It is the loss of a dear one who has gone without hope of return. It is the fear of possible absence and the fear of castration. (Weyl-Kailey, 1985, pp. 38-39).

The unconscious finds in mathematics a convenient symbolic repertoire. In a similar way to dream work, the unconscious makes connections between different forms of representation. Students and teachers of mathematics may experience this at a conscious level by associating human and mathematical relationships and processes. The result - at a conscious level - for the student and the teacher can be vehement rejection or an obsessive love (directed towards the mathematics, the teacher or the students) leading to difficulties in the classroom.

For one eleven-year-old, transfer to secondary education marked the end of her considerable ability in mathematics. She became hopeless at mathematics, with anxiety verging on phobia. As the daughter of two diplomats, one from Italy the other from Scandinavia, she attended school successfully in several countries before settling in France aged ten. The introduction to set theory in early secondary school appears to have become associated with a major crisis of identity. In her mind, the intersection of two sets was reinterpreted in denial of the mathematical rules and came to represent her own identificatory anxiety: she regarded herself as neither Scandinavian nor Italian – a nobody. It took a year of careful mathematical work with Weyl-Kailey using set theory to re-present her identity in many different positive ways before the girl came to accept and internalise the mathematical meaning of the intersection as having the attributes of both sets. The powerful affective charge, which accompanied her crisis of identity, prevented the acceptance of the mathematical rules for set theory and weakened her ability to use logico-mathematical cognitive processes to interrogate and internalise the mathematical rules. The affective charge is often strong enough to render the mathematics inexplicable.

Because the forms of mathematical symbolism and representation offer scope for the unconscious to use mathematics to represent unconscious conflicts, affective associations frequently accompany students' cognitive processes. In his book *Camille a la haine et... Léo adore les maths: l'imaginaire dans l'enseignement,* Jacques Nimier (2006) reports on the results of over 1500 questionnaire replies from school students in France, Canada, UK, USA, Morocco and Greece. Mathematics is seen and used by the respondents in various ways: as a constraint, as a system that represents and helps maintain order, something that represents a frontier, a strange boundary and a mystery, success and status, access to the real world and a source of positive energy, something that carries risks and dangers. It is used by some students to acquire and promote high status, and by others to represent phobic reactions, aggression and anxiety.

In Nimier's study students describe how they protect themselves from the sense of danger that mathematics poses. For one student mathematics produces great anxiety: it has become the gathering of fruit, but with the certain knowledge that a storm is fast approaching. The impending storm creates pressure to gather as much fruit as possible in the short time available before the storm arrives and curtails the harvesting. For another student, algebra classes are desperately tedious. The

TONY BROWN (BRISTOL)

teacher's voice reminds her of a far off sleep-inducing murmur. She connects the teacher's aggravating voice to the squabbling in her parents' bedroom next to her own. Algebra has become infected with the anxiety of her home life; the cognitive processes required for working on algebraic problems have become tightly intertwined with the affective charge of anxiety: algebra is first associated unconsciously with anxiety but then becomes the problem.

Although this chapter has drawn on data relating to students, teachers are subject to the same psychodynamic processes and stories of their symbolic and metaphoric use of mathematics to represent unconscious desires are equally numerous and valid.

CONCLUSION

This chapter has attempted to set the scene for taking up a complex pedagogical stance: one that for many readers will require an excursion into new territory. It is not the territory of the analyst or therapist, but one that teachers and learners can explore and come to own as a professional stance. Through a process of questioning what education and psychoanalysis can offer each other, we have moved towards a view of how educationists might construct a more useful account of the education project and the development of mathematics pedagogy. This is then taken up in the chapters that follow.

NOTES

[1] The Vienna Psychoanalytic Society opened its Teaching Institute in 1925, the purpose of which was to train prospective lay analysts. In the 1930s there was a desire to understand learning from a psychoanalytic perspective. Although some of the ideas developed during the interwar years continued, as émigrés worked in clinics, child welfare organizations, and schools, in the face of survival and assimilation in postwar US, an identifiable theory and practice of psychoanalytic pedagogy were largely lost. (Ascher, 2005, p. 277)

[2] Depicted in *Notes on a Scandal*, based on Zoe Heller's (2003) novel.

[3] Phantasies are the primary content of unconscious mental processes. In simple terms they are unconscious desires and anxieties.

[4] For the past two decades French writers have been more fully engaged than their British counterparts in this area of pedagogy, but see David Pimm's (1994) *Another Psychology of Mathematics Education*. For examples of three French writers on the pedagogy of mathematical, see: *Victories sur les Maths*, by Lusiane Weyl-Kailey (1985), *Malaise dans la formation des Enseignants*, by Claudine Blanchard-Laville (2000) and the various paper and online publications of Jacques Nimier. <http://perso.orange.fr/jacques.nimier/> accessed 3 June 2007

[5] Zero and Infinity. It is nothing more than a number for many children. It can be an expression of a lack, of nothing, of absence, the distressing vacuum, distressing to the point that adding 2 to 0 becomes impossible; $0+2=0$ – one can find this apparent possibility in algebra. The child may comprehend that $5 - 7 = -2$ but $0 - 2 = 0$? Worse, 3×0 cannot be equal to 0 "Since one has three, how can this three disappear?"... Worse still: 0 divided by 4: how can zero be partitioned when it doesn't represent anything? Last, the abyss, 4 divided by zero. When one divides by a number that approaches zero the quotient grows to approach infinity. Division by zero is impossible; a mystery. (1985, p. 37)

32

WHAT COUNTS AS A PSYCHOANALYTIC THEORY OF EDUCATION?

[6] A clinic médico-psycho-pédagogique, opened in Paris in 1946 to support students with learning difficulties. It includes staff like Weyl-Kailey trained in mathematics and psychotherapy. The results of her work present mathematics in a new light, which offers a starting point for the development of a psychopedagogy of mathematics teaching and learning.

[7] 'One is the loneliest number that you'll ever do. Two can be as bad as one, it's the loneliest number since the number one....' Aimee Mann, *Magnolia*, 1999.

[8] David Pimm (1994) includes a moving account of a friend's young child who adapted the counting sequence to avoid uttering 3 following the death of her father in a traffic accident.

REFERENCES

Appel, S. (Ed.). (1999). *Psychoanalysis and pedagogy: Critical studies in education and culture.* Westport, CT: Bergin & Garvey.

Ascher, C. (2005). The force of ideas. *History of Education, 34*(3), 277–293.

Blanchard-Laville, C. (2000). *Malaise dans la formation des Enseignants.* Paris: L'Harmattan.

Britzman, D. (2003). *After-education: Anna Freud, Melanie Klein, and psychoanalytic histories of learning.* New York: State University of New York Press.

Felman, S. (1994). Psychoanalysis and education: Teaching terminable and interminable. In R.C. Davis & R. Schleifer (Eds.), *Contemporary literacy criticism: Literary and cultural studies.* New York: Longman.

Fischbein, I. (1987). *Intuition in science and mathematics: An educational approach.* Dordrecht: Reidel Publishing Co.

Freud, A. (1930). Four lectures on psychoanalysis for teachers and parents. In *The writings of Anna Freud* (Vol. 1, pp. 73–136). Madison, WI: International Universities Press.

Freud, S. (1905). *Three essays on the theory of sexuality.* Standard Edition Volume VII, pp. 123–246.

Freud, S. (1911). *Formulations on the two principles of mental functioning.* Standard Edition Volume XII, pp. 213–226.

Freud, S. (1914). *Remembering repeating and working through (Further recommendations on the technique of psychoanalysis II).* Standard Edition Volume XII, pp. 145–156.

Freud, S. (1930). *Civilisation and its discontents* (1929) Standard Edition Volume XXI, pp. 59–148).

Freud, S. (1933). *New Introductory Lectures On Psycho-Analysis* Standard Edition Volume XXIII, p. 248.

Lakoff, G. (2002). *Moral politics: How liberals and conservatives think* (2nd ed.). Chicago: University of Chicago Press.

McDermott, R., & Varenne, H. (1998). *Successful failure.* Boulder, CO: Westview Press.

Nimier, J. (2006). *Camille a la haine et... Léo adore les maths: l'imaginaire dans l'enseignement.* Lyon: Aléas.

Pimm, D. (1994). Another psychology of mathematics education. In P. Ernest (Ed.), *Epistemology and Mathematics Education.* London: Falmer Press.

Piper, H., & Stronach, I. (2008). *Don't touch.* London: Routledge.

Spindler, G., & Spindler, L. (2000). *Fifty years of anthropology and education, 1950–2000: A Spindler anthology.* London: Psychology Press.

Weyl-Kailey, L. (1985). *Victoires sur les Maths.* Paris: Editions Robert Laffont.

Winnicott, D. W. (1986). Aggression, guilt and reparation. In *Home is where we start from: Essays by a psychoanalyst* (pp. 80–89). New York: Norton.

Tony Brown
Escalate
Graduate School of Education
University of Bristol.

PART TWO

RELATIONALITY AND ANXIETY FOR STUDENTS OF MATHEMATICS

TAMARA BIBBY

2. THE EXPERIENCE OF LEARNING IN CLASSROOMS: *MOVING BEYOND VYGOTSKY*

INTRODUCTION

Metaphors play an important part in shaping the ways in which we make sense of our lives. However, while they can provide us with powerful images that enable us to engage with abstract ideas, they simultaneously constrain and limit subsequent thinking generating sometimes unintended or undesirable implications. In this chapter I explore some consequences of the metaphors of learning and teaching associated with a Vygotskian perspective on education. In the first part of the chapter I will use the psychoanalytic theories of Foulkes and Bion to explore the importance and implications of the group nature of the educative enterprise. The theories of Bion and Benjamin will also be drawn upon to find different ways of thinking about the nature of a pedagogic relationship and what this might mean for the ways we conceptualise learning. In the second part of the chapter I will draw on data from a recent research project to provide some exemplification for these theories, putting experiences and events onto the bones of the theories to bring them to life in a classroom setting.

GROUPS AND INDIVIDUALS

Since the West's 'discovery' of Vygotsky his influence on teaching, teacher training and educational research has gradually increased. Of his many ideas, there are two that seem to have passed into common sense. One is that learning happens in an individual's 'Zone of Proximal Development': the idea that there exists a space between what I can currently manage alone and what I can do with the assistance of a more capable other and that as I learn so I move towards what the other can do, crossing my zone of potentiality. This idea provides an attractive metaphorical image of teaching as a somewhat gentle, benevolent, rational process of drawing the less-knowing learner towards the more-knowing teacher. As a metaphor this is redolent of the expectations of child-centred, progressive education and idealises both the learner and the teacher. Yet, as Britzman (1979, p. 13 cited in Britzman, 2003, p. 22) suggests, drawing on Bloom's introduction to *Emile*, there is a paradox at the heart of Rousseau's moral pedagogy: '*What is forgotten is that Rousseau's full formula* (for raising a child for eventual self-sufficiency) *is that while the child must always do what he wants to do, he should want to do only what the tutor wants him to do*'. Highlighting a tension about

T. Brown (ed.), The Psychology of Mathematics Education: A Psychoanalytic Displacement, 37–59.
© *2008 Sense Publishers. All rights reserved.*

whose desire is to take primacy in a pedagogic encounter raises a question about the nature of this 'zone'. The fantasy seems to be that it is a sun drenched meadow filled with flowers and the sounds of busy bees although for some it may feel more like a soaked and pitted no-man's land full of noxious fumes, unbearable noise, mud and disease.

The seductive imagery conjured by Vygotsky's metaphor of the 'zone of proximal development' leaves hanging the nature of the zone and obscures the space it occupies, it allows us to ignore the difficulties and resistances which the learner will encounter and develop. Indeed, it demonises them – any resistance must be wilful and destructive: why would anyone want to resist benevolence and kind intentions? In doing this, the metaphor encourages us to ignore any differences between the learner and the teacher and seems to suggest that the learner's differences will be unimportant and willingly subjugated to the teacher's benevolent intentions. Similarly, the metaphor locates the teacher in a place of idealised omnipotence; an impossible place from which to teach or relate, a place from which the teacher's own difficulties and resistances, perhaps difficulties with particular students, become intolerable and unspeakable.

Another aspect of this metaphor relates to the nature of the 'more experienced other'. Through my years of involvement in the initial and continuing education of teachers it has been evident that, whatever Vygotsky's original intentions, (and some people's use of his ideas to support the use of group work notwithstanding), this 'more experienced other' has generally been understood as older than the learner and preferably an adult or the teacher. Such an interpretation has numerous implications not least of which is that it places the 'teacher' at a pinnacle of knowing (Walkerdine, 1988) and, conversely, the learner in a state of perpetual deficit. As a consequence, teachers have nothing to learn, or cannot learn, from their pupils since in this interpretation a child cannot take the position of 'more capable other'. In relation to learning in higher education the uni-directional and age determined nature of the flow becomes a problematic idea. Even in schools, however, the suggestion that the teacher has nothing to learn from the pupils is deeply troubling. At the very least, and staying within modern paradigms of teaching and learning, the teacher needs to learn 'where the child is at' in their learning; the state of their (mis)understandings. From this perspective, the pupil is the 'more experienced other' and the teacher the learner. So the jobs of the 'teacher' and 'learner' are not identical but they do coexist in space and time and are (or could be) mutually constitutive. The (non)mutuality of the learning relationship is explored further below as are the consequences of choosing to *learn about* children's learning without accepting that this means *learning from* them.

Vygotsky's other important, and by now almost common-sense suggestion, is that thought is internalised action: that what happens on the internal plane, happens first in the world in speech and in actions. In essays from students on education courses (many of whom are teachers) there often occurs an elision, perhaps encouraged by lingering influences from developmental psychology, such that internalised thought/ individual working is seen as somehow more mature, more personally authentic than work undertaken collaboratively or with assistance. So we learn quickly that it is 'more grown-up' to read 'silently' in your head than to utter the words aloud. It may also help to explain the enduring power of the individually taken examination paper over the group report.

Vygotskian ideas have impacted hugely on 'the turn to the social' within education and educational research. But, as we can see from the 'common sense' (mis)representation of his ideas in some students' work, there is a continuing tendency to privilege the individual or at least to down-play and simplify the social. The social, from this perspective, is construed as an aggregation of individuals each of whom is fundamentally more important than the group. This would seem to be a rather spare and stripped down definition of the social. Such a construction aptly demonstrates Bion's (1961) observation that we are group creatures at war with our group natures. Developments of Vygotskian theories, through activity theory, move uncomfortably between the individual and the social or cultural without resolving, or satisfactorily exploring, the tensions inherent in this tussle.

PSYCHOANALYTIC NOTIONS OF THE GROUP: MOVING BEYOND VYGOTSKY

My somewhat playful exploration of the Vygotskian metaphors that have gained currency in education in the UK highlight several tensions that I wish to use this chapter to explore. I do, however, want to take seriously and explore issues raised above that are, for me, found in silences that develop as perhaps unintended consequences of our use of the metaphors associated with the Zone of Proximal Development. I am particularly exercised by the nature of this 'zone of proximal development', it suggests a space existing within a relationship between the learner and the 'more experienced other' that it leaves undefined. Later I will draw on another set of metaphors and data from a research project and use the experiences of children learning in the primary classroom to explore the nature of this space and the pedagogic relationship.

So many analyses paint Vygotsky as a central figure in these modes of thought yet there were others, contemporary with Vygotsky, who developed similar ideas but in a different direction. I am thinking particularly of Bion, Foulkes and other group psychoanalytic theorists and practitioners. Foulkes particularly saw human beings as 'social through and through'. For him:

Each individual – itself an artificial, though plausible abstraction – is centrally and basically determined, inevitably, by the world in which he lives, by the community, the group of which he forms a part. (Foulkes, 1948 cited in Powell, 1994, p. 12)

Foulkes' central concept of the matrix designates all humanity as connected through lines of influence formed within groups: the family, cultural configurations: schools, religious practices and so forth, work groups, friendship groups. He defines levels of matrix (foundational, personal, dynamic, etc.) but it is not my intention here to explore his theories. Rather I will take this idea of the individual as a nodal point in a series of interwoven matrices – fluid, shifting

TAMARA BIBBY

networks of social connections – and consider this as a starting point. Such ideas are familiar from social theories but it is his move to embrace unconscious processes within the matrix that many find more problematic. As well as standing in strange relation to individual cognitive psychologies, these ideas also stand to the side of other, more individual psychoanalytic theories such as those of Freud, Lacan and Klein. In relation to mathematics education individual conceptions of the human subject can be found in the work of, for example, de Abreu, Bishop & Presmeg (2002), Ernest (2004), and Cobb & Hodge (2007).

Working with a 'figure-ground' concept, rather like the optical trick provided by the 'is it a vase or two people facing each other?' picture, group psychoanalytic theory considers the ego and unconscious to exist simultaneously at both individual and social levels. This is a difficult idea, it is not only that the group is a collection of individuals but that the group is a thing in itself, an idea we can find unsettling:

> Foulkes repeatedly stated that the 'social' is deeply inside each one of us, and what seems to be 'outside' or 'inside' is itself a construct by ourselves and by our cultures. Individual and social, intra- and inter-personal, are like the Moebius strip, eternally unfolding and infolding. … For him (Foulkes) society is not 'outside' the person: it is internal and penetrates to the innermost being of the individual. (Pines, 1994, pp. 48-9)

In describing Foulkes' 'group-as-a-whole', Pines (1994) keeps returning to Foulkes' own reiteration that '*what we call mind arises from each individual's need for communication and for reception*', a need to be seen and heard to which I will return later. He draws on Vygotsky's 'law of proximal development' to look at the way in which, what begins as an interplay of gestures, of call and response between care-giver and infant, leads the child to enter the language and cultural practices of the groups into which she has been born. Again, I will return to the idea of call and response in primary care-giver/child relationships later but note that this is a very different context within which to draw on this aspect of Vygotsky (and is perhaps closer to his original intentions).

Yet we are still left with the difficulty and discomfort of thinking at different levels at once: of accepting simultaneously one-person psychology (*what goes on inside a person*), two-person psychology (*within reciprocal relationships*) and three-person psychology (*the relational field of the basic family constellation – and with social roles and social relations derived from it*) (Schlapobersky, 1994). I cannot offer a solution to this difficulty but living and working with it seem important, especially in the context of education in formal institutional settings. The notion of a 'basic family constellation' may appear hetero-normative and sit uncomfortably for some readers. My understanding is that the family referred to (mother, father, child) is, from a psychoanalytic perspective, the Oedipal family. As such it might take some other form but the roles of primary carer, secondary law-giver/carer and child remain important. Benjamin (1986) and Mitchell (2003) have discussed some of the affects of this 'constellation' and its foundational role in psychoanalytic thinking.

THE EXPERIENCE OF LEARNING IN CLASSROOMS

The analysis offered in this chapter takes seriously the effects of group and individual unconscious processes and I begin by exploring what I mean by this. I will suggest that, as learning takes place in relationships, rather than in the minds of individuals, it is important to have some ways of thinking about these relationships. It is also important not to idealise relationships; while they can be warm, caring, generative, thoughtful and nurturing they can also be cold, distant, hateful, envious and destructive. In thinking about the relationships between peers and also between children and adults/ teachers it is important to consider both what is and what might be. To do this I will draw on data from a research project (described below) and the theories of a range of psychoanalytic theorists, particularly Bion and Benjamin. My interest is not in suggesting a 'fix', while I will suggest that there are ways in which pedagogic relationships might be changed I believe we already know much of this, my aim is to provide a conceptual framework and a set of metaphors, a vocabulary that may enable us to think differently about what we may already know.

GROUPS AND LEARNING: A PERSPECTIVE FROM BION

In considering educational contexts it seems particularly important to think about the nature of groups and about activities such as thinking and learning. To do this I turn to the founder of group psychoanalysis, Bion, whose work has precisely these foci. His theories, also founded on group actions and being, are not identical with Foulkes' but their differences are not significant to this chapter; indeed I will use them to complement each other. Bion made two important contributions to the way we conceptualise thought and thinking. The first concerns the nature of groups and group processes (Bion, 1961; Jaques, 1991; Nitsun, 1996). While these ideas are important and have much to offer teachers, it is his theories on the development of thought and thinking (Bion, 1970) and their nature as relationships that I wish to focus on here. Bion reverses the more usual notion that thinking generates thoughts:

> The problem is simplified if 'thoughts' are regarded as epistemologically prior to thinking and that thinking has to be developed as a method or apparatus for dealing with 'thoughts'. (cited in Britzman, 2003, p. 25)

Thinking, for Bion, is a way of dealing with the discomfort of thoughts. However, before we can process and modify thoughts through thinking we first have to decide to tolerate, rather than evade, the pain of those thoughts. Of course, any such 'decision' is not likely to be consciously taken. Being in a group causes further difficulties in the shape of our anxiety about other people's expectations and their reading of our own behaviour/ performance. This exacerbates the difficulties associated with thinking about our thoughts. In placing this ability to tolerate anxiety and frustration at the heart of our ability to learn and develop, Bion moves away from Freud. Bion's suggestion is that we need to be able to tolerate the discomfort of not understanding why that picture is of 3/5 rather than 2/5 (or anything else) and be willing to take the risks required for us to develop that

41

TAMARA BIBBY

understanding. These risks all relate to our relationships: there are familiar risks associated with answering questions wrongly and of being seen not to know, but there are also the risks associated with knowing and of understanding – of being seen as one who knows and understands. Both knowing and not knowing, and being seen as such, have implications for our sense of self and of our relationships. Learning involves risks on many levels, not just the risk of public exposure to humiliation.

For Bion, knowledge, coming to know, is an emotional activity. Along with love and hate it forms the six basic emotional experiences: knowledge (K), love (L) and hate (H), and their negatives -K ('Minus K'), -L and –H . These 'minus' links are not an absence of the emotional activity, nor are they its opposite. Rather, they represent a block to it, a refusal to engage, or a repression. If a minus link is experienced as dominating a relationship then *'the process of understanding within the relationship is stopped and reversed; meaningful experience may be destroyed'* (Symmington & Symmington, 1996 p. 29). For our purposes it is the K and minus K links that will be the focus. The K link is the linkage formed between thought and person in the emotional act of coming to know:

> K stood in both for the problem of realizing 'knowledge' and for accepting new ideas and new people as valuable and worthy. 'Minus K' is a destructive attack upon links between ideas and people. (Britzman, 2003, p. 25)

As we will see later in relation to the data, experiencing a –K link with respect to those who teach us mathematics might mean loosing a sense of oneself as a knower of mathematics as well as the loss of mathematical knowledge worked on within that relationship.

It is important to distinguish the K link and the kind of learning/coming to know that develops in such a relationship from acquiring knowledge about a person or thing. In this sense it is different from curricular or school knowledge, which Bion likens to 'cannibal knowledge' (Symmington & Symmington, 1996, p. 28), knowledge that is gained without the cost of giving. As an example, this might relate back to the teacher making judgements about a child's level of understanding by *'learning about'* their knowledge through a test rather than by *'learning from'* the child her or his own understanding through discussion. Yet, it appears that developing knowledge about a thing can also only happen within a relationship based on a secure K link; that is to say, a relationship characterised by a secure K link is also the foundation for coming to know in other, more academically familiar ways (Bibby, forthcoming a). I want to make a connection between this idea of knowledge only being available inside relationships characterised by a positive K link and Benjamin's *intersubjective third* which I discuss below.

> The (K) link is a crucial activity in which emotional experience of learning takes place. Hatred of learning, … leads to an attack on the link, resulting in the process being stopped of even reversed. Thus, instead of meaning developing or thinking being promoted, there occurs a reversal of the process so that any meaningful units become stripped of meaning. … If a negative link is dominating, the process of understanding within the relationship is

stopped and reversed; meaningful experience may be destroyed. (Symmington & Symmington, 1996, p. 29)

Learning in a relationship characterised by a minus K link is much more destructive than a mere 'inability to think'; Buxton's (1981) maths-phobic panic resulting in paralysis or turmoil hides much more poisonous emotions and states of being. Both manifestations of panic are portrayed as uncomfortable stutters in the otherwise continuous flow of experience and learning, however the experience of a minus K link constitutes something closer to a diversion, break or blockage in the flow, nothing is the same again. The destroyed learning-relationship, the minus K link, results in the loss of knowing: loss of self to group and loss of knowledge to self. What this might look like and mean in the classroom is explored more fully below but, if a minus K link is suggestive of a destructive learning relationship, is there a way of thinking about this in more relational terms? Is there some handle on the theory that might be less abstract? How can we recognise the kinds of relationship that might result in a minus K link?

LEARNING RELATIONSHIPS: A PERSPECTIVE FROM BENJAMIN

Above I suggested that the notion of a 'zone of proximal development' assumes enough mutual goodwill for progress in learning to be made but leaves silent the nature of the pedagogic relationship. When researchers have looked for empirical evidence of teachers' uses of such a 'zone' they have struggled. Some evidence has been found in the dyadic early learning relationships of very small infants and their carers, but in the context of more complex groups (such as a classroom) and older children, despite teachers' stated intentions, evidence has been less forthcoming (see for example Askew, Bliss et al, 1994). This suggests a need to consider more carefully the nature of pedagogic relationships: both the generative and the destructive.

A Third, Intersubjective Space Between Us

Jessica Benjamin (2004) posits the possibility of developing relationships, which she characterises as forming a 'third space' of intersubjective recognition and experiencing. As she explains:

> To the degree that we ever manage to grasp two-way directionality (*that in a relationship, I impact on you as much as you impact on me*), we do so only from the place of the *third*, a vantage point outside the two. However, the intersubjective position that I refer to as *thirdness* consists of more than this vantage point of observation. (This can refer to) anything one holds in mind that creates another point of reference outside the dyad. My interest is not in which 'thing' we use, but in the process of creating thirdness – that is, in how we build relational systems and how we develop the intersubjective capacities for such co-creation. ... Thus I consider it crucial not to reify the third, but to consider it primarily as a principle, function, or relationship,

rather than as a 'thing' in the way that theory or rules of technique are things. (p. 7)

For Benjamin, our ability to co-create and surrender to thirdness is rooted in our earliest experiences with our mother (or other primary carer). Firstly, there is the experience of having our hungry anguish held, tolerated and relieved. The mother is able to hang onto the fact that the baby's distress will pass and, while she is able to recognise and empathise with its pain and frustration, she is not overwhelmed by it, nor does she run from it. She is able to ...

> hold the tension between the identificatory oneness and the observing function. This mental space of thirdness in the carer must, I believe, be in some way palpable to the child. As a function, in both its symbolic and soothing aspects, it can be recognised and identified with, then made use of by the child. (p. 14)

For the teacher and learner in the classroom to recreate this ability to surrender to a third space the teacher would need to be able to hold the learners' tensions and anxieties knowing that they will pass. This teacher would be able to let the difficulty exist and facilitate the struggle and would be able to let the learners know, at some level, that their struggles were okay, survivable and, with time and effort, surmountable.

A Position of Complementarity: You or Me, Doer or Done To

In tolerating the child's (or learner's) discomfort the mother/teacher processes its pain and frustration, thinks the thoughts, and returns them to the child/learner in a manageable form. However, if the mother/teacher is not able to hold the child in mind, if she over-identifies with the child she may either swamp them (by *giving from a position of complementarity*, an act of over-identification in which she and the child are assumed to be one), leaving them unable to learn to think their own thoughts, or abandon them, leaving them alone with the unmanageable feelings and similarly unable to process their thoughts/feelings.

> if she gives from a position of pure complementarity (the one who knows, heals, remains in charge), the patient will feel that because of what the analyst has given him the analyst owns him ... Further, the patient has nothing to give back, no impact or insight that will change the analyst. The patient will feel he must suppress his differences, spare the analyst, participate in pseudo-mutuality or react with envious defiance of the analyst's power. (Benjamin, 2004, p. 14)

A position of complementary two-ness in which one is active and the other passive is characterised by a pattern of action-reaction and is one-directional, moving from to doer to the done to, from the one in control to the controlled, from the mother to the baby, from the teacher to the learner. *By contrast*, Benjamin points out, *a shared third is experienced as a cooperative endeavour.* (2004, p.18)

THE EXPERIENCE OF LEARNING IN CLASSROOMS

The other extreme, of abandonment, is also associated with not feeling seen or valued and can have problematic consequences.

If the patient does not feel safely taken into the analyst's mind, the observing position of the third is experienced as a barrier to getting in, leading to compliance, hopeless dejection, or hurt anger. (Benjamin, 2004, p. 28)

Shifting the context from patient/analyst to learner/teacher we can recognise in the description of complementarity the teacher who would make things easier for the learner through an over identification with her struggling pupils; the 'I know, I found it hard, I couldn't do it either, push these counters together and recount them then you'll have the answer' or 'As a teacher I would never do to children what was done to me in school'. For the pupil caught in this gaze and over protective containment there is no room to move or to think. From this position maintaining the tension of holding the learner's discomfort while helping the child to process its experience is avoided, the tension is expelled in an act of identification. But while the teacher may feel relieved that the tension they experienced has been dispelled, the child is left with their difficult feelings of not understanding the work, and now also not understanding why the teacher has 'rescued' them. Holding tension is never comfortable, helping a learner to understand why they are struggling and watching the painful process of learners developing understanding is much more difficult than solving the problem for them – but this is about the release of tension for the teacher, not the learning of the learner.

A key aspect of this complementarity is the way in which the structure of the doer/'done to' becomes coercive and, Benjamin suggests, it is an important characteristic of the impasse that is created that the relationship is characterised by 'coercive dependence that draws each into the orbit of the other's escalating reactivity. Conflict cannot be processed, observed, held, mediated, or played with. Instead, it emerges at the procedural level as an unresolved opposition between us, even tit for tat' (2004, p. 10. See also Mendick, 2006, for the operation of other, and especially gendered dualities within mathematics).

It would be in maintaining a sense of sharing and collaborative endeavour and managing to hold onto these tensions for each other that a space of thirdness might be created. However, the development of systems of sharing and mutuality may be antithetical to the atmosphere in many of today's classrooms dominated as they are by test results and the need to be doing better every day (Ball, 2003). The co-creation of processes that will be struggled for over time might feel too difficult, too demanding of time. Perhaps the process is even dangerous if your thoughts and movements are monitored through everything from your planning documents to the children's test results. In a climate in which the demand for control that permeates down from government to the classroom is extreme and unrelenting, letting go might feel impossible.

Despite this I suggest that a place to experience and learn about each other is key to other forms of learning. It is through the learner's engagement with a teacher they know and trust and who knows and trusts them that both can come to know about each others' passions (loves and hatreds), and that through this interest in the teacher and their passionate engagement with the things we must learn that we learn the subject too:

> Sally   The teachers make a big difference when its subjects so I hardly have Miss Daniels ever but I had her once in maths and she wasn't the best. But when it comes to subjects I um don't like but I have a teacher that I like then I would have a good standard. But if I had a teacher that I don't get along with, then I wouldn't get it

However, as we have already seen, holding the learner's anxieties and fear, tolerating their pain so that the K linkage or a place of intersubjective awareness (of thirdness) can form and be maintained is not easy and can quickly founder.

BEING IN THE CLASSROOM – WHAT IS

In the first part of this chapter I described three interrelated psychoanalytic theories. The first of these (Foulkes) focused on the importance of an acknowledgement of the group. While I have not pursued this aspect in detail, it is foundational to a move away from individualised notions of learning and teaching. More obviously I have drawn on the strongly related theories of Bion and Benjamin. I have suggested that there is a connection between Bion's notion of knowledge as an emotional activity and Benjamin's relational psychoanalytic theories. Further, I have begun to draw a connection between the existence of a minus K link and a doer/'done to' dynamic in which the overwhelming experience is of a reactive impasse characterised by complementarity (over-identification) or abandonment. The other side of this, a K link, might then be thought about as coming about and existing in a place of surrender to an intersubjective third. In these ways I have begun to explore the space that might lurk beyond a 'zone of proximal development'.

In the second part of the chapter I will turn to data from a research project to explore what these theories may look and feel like in the classroom. I will begin by saying something about the project and then move on to the analysis.

THE RESEARCH CONTEXT

The data drawn on here comes from an intensive study undertaken with one class of primary school children across five terms spanning three academic years: from the summer term in Year 4 (pupils aged 9 years), throughout Year 5 and to the end of the first term in Year 6 (pupils aged 10-11 years).

The school is a primary school in England located in a working class, inner-urban multicultural community. The ethnic make up of the school reflects well the community in which it is situated being 50% Bangladeshi with 30% white (UK) working-class and the remaining 20% being of Black Caribbean, African, Chinese and Indian heritages. At the time of the research over 70% of pupils were eligible for free school meals, a social index of poverty commonly utilised within the United Kingdom. It has consistently done well in the local school league tables coming in the top five and generally performs above national expectations. For a school with this make-up and coming from this urban environment, these are significant and noteworthy achievements although we might want to question the cost that such success comes at (Bibby, forthcoming b).

The data used below comes from formal and informal interviews and discussions with pupils undertaken either singly or as part of friendship groups. Some field notes record work undertaken with groups of ten when the children undertook their own research with research training and supervision from myself. As part of this process some children became very interested in interviewing peers and teachers – those interviews are also drawn on. While the research team chose the adults' pseudonyms, the children chose their own so although they have chosen what might be thought 'gender appropriate' names, their pseudonyms do not necessarily reflect their ethnicity. Each year group exposed the children to three teachers: their class teacher, the parallel class teacher and a support teacher, all three shared the teaching for the year and the children were mixed and split differently for different subjects. Three researchers interacted with the children: myself, Sheryl Clark and Alice Haddon.

Looking at the observation and interview data it is easy to find examples of the difficult feelings engendered by mundane classroom exchanges. These exchanges, which were perhaps lost to the teachers in the heat and bustle of the one-to-thirty-ness of their classroom relationships, were seen and felt acutely by the children. The extent to which this happened and the acuteness of the children's experiences came initially as something of a surprise to the research team.

Despite the benign images conjured by the notion of the 'zone of proximal development', real classrooms are often better characterised as places where learning is fought over and where individuals (adults and children) behave in defensive and resistant ways which will include attacking and hiding. So the ZPD's reliance on willing compliance leaves us with no way to think about more troubling classroom processes other than to split them off from learning and to deal with them as something else (as 'behaviour' for example).

From Bion: A Pedagogic Relationship Characterised by a Minus K Link

While much of what follows are events and experiences borne out of relationships characterised by a –K link, the resilience of the children in seeking reparation remains a remarkable testament to their hopefulness. Unfortunately, towards the end of the Autumn term in Year 6 some children were beginning to despair of improvement and were learning to habituate themselves to the impoverished classroom relationships that were all that was on offer. I have no evidence for the long-term consequences of such capitulation, however, the theory would suggest that they are neither pleasant or hopeful.

As I suggested earlier, the destruction of thought and thinking brought about by the existence of a relationship founded on a minus K link can be experienced as catastrophic and result in the loss of knowing: loss of self to group and loss of knowledge to self. As a year 6 boy explained to a researcher and his friends during a group interview:

SC   How do you feel if you get put in the lowest (maths) group?

Muhi   It feels not good because I don't feel good. It looks like all the medium stuff went to the lowest, it feels like my brain is going down, like we are doing Nursery work and I'm back in Reception

Such loss of knowledge is more personally threatening than the temporary 'blindness' or 'inability to think straight' often described as accompanying fear of mathematics (for example, Buxton, 1981). Muhi's description is of feeling diminished and infantilised by a teacher who cannot or will not recognise him, his efforts and what his efforts mean to him and to his relationship with her. It is more than the 'content of his brain' that has sunk and been lost (*the medium stuff went to the lowest*), in his analysis he has also lost his position in the school and his peer group (*I'm back in Reception*), and his self respect (*I don't feel good*). This is a catastrophic event. His turmoil is evident throughout this interview and also in his distressed (and distressing) attention seeking actions in lessons. As he explained when the researcher asked him in a lesson why he kept calling out to tell the teacher what number he was on in a mathematics exercise: 'because sometimes she doesn't care what number I'm on'. The teacher was experienced as having no interest in his progress through the very tasks she had demanded he perform; she seems to have abandoned him to his fate in his learning yet she continues to judge and act upon those judgements. Muhi appears to be stripped of any ability to work to influence her behaviours towards him. Her taking of knowledge *about* him is experienced as devouring. Perhaps if she were to spend time understanding why he has become so irritating in mathematics lessons, taking time to learn *from* him, the lessons might be experienced differently by both of them.

From Benjamin: Being Suffocated in Over-Identification

One possible configuration for a relationship in which a space of thirdness cannot be managed is a position of complementarity, a relationship that is very familiar from work in and with schools. As I suggested above, an act of complementarity enables the teacher to relieve her own uncomfortable unpleasant feelings and anxieties through an act of identification with a student or group of students. This position allows the person in control to control completely in the certain knowledge that *they know* what the other person is feeling and thinking. This, Benjamin suggests, amounts to a theft of self by the other. The relief is all the teacher's and the student can be left with the original difficult feelings associated with not understanding the work/ ideas and with the added burden of wondering why they needed rescuing: what was it about their lack of understanding that the teacher could not bear? Are they unbearable? Not survivable? Do they need to hide their impossible ignorance to protect the person who is supposed to be there to help

THE EXPERIENCE OF LEARNING IN CLASSROOMS

them? Pushed to these places we can begin to see how the position of the learner could be very difficult in such a context.

In our research this dynamic was exemplified by Miss Middleton's own relationship with mathematics and her mathematics group. Interviewed by the children, she identified mathematics as the subject she least liked teaching: '*I hate it*' she told them. Some reacted to her style of teaching mathematics well, they hated mathematics too and colluded with her through a '*pseudo-mutuality*' to make it unnecessary to engage with the subject. Others found her lack of teaching more problematic. Muhi and his friend Matthew struggled to make sense of why they had both been moved from the 'middle' mathematics group: Muhi into the 'bottom' group and Matthew into the 'top' group. They explained first that they'd been working together and thought they were getting the same marks in their work and tests:

Muhi Yeah, and we were just opposite each other on our table. ... We (got) our work done, we finish it, every sheet. But I don't know why I got kicked out from Miss South's class. Because um, I don't know, because –

Mat. Maybe you had a low level score

Muhi I had a level 4, so was his. And I got kicked out. ... And Frank said I got kicked out because I keep on talking to Matthew. But we don't really talk, we just talk about our work

SC So then you got put in another group as a result?

Muhi Yeah, I got to the lowest. And Miss Middleton hates maths, so guess what she does? She says 'right, get all your times tables done' and then she gets paper and we just have to colour, like reception.

Mat. Miss Middleton is fun. I wish I was in her maths group

Muhi But she hates maths. She doesn't even learn us maths. It's (very) boring, we just had to colour like reception (...)

Emran When Miss Middleton took us just for a bit she never taught us it and I think it was just a waste, I don't know, of teaching. Because I learned more from when we had to do sticking to make a collage

Matthew seems to try to make it okay for Muhi to be in Miss Middleton's bottom mathematics group: it must be fun. But for Muhi there is only frustration, he is left not learning a subject he used to enjoy and he is diminished by the experience. Eventually Emran confirms his interpretation of the lessons, little learning happens. In relation to her assuming a position of complementarity Muhi feels helpless and angry or frustrated: how can he know how to behave with this teacher? Here, in the face of a minus K link, his understanding of himself as a collaborative and successful mathematics learner has been stripped of meaning and he is left empty. His energies, once focused on learning mathematics, are now taken up with trying to make sense of his sense of loss, disappointment and bewilderment: who am I now that I have been demoted to this non-maths mathematics class?

So, how can we characterise what was happening among the children we spent so much time with? While the analysis here is somewhat gloomy, it is worth holding onto the determination and continuing efforts of the children, the optimism of their will.

From Benjamin: Feeling Abandoned, Wanting to Abandon

Foulkes' suggestion that *what we call mind* arises from our *need for communication and reception*, for being seen and heard, gives us some indication of the fundamental importances of these experiences. Benjamin underlines this importance with her suggestion that feeling *taken into the mind* of the other is central to the development of an intersubjective thirdness in a relationship. The kinds of experiences that can result in feeling unseen and not having been taken safely into the teacher's mind are legion (see also Spindler, 2006), they include being overlooked in the classroom when you have put your hand up to answer a question...

> Minnie The people that don't put their hand up, she's always choosing them. And the people that we wanna say it and we stretch our arm up so high and then your arm starts to hurt. ... There's no point putting your hand up

... and extend to having a contribution misunderstood and/ or passed over, or to feeling misrepresented in some other way. The anger of the children in being overlooked, or of feeling invisible, generated mistrust in the teachers and of their intentions. In another interview Sally and Minnie explained their reasons for mistrusting their teachers' claims, at the start of the new school year, to good will and liking the class, they carried this mistrust forward into their other dealings with Miss Warner:

> Sally Miss Warner, when she saw us she said she'd heard we were a really good class but I don't know if she believes that. We had to make little books introducing ourselves. What she did was she just put them in this box, like a scrap box and I'm sure I saw Fatima's ripped and Muhi's ripped so she doesn't exactly take care

> Minnie I think on the outside she likes us and she's just saying, I think she's lying, but inside I think she's saying 'I don't like this class'

The teacher's actions and her words told different stories leaving the girls uncertain which to believe but tending rather to trust the actions over the words. The teachers insisted that lessons were worth doing because they were interesting. Yet these sentiments were belied by actions and experiences. As Rezwana commented: 'I don't think they even care. All they care about is to do work, blah blah blah'. Rezwana's comment seems to indicate that she feels there to be a lack of caring about the children as individuals. This personal invisibility and felt lack of caring about the whole individual sometimes resulted in some children feeling their teachers did not like them. Sally vividly explained her frustration and she and her friends Sabrina and Sophie explored their feelings with the researcher (AH):

> Sally   I put my hand up and she (Miss South) never chooses me, especially in maths. She loves the other Year 5 class and then like um she blames me if I've got it wrong. It's like 'Sally, you don't understand' but it's her, she doesn't understand and then when I'm ignored I don't like it. I feel left out and nobody ignores me! But then she says I only ignore you it's because you're so clever, but then that's not true. … I think it's just that she doesn't like me. No Alice it's true, I don't think she likes me that much.

They described the effect this had on their learning. Like much of the interview data, this extract has an 'us and them' ('done to'/'doer') feel about it and a feeling of frustration and anger can be sensed coming through from the children's descriptions of what it was like being in the classroom:

> AH   And what happens to you when you're trying to get on with learning things and you feel the teacher doesn't like you? Does that make a difference?

> Sally   Yes, it's a bit difficult to concentrate and then she's like 'you're not concentrating properly', but when you tell her that 'you're leaving me out' then she doesn't know how you feel because its not happening to her!

> AH   Because she's not being left out?

> Sally   Yeah cos she's being like, everyone's surrounding her going 'Miss South, Miss South!'

> Sab.   If I was Miss South yeah, and Miss South were me yeah, I'd just squash her like a fly! (laughter from all three)

> AH   And what would you do Sophie?

> Sop.   I'd ignore her as well

> AH   Yeah but you can't really ignore a teacher so well, it doesn't work so well that way round

> Sab.   Send her to the head teacher

> Sally   I would ignore them or this is what I feel like to do with this boy in my maths group, getting a ruler and whacking it on his head … yeah that's what I feel like to do with Miss South 'cos teachers need things like that.

TAMARA BIBBY

Given their relative powerlessness there is little that the pupils can do in the face of their perceived persecution by a relentless 'doer'; they have little ability to deliver the tit-for-tat responses they might secretly want to make. Their resentment of this teacher suggests a blocked or broken relationship (a minus K link), in which they cannot know or be known by their teacher, instead they have to defend themselves against her lack of empathy. The need to comply with her demands has led to hurt anger and the violence of their revenge fantasies is powerful. Elsewhere, and in the context of having *'The lion, the witch and the wardrobe'* as a class reading book, they express a desire to *'push her into the wardrobe'* and so to banish her to another reality.

Given the difficulty of banishing and 'disappearing' ones' teacher, that some children effectively make themselves 'disappear' is perhaps not completely surprising. Indeed, this is a very compliant, well-behaved class and the simmering resentments and anger remained largely hidden from adult eyes. Any serious and long-lasting fallings-out tended to be conducted privately. There were few public demonstrations of fury or hurt with their peers, let alone their teachers. Indeed, this is ironically part of the reason the class were chosen to work with the project. Earlier I suggested that the metaphor of the zone of proximal development encourages us to ignore any differences between the learner and the teacher and that it seems to suggest that the learner's differences will be relatively unimportant and willingly subjugated to the teacher's benevolent intentions. The extent to which the children looked beyond themselves for validation was remarkable but perhaps, if they were experiencing complementarity (being 'done to') then their lack of learning of how to experience themselves for themselves might make this more predictable. Perhaps, feeling at the whim of seemingly capricious adults increases the need to please them, to propitiate themselves:

> Rhatul   Mr Leader (Head teacher) tells us if you're good at reading and if you are (he) read(s) out the questions and you have to write down the answer to each question … and Mr Leader gave us a prize. (…) And if we can do it, if we've got all of them right, he'll give you a prize. Mr Leader gave us the prize and he was so happy that we could do our times-ing.

It is for the head teacher that Rhatul and (he suggests) his peers learn, their success is offered to him for his approval and his happiness; their pleasure is in his happiness, not their own achievements. For some, however, getting positive attention was experienced as difficult: what could be seen and celebrated felt beyond them. Emran (being interviewed in Year 5 with friends Matthew, Muhi and Jack) explained the inequity of the 'table points' system in which the tables (seating was arranged by the class teacher) were rewarded with yellow slips, ostensibly for working well, and individuals were punished with red ones:

> AH   And is table points a good idea do you think?
>
> E   sometimes they (the teachers) don't even expect us (boys) to be doing hard work, they go to another table and just give (the reward) out

THE EXPERIENCE OF LEARNING IN CLASSROOMS

AH	So it's not to do with whether you're working hard
E	No
AH	What do you think its to do with?
E	Tidying up

There was a great deal of ambivalence and confusion about who was 'doing' what to this group of boys. As the discussion continued where the persecution was coming from shifted:

Muhi	And the golden slip thing, I don't want it! All the girls, especially Beyonce they just help because they want to win something and when we say, can we help she goes 'Nooo' and it ain't fair
Emran	They just do it to get rewards and yellow slips (…)
AH	Do you think the girls get more rewards than the boys?
E	Yeah. And Bobby, because he's quiet he gets a yellow slip
Mu.	Just because Bobby's quiet it doesn't mean he should get a yellow slip and lots of things
AH	So he gets lots of things because he's quiet
E	But when the teachers aren't looking he bosses everyone!
Mat.	Yeah he does
Jack	He doesn't boss me because I've never given crisps
E	AND he never gets his own crisps, he just wants more and more from ours

Here we begin to get a sense of the complex social and emotional economy of the primary school peer group and the way that they looked to each other and their teachers to see and be seen. We can hear Muhi resisting what he seemed to read as the manipulative quality of the table points/yellow slip system and the boys' shared disgust at Bobby's apparent duplicity and the teachers being taken in by this. They grapple with key questions: Who is judging who and how? What is valued? How can I be seen and valued? Who is in control? Do they use their power fairly? In this exchange too we begin to see *the intense jealousy, rivalry and envy* that first takes place among siblings and later schoolchildren *reversed into demands for equality and fairness* (Mitchell, 2003, p. 11).

What was notable was that, in over a year spent with this class, at no time did we see or hear of issues like this being picked up or discussed. The teachers seemed happy to remain in control, the children's compliant behaviour and success with SATs (compulsory 'Standard Assessment Tests') meant that they were not forced to consider the status quo within which they operated. That the children felt persecuted did not result in the teachers experiencing their half of the dichotomy;

the persecution they experienced was projected outside, onto government and their tools: the relevant departments, inspection regimes, the league tables, policy writers and so forth. It is my belief, however, that the doer-done to dynamic was very much alive and well in this classroom and this school. The adults and the children were certainly stuck in an impasse in which the children subjugated their desires and needs to the pleasures of the teachers and the teachers continued to control and dominate from a position of misplaced omnipotent benevolence. Schools and classes in more challenging circumstances may not be so quiet.

In a classroom landscape such as this the safe flower-filled, meadow-like 'zone of proximal development' is shown for a sham. This is a far more dangerous place to be: filled with shifting and ambivalent relationships and unstable booby-traps with paradoxical qualities. This is a friendless place of hard existential uncertainties to be managed alone and with few allies.

BEING IN THE CLASSROOM – WHAT MIGHT BE

If these are the difficult feelings that the children in the class experienced, do we have any sense of what they felt the wanted? What was felt to be missing?

Wanting to be Seen and Heard - Reaching Out for an Intersubjective Thirdness

If the teacher is to remain in control all the time and to always be the 'more experienced other' then developing reciprocally educative relationships is not going to be possible; the dynamic will always be one of mutual antagonism, an impasse of doer and done to duality. The non-mutual learning described above and experienced by the children as acutely unsatisfactory left them wanting something more mutual and interrelated, something more nurturing and sustaining.

In the children's own research it became particularly clear that there was a desire on their part to open channels of communication with their teachers – to establish a different kind of communication redolent of a K link, a getting to know that would involve mutual trust and a dialogue, a space that we might characterise as intersubjective. Of the three research groups two generated data on the effects of their relations to teachers ('What do we mean by "fun and "boring"?' and 'Why do we feel different when we do tests and challenges?') and one group specifically interviewed teachers in an attempt to get to know them better. In the preparation, conduct and analysis of this research it was remarkable the extent to which the children made efforts to hold the teachers in mind, to offer opportunities for reciprocal and mutual understanding and to manage and transform what they thought they knew would be the teachers' anxieties. It was also notable that in this school the children were so little considered that their efforts to see, understand and value their teachers did not touch the adults; what the children had to offer could not break through the teachers' deafness to anything but the clamour of the demands of the outside (OfSTED, DFES, league tables etc).

It is not unusual for children to be curious about their teachers and to entertain fantasies about their lives beyond the 9-3.30 that is shared: do teachers really live in school, sleeping in cupboards or the staffroom? However, it is less usual for pupils to be given an opportunity to interview teachers and to explore their own motivations for wanting to do so. The first event of note to me as a facilitator of the children's research project was the hostility, suspicion and anxiety raised by their initial letters asking whether teachers would be prepared to be interviewed. Interestingly none of the teaching staff felt able to refuse the requests for interviews (one member of the support staff did) but it was apparent that the interview was resisted in action by at least one teacher; a disturbing experience for the child interviewer. Nor did the hostility get directed at the children, it was directed towards me. There was a suspicion that I had directed the pupils and that I was using them to interview the teachers as a sneaky way of getting to more of them. This was an unpleasant experience and seemed to speak volumes of the lack of trust within the school and also a lack of seriousness about the children as people with interests and opinions. In times of OfSTED and constant surveillance it is perhaps understandable that this reaction might be a possibility; that does not lessen the shock of its reality. More importantly, the teachers' denial of the children as people more than learning-taker-ins-and-test-performers raises issues about the kinds of relationships that they can countenance; they seemed intent on remaining the *doers* to the children's *done-tos*, of remaining in control.

> One-way recognition misses the mutuality of identification by which another's intention is known to us. To separate or oppose being understood from self-reflective understanding or understanding the other misses the process of creating a shared third as a vehicle of mutual understanding. (Benjamin, 2004, p. 27)

During the analysis of the data from the teachers' interviews the children noticed and reflected on what they identified as anomalies. For example, they noticed that, when asked what subjects they liked teaching, all the teachers mentioned either literacy or mathematics. Other areas of the curriculum were only mentioned in terms of subjects the teachers did not like teaching. This rang hollow to the children, surely some must like teaching other parts of the curriculum best? And was it really possible that they all spent all their time outside of school eating? But perhaps the most troubling aspect of the interviews was a rather different silence, again identified by the children. Two of the teachers who had been interviewed had talked about doing things at the weekends and in holidays with their daughters but the fact that they were married to each other and that the children belong to both of them was not acknowledged despite this not being a secret. This was noticed and talked about by the children as if it was some kind of betrayal. The children talked for a long time about whether, if I had asked the questions (as an adult) or if they asked them again, we would get the same responses. While they understood, and reminded each other, that the teachers might want privacy about their lives, the way they had chosen to draw boundaries was troublesome to the research group and read as inauthentic and also as a slur on the children: they don't trust us.

The desire for a 'we', for closeness and mutuality, for a different, more reciprocal relationship also came through in other, less overt ways; for example, in their continuing to seek approval after many felt rebuffs and rejections. The extent to which the physical and psychic space of the classroom was out of their control was struggled with throughout our time of listening to the children. It was a theme they all (boys and girls) returned to in a variety of small and large ways. The loss of the carpet space in Year 6 was particularly mourned and, felt with the physical distance from friends generated by the teachers deciding who was to sit where, led to very complex and painful feelings of isolation and loneliness. Rani particularly struggled with her feeling of isolation from her teacher and her peers. Now they had lost the close physicality of the carpet, of being able to lean a little to one side and make contact with a friend, of being able to whisper a comment while the teacher read. Now, sitting on chairs around tables, everyone was far away, there was no physical contact and a whisper might be misconstrued, reaching out with warmth might be punished. The loss of intimacy and trust was experienced as a kind of ache but, like a lost tooth, something to learn to live with.

DISCUSSION AND CONCLUSION

Benjamin suggests that the only way out of the doer/ 'done to' impasse is to recognise our own participation in the dyad, she suggests that we need to 'surrender our resistance to responsibility, a resistance arising from reactivity to blame'. That is, we need to stop feeling stuck and reacting with tit-for-tat behaviours and to do this we need to own our complicity.

> Once we have deeply accepted our own contribution – and its inevitability – the fact of two-way participation becomes a vivid experience, something we can understand and use to feel less helpless and more effective. In this sense, we surrender to the principle of reciprocal influence in interaction, which makes possible both responsible action and freely given recognition. This action is what allows the outside, different other to come into view (Winnicott, 1971). It opens the space of thirdness, enabling us to negotiate differences and to connect. (p. 11)

What would this look like? How can groups (schools, other groups) move beyond a doer/'done to', submit or fight, win/lose or continue to confront/fight dynamic? And what would this look like in mathematics lessons? Would it be any different to other lessons? As stated above, the difficulty here is that the dynamic is demonstrated in the words. If the solution is seen in terms of winners and submission then the power imbalance that has started the difficulty is maintained: the two-ness of the relationship (us and them, good and bad, right and wrong) and the uni-directionality of the communicative endeavours is perpetuated. However, surrender, Benjamin suggests, provides a different space. In surrendering I am not submitting to your demand, however, I am suspending my demand that you listen to me so that I can listen to you and so that we can think together. It is, she suggests, in the act of surrender that a third space can be created.

THE EXPERIENCE OF LEARNING IN CLASSROOMS

But is this a state of being that might be desirable in schools? What would it mean for the adults to surrender control in this way and to own their complicity in the blocked relationships of the classroom and school? This is the hard part – for teachers to 'recognise that the object of our feelings needs, actions, and thoughts is actually another subject, an equivalent centre of being, is the real difficulty'. (Benjamin, 2004, p. 6) The difficulty of this demand is not immediately obvious; of course teachers know that children are individuals. But this cognitive knowing is not enough. All of the teachers interviewed as part of this project were clear with the research team that they valued the children and their contributions, the school thought of itself as a 'listening school', yet this is not how they were experienced by the children. And the real test is that they had no idea and no way of coming to know this. The cognitive model of teaching and learning founded (however loosely) on benign Vygotskian principles of 'leading the children' to a state of knowing and of 'assessment for learning' (Black & Wiliam, 1998; Black, Harrison, Lee, Marshall & Wiliam, 2003) as a guide to letting the children into the secret gardens (labyrinths?) of assessment and the curriculum was backfiring and only the children's good intentions and polite acceptance of adult authority kept the lid on the feelings. The learning that was taking place was that one had to come to terms with an impoverished view of oneself, that how one felt was unimportant as long as you kept doing the work, and that pleasing the teacher was the key to success and provided a thin form of nourishment. The children were learning to be what the teachers expected them to be, they were learning to *want to do only what the tutor wants [them] to do*, and that was very little.

> In a world without shared thirds, without a space of collaboration and sharing, everything is mine or yours, including the perception of reality. (Benjamin, 2004, p. 22)

In the classroom both teacher and child are learners. However, the things that they do not know, while connected, are different: among other things, for the teacher what is unknown is how each child will come to understand and make sense of the mathematics they are teaching while for the child the unknown is the mathematics. But for both of them their shared unknown is how they and the other will react to their coming to know of their unknowns; this is the intersubjective work that underpins the pedagogical work in mathematics and in other curriculum areas.

So drawing on Benjamin and Bion, a functioning pedagogic relationship might be thought of as a place that can tolerate thinking, that can contain anxiety so it does not overwhelm and stop thinking. It is a relationship that can enable both learners (teacher and pupil) to bear not knowing, that can enable us to take the journey from familiar, known places (of not-knowing) to a new place (of knowing) and to do the identity work that would enable the learner to rethink herself and to adapt to her new sense of 'self as knower'. Such relationships might underlie the apparently ideal mathematics classrooms of writers such as those reported by, for example, Lampert (1990) and Ma (1999) and Watson, de Geest & Prestage (2003), although there is no space here to undertake that investigation.

TAMARA BIBBY

Enabling these relationships to develop is the ethical work of the teacher. And this is a non-trivial task for it involves being the 'grown up'. That is to say, it means containing one's own anxieties, fears, desires and furies and not projecting them onto the children; not acting out when to do so seems like the only bearable course of action. It means being able to take a position of vulnerability, of *taking the side of the child rather than the side of the law* (Matthews, 2007), of exploring ones' own desire for punitive vengeance rather than only the child's resistance to our mathematics (Taubman, 2006). Ultimately, the nature of any 'zone' between the teacher and learner or better, amongst learners, will need to be continually contested, struggled over and nurtured, not assumed and left to its own devices.

REFERENCES

Abreu, G. de., Bishop, A., & Presmeg, N. (Eds.). (2002). *Transitions between contexts of mathematical practices*. Dordrecht: Kluwer Academic Publishers.

Askew, M., Bliss, J., et al. (1994). Scaffolding in mathematics, science and technology. In P. Murphy, M. Selinger, J. Bourne, & M. Briggs (Eds.), *Subject learning in the primary curriculum* (pp. 209–217). London: Routledge in association with The Open University.

Ball, S. J. (2003). The teacher's soul and the terrors of performativity. *Journal of Education Policy 18*(2), 215–228.

Benjamin J. (1990/1988). *The bonds of love: Psychoanalysis, feminism, and the problem of domination*. Reading: Virago.

Benjamin, J. (2004). Beyond doer and done to: an intersubjective view of thirdness. *Psychoanalytic Quarterly, LXXIII*, 5–46.

Bibby, T. (forthcoming a). How do children understand themselves as learners? Towards a learner-centred understanding of pedagogy. *Pedagogy, Culture and Society*.

Bibby, T. (forthcoming b). The new managerialism: A view from the carpet.

Bion, W. R. (1961). *Experiences in groups and other papers*. Hove, East Sussex: Brunner-Routledge.

Bion, W. R. (2004/1970). *Attention and interpretation*. London: Karnac.

Black, P., Harrison, C. Lee, C. Marshall, B., & Wiliam, D. (2003). *Assessment for learning: Putting it into practice*. Maidenhead: Open University Press.

Black, P., & Wiliam, D. (1998). *Inside the black box: Raising standards through classroom assessment*. London: King's College, School of Education.

Britzman, D. (2003). *After-Education: Anna Freud, Melanie Klein, and psychoanalytic histories of learning*. Albany, NY: State University of New York Press.

Buxton, L. (1981). *Do you panic about maths? Coping with maths anxiety*. London: Heinemann Educational Press.

Cobb, P., & Hodge, L. (2007). Diversity, equity and access to mathematical ideas. In N. S. Nasir, & P. Cobb (Eds.), *Improving access to mathematics: Diversity and equity in the classroom* (pp. 159–171). New York: Teachers College Press.

Ernest, P. (2004). Postmodernity and social research in mathematics education. In P. Valero & R. Zevenbergen (Eds.), *Researching the socio-political dimensions if mathematics education: Issues of power in theory and methodology* (pp. 65–84). Dordrecht: Kluwer Academic Publishers.

Jaques, D. (1991). *Learning in groups*. London: Kogan Page.

Lampert, M. (1990). When the problem is not the question and the solution is not the answer: Mathematical knowing and teaching. *American Educational Research Journal, 27*(1), 29–63.

Ma, L. (1999). *Knowing and teaching mathematics: Teachers' understanding of fundamental mathematics in China and the United States*. Mahwah, NJ: Lawrence Erlbaum Associates.

Matthews, S. (2007). Some notes on hate in teaching. *Psychoanalysis, Culture and Society, 12*(2), 185–192.

THE EXPERIENCE OF LEARNING IN CLASSROOMS

Mendick, H. (2006). *Masculinities in mathematics*. Maidenhead: Open University Press.

Mitchell, J. (2006/2003). *Siblings*. Cambridge: Polity Press.

Nitsun, M. (1996). *The anti-group: Destructive forces in the group and their creative potential*. Hove: Brunner-Routledge.

Pines, M. (2000/1994). The group-as-a-whole. In D. Brown & L. Zinkin (Eds.), *The psyche and the social world: Developments in group-analytic theory*. London: Jessica Kingsley.

Powell, A. (2000/1994). Towards a unifying concept of the group matrix. In D. Brown & L. Zinkin (Eds.), *The psyche and the social world: developments in group-analytic theory*. London: Jessica Kingsley.

Schlapobersky, J. (2000/1994). The language of the group. In D. Brown & L. Zinkin (Eds.), *The psyche and the social world: Developments in group-analytic theory*. London: Jessica Kingsley.

Spindler, G. (2006). Living and writing ethnography: An exploration on self-adaptation and its consequences. In G. Spindler & L. Hammond (Eds.), *Innovations in educational ethnography: Theories, methods and results* (pp. 65–82). Mahwah, NJ: Lawrence Erlbaum Associates.

Symmington, J., & Symmington N. (2004/1996). *The clinical thinking of Wilfred Bion*. Hove: Bruner-Routledge.

Taubman, P. M. (2006). I love them to death. In G. M. Boldt & P. M. Salvio (Eds.), *Love's return: Psychoanalytic essays on childhood, teaching and learning*. London: Routledge.

Walkerdine, V. (1988). *The mastery of reason: Cognitive development and the production of rationality*. London: Routledge.

Watson, A., Geest, E. de, & Prestage, S. (2003). *Deep progress in mathematics: The improving attainment in mathematics project*. Oxford: University of Oxford.

Tamara Bibby
Department of Learning, Curriculum and Communication
Institute of Education
London

ROBERTO RIBEIRO BALDINO AND
TÂNIA CRISTINA BAPTISTA CABRAL

3. I LOVE MATHS ANXIETY

INTRODUCTION

In this study of young adult mathematics learners, we introduce the notion of maths anxiety by reporting on a Google-count in which we sought to locate occurrences of 'math anxiety' together with others such as 'stress', 'achievement', 'overcoming', etc. It would appear from this count that maths anxiety is widely considered to be a significant hindrance to learning and that research on this phenomenon is typically aimed at freeing students of this or, at least, reducing anxiety to acceptable levels. It also appears that research primarily employs quantitative methods and proposes psychiatric solutions. In this chapter we consider an alternative approach to this phenomenon through the theoretical apparatus of Lacan's psychoanalysis. In order to justify such an approach we argue for the fundamental role of language in mathematics teaching and learning through the following steps. 1) We characterise arithmetic as a social phenomenon rooted in language, not in biology. 2) We characterise mathematics as the realm of language that accepts the identity A=A as a triviality, and thereby we try to provide an answer to the question: 'what is mathematics?' 3) We characterise mathematics teaching as the introduction of students into a realm that severely restricts the language they are able to use. We leave aside the important question of the relations of thoughts to language; in this chapter the word 'thought' has the common sense meaning, except in an excerpt of Freud. From this approach we seek to explain why anxiety is associated with mathematics teaching and infer that the undesirable effects of anxiety can be avoided not by avoiding anxiety itself, but by using anxiety itself to reshape the subject's sense of self in relation to mathematical activity and the social demands associated with this activity. In our argument maths anxiety is not to be avoided, but rather to be loved. We describe how certain forms of classroom organisation can allow us as teachers to achieve closer contact with our more anxious students. We report on two episodes where anxiety is explicitly addressed in actual classroom situations. In an attempt to make Lacanian psychoanalysis more accessible we have constructed an imaginary character, transparent to her own desire, and so able to present the theory as if she were actually living it. Such a character is impossible, however, since, according to Lacan, the individual is shaped by a desire but a desire that misses its object, in the sense that what appears as desirable is always a mirage produced by a certain need, by a certain hunger, a certain expectation, by a *lack*, a lack that *causes* desire. Also,

---

T. Brown (ed.), The Psychology of Mathematics Education: A Psychoanalytic Displacement, 61–92.
© *2008 Sense Publishers. All rights reserved.*

to avoid excessive mathematical complexity for the reader and any potential fear of the subject that he or she may possess, we have avoided college mathematics except in a short appendix intended for calculus teachers.

COUNTING ON ANXIETY

From Wikipedia we learn that 'anxiety is an unpleasant complex combination often accompanied by physical sensations such as heart palpitations, nausea, chest pain and/ or shortness of breath, tension, headache and feelings of inner nervousness'. This undesirable psychological state affects many people: 'anxiety' as a signifier occurs over 56 million times in Google. Here we are concerned with a particular form of this phenomenon known as *math/s anxiety*. As a signifier it occurs 199 000 times according to our own count in April 2006. Even taking into account that Google counts repetitions, this number is too high to allow a comprehensive survey of literature. From such Google-counting we have some indication that maths anxiety is a form of anxiety specific to mathematics and related subjects. Indeed 'physics anxiety' occurs only 102 times and 'biology anxiety' 45 times. On the other hand, subjects that get closer to mathematics seem to be more at risk: 'computer anxiety' occurs 19,000 times and 'statistics anxiety' 11,000 times. Other designations of the same phenomenon also appear: 'mathematics anxiety' (41,000 times) and 'math phobia' (35,000); new designators have also been created: 'mathanxiety' (850) and 'mathphobia' (620). Where does all this anxiety and phobia happen? Proceeding with our search we discovered that maths anxiety emerges 'in school' (30,000 occurrences), or more specifically, 'in elementary school' (564), 'in high school' (17,000), 'in college' (26,000), and 'in university' (1,000). We could go on ...

It would seem from these enquiries that maths anxiety is widely considered as a problem that needs to be solved. Fumbling over remaining occurrences we find the works of Evans (2000) and Brown and their collaborators (e.g. Brown, Atkinson & England, 2006), mixed with books, university catalogues and works that also mention 'Psychiatry', 'overcoming', 'reducing', 'conquering' and other categories somewhat alien to Lacanian psychoanalysis.

So in summary maths anxiety is considered to be a negative attribute, which inhibits both social functioning and school performance. It is generally analysed by quantitative methods and overcome by corrective procedures from within mathematics education and psychiatry. But since maths anxiety is not usually conceived of as a disease, the connection with general states of anxiety is not well characterised in the literature. As a result, treatment consists of *ad hoc* therapies targeted at suppressing anxiety as a symptom. In this chapter we seek to explore an alternative approach.

WHY PSYCHOANALYSIS?

Whenever a fresh theoretical insertion into an old problem is made, people invariably ask: why? How do you justify the necessity of your view? The most comfortable answer for us would be: wait and see. But psychoanalysis and especially Lacan do not ordinarily command much patience from the general reader. So we feel some obligation to venture into critically commenting on some of the research done so far on maths anxiety. Fortunately Evans has preceded us in this task. His substantial book, *Adult mathematical thinking and emotions,* comprises an effective treatise on mathematics education and affectivity. Although his research is not strictly based on psychoanalysis, he surveys the main literature on maths anxiety, including 'approaches informed by psychoanalysis'. (Evans, 2000, p. 113)

By adjusting some of his statements we will be able to introduce our own ideas. First of all, anxiety is not an unconscious process as one might infer from the following passage:

> Since in the psychoanalytical view anxiety may be unconscious, it therefore cannot be assumed to be *reportable* by the subject. Nor can it be assumed to be *observable* in a dependable way. Only some of its symptoms may be observable, and because of defences, these may appear in distorted form: as 'no feeling' at all, or indeed as the opposite of anxiety. (Evans, 2000, p. 45)

Yes, we cannot assume that anxiety would be reported by the individual. Such an assumption would provide the ground for quantitative approaches through questionnaires such as the MARS scale, which provides the foundation of most research on maths anxiety; anxiety may be observable in unpredictable ways. When we say that anxiety is not unconscious, the common-sense opposition conscious/unconscious may jump to the conclusion that we are saying that 'anxiety is conscious'. Such opposition is a retention from the early works of Freud. We must transcend this opposition in order to clarify the concept of anxiety that we adopt here. We start by noticing that the idea of an 'unconscious' anxiety is directly opposed to Freud's own position:

> With the thesis that the ego is the only seat for anxiety – only the ego may produce and feel anxiety - we have established a new and stable position from which a number of things assume a new aspect. It is truly difficult to check in what sense one could speak of 'anxiety of the id' or to assign to the superego the aptitude to feel a state of apprehension. (Freud, 1933, p. XXXII)

That is, whilst Freud locates anxiety in the ego, Evans suggests that anxiety may be unconscious and thus not available to the ego. However, Evans' statement finds support in a partial reading of Laplanche & Pontalis, (1973, p. 110), which he quotes, who suggest 'defence can be directed not only against instinctual claims, but also against everything which is liable to the development of anxiety'. However, the concepts of 'defence' and 'repression' should not be confused. Indeed, at another point we read in Laplanche & Pontalis: 'one should not argue ...that repression and defence may be treated as synonyms. Repression is ... a moment of the defence operation – and this in its precise sense of repression into the unconscious'. (ibid. 392) So, for Freud, anxiety is not unconscious; it is present in the conscious ego. Together with this assertion Freud sustains two other ones as milestones well established in his 'mature works', that is, the works after he introduced the so-called second topography (ego, id, super-ego) in place of his first version (unconscious, pre-conscious and conscious). Briefly, for Freud, anxiety is a process of the ego:

> It was anxiety that produced repression and not as I formerly believed the repression that produced anxiety. (Freud, 1936, p. IV; 1933, p. XXXII)

> Anxiety as a sign that announces a situation of danger assumes priority with the new point of view (ego, id, super-ego). (Freud, 1933, p. XXXII)

Anxiety was there *before*. This means that anxiety is not a result of repression, it is not a symptom to be 'overcome' as the doxa maintains. It produces repression of drives and the repressed material emerges as the symptoms. Besides, if anxiety is a sign, warning the ego of an imminent danger, there can be no point in trying to avoid, suppress or overcome this 'sign'. Lacan reinforces Freud's position saying that anxiety 'is what does not deceive'. (Lacan, 2004, p. 92)

Since anxiety is felt only by the ego it may be assumed that it is a consciously experienced feeling. The subject knows very well whether s/he feels anxiety or not. Therefore, contrary to Evans' claim (2000), anxiety *is* observable. By whom? By the subject who feels it. However, in order to observe it, the researcher will have to rely on the subject's report. And this is the main point: is anxiety *reportable* by the subject to the researcher? The subject may simply *not report* any anxiety, as Evans rightly foresees. It is in this sense that anxiety may be *unreportable*.

We will first focus on a quantitative approach through questionnaires such as the MARS scale, which provides the foundation of most research on maths anxiety.

Quantitative treatment of data collected via questionnaires presupposes a transparent subject who could evaluate, without mistake or remainder, his or her objective situation about maths anxiety. Such an approach produces a useful and necessary comparative knowledge but, since it *evaporates the unconscious*, it loses the constitution of human subjects in language, and departs from psychoanalytical considerations. If we assume that two desires are already implied in the encounter of two subjects in a situation that common sense calls 'communication', such as the student and the teacher, or the interviewer and the interviewee, or the questionnaire and the respondent, we are obliged to bring the unconscious into play. Psychoanalysis as a theory of the clinic where nothing else besides language is implied, is certainly a promising path to follow. What MARS and maths anxiety scales based on questionnaires can be sure of, is that they correlate *answers*, not necessarily *levels* of anxiety. Absence of report does not mean absence of anxiety itself. Against such a simplified view that knowledge may be out there waiting for us to pick it up, we quote Jacques-Alain Miller, the heir of Lacan's copyrights who criticises the medical conception of the anxiety phenomenon. He refers to a book published by the *Institut national de la santé et de la recherche médicale* (INSERM, 2004):

INSERM does not only say that there is knowledge in the real, it imagines that this knowledge is reduced to the accountable signifier. This point of view, which comes from a sort of positivism, is that the real is reduced to this knowledge and thus evaporates in this knowledge. (Miller, 2005, p. 19)

WHY LACAN?

We also wish to suggest possible shortcomings in much literature on maths anxiety: the absence of a characterisation of mathematics anxiety as properly mathematical. Most everything said in the literature could equally refer to physics or biology anxiety.

In order to characterise maths anxiety as a form of anxiety we have to pass through the difficult question of characterising mathematics itself. We approach this question via a previous one: What distinguishes mathematics from other sciences? The naïve answer is that deciding right or wrong in mathematics does not require external information. The counting process is apparently internal to the counting subject. Inner/outer of a human subject implies a biological perspective. So, a variant of this answer goes up to postulating that the decision process has a biological root. Focusing on the narrowest possible situation, 'one plus one makes two' would be a condition written in the DNA structure, just as talking might be seen as a condition to being declared human. If we try to disrupt this position, for instance, by invoking the fallibility theses of mathematics, people might think that we are insinuating that some day, perhaps, one plus one will cease being two. However, what we are trying to draw attention to, is the process through which people become so sure that 1+1=2. This is not obvious to everyone. It is the result of a long historical and educational process. For instance, one python plus one duck is certainly one python, so 1+1=1. One father plus one mother, this makes 3 and one arrow plus one arrow may well be zero, if I miss both shots. These are meaningful responses among Brazilian Indians (Ferreira, 1997).

People who contend that 1+1=2 is an eternal and universal truth of human spirit will certainly argue that it is not this that we are talking about. Then, what precisely *is* it that *we are talking about*? In order to agree that 1+1=2 we first have to *rule out* some situations. And in order to rule out situations without first ruling out people, we have to argue, we have to engage in dialogue and we have to educate. So, 1+1=2 is a cultural truth. Arithmetic is a social phenomenon rooted in language, not in biology. It is a phenomenon as old and as basic as language itself.

Apparently, our conclusion is that if we want to characterise the specificity of mathematics we have to take language as it is generally considered, as a 'communication' device between 'human subjects'. We take this statement as temporarily true in order to conclude that, since we are using a model based on a practice that involves only two people and relies exclusively on spoken/heard words in the context of a psychoanalytical clinic. Psychoanalysis is a theory of this practice. But what do such theories have to say about our science and our teaching? And we need to remember that these theories have shifted through time, even in the minds of certain key individuals. Freud and Lacan each changed substantially during their lives, reinventing themselves repeatedly.

Since we need to go down to the root of a phenomenon as old and basic as language itself, we 'choose' to rely on a theory that inverts this formula: instead of considering language as a human phenomenon it considers *humans as a language phenomenon*, in other words, we choose a theory that assumes, as a fundamental point, that language is constitutive of human subjects, of their choices (transference), desires (unconscious), commitments (drives) and enjoyments (repetitions). According to this theory, human beings do not 'communicate' through language, they become human as they talk; communication is an accident. This theory is Lacan's psychoanalytic theory; this is our 'choice'.

Warning to the Reader

Dear reader, at this point, to be honest, we feel compelled to address you directly. The argument in the above paragraphs might be seen as a hoax intended to facilitate your understanding. Indeed, we assume that you are interested in mathematics education and, perhaps, you are also a mathematics teacher. We assume that you are curious about psychoanalytical perspectives and what they have to offer to mathematics education. Perhaps you are asking yourself: 'can this help me?' More specifically, you may be considering whether you should add Freud and Lacan to your bookshelf, or even place them among your favourite authors.

We would like to say 'yes, do this' and we would like to assume the responsibility for your choice. Yet, in terms of psychoanalysis this would be called a strong transferential relationship. There is nothing wrong with that as such. Transference is the initial point in any psychoanalysis and it is also the initial point of the teacher-student relationship. Such a relation, however, must be worked out through a psychoanalytical process but this is certainly out of the question here. We are thus obliged to pursue another course. Instead of *assuring* you, we prefer to *warn* you: beware of your decision! Why? Because you are a human subject who is contemplating a theory about human subjects! Before you can look at Freud-Lacan's theory, the theory itself will be looking at you. How? Through the unconscious. Freud would say that your decision is not as free as you would like to think it to be, it is conditioned by the conscious. To this you could reply: 'yes, I know; everybody has an unconscious and *my* decisions are certainly affected by *my* unconscious. Yes, there is nothing very serious about our warning thus far, the unconscious, according to Freud, it is still yours, it is inside you. Lacan, however, would say: 'no, the unconscious is not *yours*, it is not inside you, it is the discourse of the Other made through you, it is *outside*. As is the case for everybody you too have been taught what to choose, you have been taught what to *desire*. Thus Lacan is more difficult to deal with.

So, dear Reader, you have two options. You may say: 'ok, I have been warned, I know all that, but...'. That is, you decide to think of yourself as an autonomous ego, a seat of freely made decisions. In this case, we should warn you that this path has already been followed by many people. Such people make occasional reference to Freud's texts. They participate in the reading of one or the other of Lacan's seminars. They insert sharp quotations of these authors into their papers. They lead this new fashion of mathematics education that seemingly produces deep impressions in so many people. Such a position, however, one that supposes that we could 'choose' Lacanian theory from among other theories amounts to a position that falsifies this stance from the outset. Similarly, all attempts to call Lacanian theory to the assistance of any positive enterprise, be it of practice, such as teaching or of theory, such as understanding, are doomed to fail. It is foreseeable that in a decade or so, today's pioneers will declare that psychoanalysis has already done what it could for mathematics education, new authors will be brought in, new fashions will come up, new trees will be transformed into books, new books will boost the editorial market and new research trends will be looked for. In order to keep searching one must not find.

There is however an alternative route where one starts asking: 'what does this theory have to say about me?' From this point on, there is no possibility of return, because the first effect of the question is a change in the question itself. You will hear yourself asking: 'what does this theory have to say about 'Me'? In this case, as you go deeper into this theory you soon discover a kind of reflective effect that has been so well exposed by the Dutch painter M. C. Escher. You follow the water downstream and you suddenly realise that you are back upstream where you started or you look closely into a picture and you find your action of looking already depicted there in the picture. There is no way back from this instability, as this version of 'Me' who could make the decision of going back is now under the focus of the theory. The decision itself is being considered by the theory. Researching, writing and publishing, all come under the focus of the theory being generated through this. As subjects of language humans insert themselves into realms of meaning that escape their control. So, we must sincerely warn you that this is not a short cut into happiness.

The reader could ask: 'What about the authors? How did they get where they are? Why did they choose the second route?' Like many others we raised the question some years ago: what is this theory about? We did this honestly, as we do when we study mathematics. We did not ask 'what can we do with it?' Somehow we discovered that it was a *theory about ourselves*. At this point we experienced the impossibility of returning. So, in his chapter, our 'choice' of Lacan has to be understood as a declaration of commitment. To 'understand' Lacan is already to embrace Lacanian theory and its consequences. We would not know how to organize our thoughts differently. Here we face the major difficulty of this chapter: how do we produce a survey of Lacanian theory without distorting it? We draw on the following expedient. Lacan alerts us to 'the impossibility of the subject, at the level of desire, of finding himself, as a subject, her cause'. (Lacan, 2004, p. 381) So, we imagine a character who could violate this impossibility, 'a being to whom her cause would not be foreign' (ibid.) and who could report us her desire upon the scene; we introduce Diaphany. The aberration produced by the following hypothetic monologue of a student who would be *transparent* to her desire proves the impossibility of such a human being; however, this expedient will allow us to shorten the reader's path into Lacan. Some effort will still be necessary, but we know of no shortest route.

DIAPHANY'S MONOLOGUE

Diaphany: Mr. Smith is my high school mathematics teacher. I participate in his class as if I were a player in a game, judged merely according to whether I win or lose. I watch carefully for a slip in his expression revealing that he may be not so sure himself, suggesting that he has lost my line of thought such that he will need to consult his copybook to check my answer. In such circumstances I become proud of myself, and that produces in me a special kind of enjoyment (jouissance). It was not my grades, the praise from my parents or the perspective of a certificate that made me work hard on my exercises. My true object of desire was behind all this. It was the principle that made me the desirer of a lack situated precisely in Mr. Smith's face when he vacillated. It was a lack in his enjoyment that produced mine. I apprehended this lack in his discourse. In the very intimation he made me I could anticipate the moment of his failure. Such was my playing strategy as a good maths student. But all this was only the exteriorisation of something deeply rooted in me. What if he does not find the answer in his copybook? What if he becomes unable to decide if my answer is right or wrong? What if I surpass his mathematical abilities? Can he lose me? This was the always-present question that caused my desire. The game had to go on. (See Lacan 2004, p. 383, 1973, p.194).

In this brief monologue and quotation we have already the essence of Lacan's theory, a dialectics constitutive of the subject and the other. Diaphany has to find her place in the world as a human subject according to the demand defined by her teacher. Mr. Smith entered not as an individual, but as a social agent: the big Other. Let us take another example, this time examining the question of maths anxiety and gender.

Diaphany: Mr. Smith is asking for $a+b$. I think the answer is c. I have just raised my hand and he *marks* me as a possible respondent; but now I regret having raised my hand, as suddenly I become less sure. He calls my name and I have to introduce myself through the signifier c to the class. If my answer is right, our team will score one point. I will produce myself as *meaning* 'the girl who played well'; if it is wrong, I will have to explain my reasoning before the class and produce myself as meaning 'the girl who can't add'. I wish I had not raised my hand, and remained in quiet seclusion perhaps waiting for a later opportunity. It seems that this game condemns me to such a division: should I have raised my hand? It is always too late to go back and too soon to give up. Either I efface myself or I produce myself as 'the one who said so'. I have the strange feeling that both situations occur simultaneously and I cannot avoid them (See Lacan, 1973, p. 191).

Diaphany: I do not feel at ease when I am faced with the decision of crossing the Rubicon; boys are more eager to break through; it is their role. As a girl, I prefer to sit back and wait for their desire to take hold of me. This makes me all the more anxious, since I do not know their desire; I never know how far afield they are willing to take me. This is why Mr. Smith's questions make me anxious. Will he order me to take the stage? Of course, as a woman my position is perhaps more comfortable. The business is already done, their desire has to come out after me and I am not an enjoyment naturally promised to their desire. This makes of me a special prize (See Lacan, 2004, p. 383).

What one has to do as a man or as a woman is wholly learned from the Other. 'Man' and 'woman' are social roles defined from positions in the relation of desire to *jouissance*: either desire has to go after jouissance or jouissance waits for desire to reach it. We can only say that such roles are biologically grounded only in so far as they are *culturally imposed* upon biological differences. They encompass all social actions, including mathematics, at school or elsewhere. Women are perhaps a little more anxious due to their position or role with respect to desire/jouissance. So the results of Evans (2000) and much other research about maths anxiety and gender could be usefully modified to take into account how far physical appearance departs from social roles.

He is saying this to me, but what does he want? (Lacan, 1973, p.194)

This is indeed why Kierkegaard can say this singular, and I believe, profoundly correct thing that the woman is more anxiety-ridden than man. How would this be possible, if at this central level anxiety was not constructed precisely, and as such, from the relationship to the desire of the Other. (Lacan, 2004, p. 383)

Diaphany: I would like to say something about anxiety as well. I recall that I first felt anxiety when I was born. No, I did not long for the hushed environment of my mother's womb. Rather, I became anxious at the moment when I realised that I was in process of being born, because I knew that once it started I would not be able to stop it. It would lead me into a beginning that would also have an end: breathing and sucking. I imagine that one may feel anxiety on the verge of bungee jumping. Some people, it seems, even look for this kind of anxiety because they know that the danger is only apparent. But, suppose there is no rubber band... All forms of anxiety reduce to this basic fear. They are warnings against an imminent danger, actual or imaginary. I suppose that death is something like this too, a process that you will not be able to stop, except that it is too general to be so unpleasant, I think. And after that... Gee, I don't know. According to Joyce there is no 'after'; the end is the beginning. The first line of Finnegan's Wake is a continuation of the last one, so that you can start reading the book at any page. In fact, how could I feel anxious at my birth if I did not already know the process? Indeed, Freud says that 'mental processes are not time-ordered, time does not modify them and the idea of time cannot be applied to them'. (Freud, 1950, p. IV) When I radicalise this statement, I conclude that birth and death are the same and life is a time-less dream. This makes me more anxious. So I try to avert my thinking and do what Freud did: I do not apply this statement to my own mental processes. I say with him that 'the objective of life is death' (Freud, 1950, p. V) and that 'inanimate things existed before the living ones' (ibid.), so that I can rebuild the time interval between birth and death and recover it as my *life-span* where I can act, where I can go to work every morning and where I can lose myself into life. I only feel anxious when Mr. Smith's threats remind me of the danger of life in his mathematics class. Then I realise that anxiety is deeply rooted in my human nature and that trying to 'cure' it amounts to 'curing' life itself.

> The ego recognises that the satisfaction of an emerging driving demand would recreate a dangerous situation still vivid in the memory. (Freud, 1933, p. XXXII)

> Anxiety (*Angst*) has an undeniable relation to *expectation*: it is the anxiety in face of something (*vor etwas*). (Freud, 1936, p. XIB)

> It is not nostalgia for what is called the maternal womb, which engenders anxiety, it is its imminence, it is everything that … will allow us to glimpse that we are going to re-enter it. (Lacan, 2004, p. 67)

From these three fragments we infer the main proposition that joins mathematics and anxiety: the danger is the anger of not being able to stop giving something out being elevated to the dimension of a vital danger: consummating life and re-entering the womb through death. We think that this is what Freud called the death drive.

Diaphany: Now, as for maths anxiety. It is all the same: once you start a calculation, there is only one way to finish it correctly. You cannot deviate from the multiplication tables. The end is identical to the beginning. I remember that my mother used to take me to elementary school every day. She seemed very eager for me to succeed, perhaps because she did not complete high school herself. She almost came into the classroom with me. Then she would leave me at the mercy of Mrs. Smith's desire. She was my elementary school teacher for many years. When I got my answers right she would make the questions more and more difficult until I got one wrong. Then she would tell me to sit down. I could never guess what she finally wanted from me. Whenever she called me I knew that this situation would repeat itself. If I did well I would get a crumb of her love. But did I really want it? I felt squeezed between the beginning and the end of the situation and there was no space left for me to act out some diversionary strategy. She looked so perfect… and whenever I thought of an answer she would already have it in her mind so she would never lose track of what I was thinking.

> What is most anxiety-provoking for the child, is that precisely this relation of lack on which she establishes herself, which makes her desire, this relation is all the more disturbed when there is no possibility of lack, when the mother is always on her back, and specially by whipping her bottom. Anxiety is not the signal of a lack but of something that you must manage to conceive of at this redoubled level as being the absence of this support of the lack. (Lacan, 2004, p. 66)

If Mrs. Smith had posed her questions in such a way that Diaphany could think that she was asking for help in order to find the answers, Diaphany would have a chance to adjust her own vacillation to Mrs. Smith's and to work out the problem together with the teacher. But if the Other's demand is sharply a 'how much is it?' and everybody around knows the answer, there is no lack, no vacillation in the desire of the Other, and the subject has to come out and produce herself as meaning. It is the lack of the possibility of dropping out from the scene. (Lacan, 1973, p. 199)

> One lack is superimposed on the other. The dialectic of the objects of desire, in so far as it creates the link between the desire of the subject and the desire of the Other ... now passes through the fact that the desire is not replied directly. It is a lack engendered from the previous time that serves to reply to the lack raised by the following time. (Lacan, 1973, p.195)

Briefly, when the lack lacks, anxiety starts. Indeed, the object of desire is waiting for Diaphany at the end of the path made by Mrs. Smith questions. But was it success? Was it a crumb of love? Or was it something else that Diaphany could not identify but that it made her anxious whenever she got too close to it? What causes anxiety is not so much the loss of a object of desire, but the proximity of a true unknown one. Sexual drives are implied here.

> And to pass to the love of the super-ego with everything that it is supposed to impose along what is called the path of failure, what does the fact that objects are not lacking mean if not that what is feared is success, it is always the 'it is not missing' (*ça ne manque pas*). (Lacan, 2004, p. 67)

Diaphany: I envied the boys who could cope with the maths teacher's desire. They certainly did not repress what Freud called 'life drive'. When they made a mistake, they could deal with their doubt: they stopped, checked and corrected the error. Through acting they could avoid anxiety. For me it felt different, I avoided raising my hand or going to the chalkboard. I did not realise that I was repressing my phonetic and scopic drives: I should not speak, I should not be seen. Very soon the repressed material returned under the form of a symptom: I became unable to carry out calculations in public. When I made a mistake I became paralysed and could not express myself. This symptom extended to other situations in my life and I had to resort to psychoanalysis to be able to express all I am saying here.

> Doubt is there only to combat anxiety and precisely all the effort that doubt expends, is against lures. It is in the measure of that what it is a matter of avoiding is the dimension of appalling certainty that is in anxiety… To act, is to tear its certainty from anxiety. To act is to operate a transfer of anxiety. (Lacan, 2004, p. 92)

Once a certain amount of anxiety is installed at the beginning of a maths course, whatever the student does to deal with the subject matter, to solve the exercises and study for the final exams, all the questions s/he makes in class or privately to the teacher, in one word, his/her *strategy*, may be understood as a way of dealing with anxiety. 'In this essential economy of desire, what does this sort of privileged desire which I call the desire of the analyst represent?' (Lacan, 2004. p. 68)

Diaphany's monologue allows us to lay the basic lines of our approach to maths anxiety in the classroom. In Evans (2000), in spite of the extension of the treatment given to emotions, there are only a few pages about pedagogy and practice and he suggests an approach based on the building of a 'friendly environment'. This suggests that some empathy and certain styles of behaviour are expected from the teacher. Breen's (2000) report of his response in a course is evocative here. In some friendly environments students are asked to speak about their feelings of anxiety and to share their emotions. Such strategies however echo the procedures of maths anxiety questionnaires such as MARS. In psychoanalysis this is called *acting out*. When it happens on the couch, the analyst simply says: all you are saying is true, but it does not touch the question. Breen (2000) and all attempts that we know to deal with maths anxiety in classrooms are based on one idea: *love*. According to J-A Miller there are two paths between desire and jouissance: one passes through love, the other through jouissance.

> The path of love is, classically, in Freud, as Lacan pointed out, a path of deception, inasmuch as love is entrenched in narcissism. It is on this base that Lacan's aphorism, according to which anxiety is what does not deceive, stands out. ... On the horizon, one finds a perfect love, whose realisation is accomplished through an intersubjective agreement imposing its harmony on the thorn nature that supports it. On the slope of anxiety it is not a question of intersubjective agreement, or of the imposition of any harmony. ... It is thus not agreement that counts, but rather what anxiety means, namely strangeness, disaccord, perturbation. (Miller, 2006, pp. 29-30)

Diaphany: I recall that when I was very little, I was afraid of the dark. Instead of leaving a dim light on during the night, my mother used to take me in her lap and walk with me across the room, asking me to touch and recognise objects and shadows. When I grew a little more, I enjoyed myself playing this game alone.

If maths anxiety has already been generated along the history of the subject and symptoms are already present, it is useless to try to suppress them following the path of love because anxiety will maintain its repressive force and the repressed material will emerge as symptoms. What we have to do is to reopen the situation that produced the anxiety and support the subject in redressing his/her dealing with the Other's desire. As a consequence we face a completely different perspective. We contend that maths anxiety as 'a route of access to the real' is not to be suppressed as a symptom but to the contrary, it is to be used to provide access to genuine mathematical *jouissance*. For Lacan, love does not short-circuit Miller's two paths from desire to jouissance. In one aphorism: *maths anxiety is not to be avoided, it is rather to be loved.*

WHAT IS MATHEMATICS?

The formula that we have proposed 'to love maths anxiety' has to be carefully digested. Anxiety about what? What precisely is the source of this anxiety that has to be 'loved'? Of course, it is anxiety about 'mathematics'. But what do we actually mean by 'mathematics'? The question 'what is mathematics?' has often been treated in the literature. For instance, Restivo (1992) takes this question up and surveys some other positions about it from a sociological point of view in a chapter entitled 'mathematics as representation'. Since we are making an effort to approach this question by way of Lacanian theory, the word 'representation' will have a different and specific meaning that we have to make clear from the beginning. For us, it is not 'knowledge' or 'mathematics' that is represented, it is the person, the self, the *subject* who is constituted in so far as he/she makes himself *represented through signifiers*, briefly, insofar as he/she talks; and talking presupposes a community of listeners. This point is important if our attempted answer is expected to make any sense.

We approach the issue from a teacher's perspective. What are we asked to do as mathematics teachers? Are we not supposed to 'teach' the students that one arrow plus one arrow make two arrows even when I miss both shots? And that a python and a duck make two 'animals' despite all contrary evidence? Mathematics teaching is without doubt the introduction of students into a severely restrictive type of language. When students get a feel of our intentions, anxiety is a normal consequence. They foresee a process that they will not be able to stop once it has started. They are supposed not only to believe and abide by the results of processes like finger-counting, but they are expected to make the introduction of their own selves into social life to depend on such processes. We expect them to be sure, we expect them to say: 'I know it is right because I checked it'.

However, what is this 'checking' that appears to be so precious in the world of mathematics? We think of it as a series of tautologies, one goes from line to line, step by step, just checking that indeed the 2+2 on the left is the 4 on the right, that the A that we wrote earlier is the same A that we have written now. To be blunt, checking reduces to checking that A=A. Common sense is so used to this identity that it may seem that we are saying that Mathematics is the art of stating the obvious. However, let us briefly consider the abstraction process that led to such a feeling of obviousness. We smile if somebody says: 'I have three brothers, John, Philip and I'. But the statements 'God is God', 'I am myself', 'I am I' and finally I=I sound less and less strange. So, A=A is not an eternal obviousness; it is as cultural as 1+1=2 and by no means trivial. From this perspective it appears that, as mathematics teachers we are expected to raise the students into the 'normality' of understanding the tautology A=A, so that they feel confident making themselves represented as subjects by this new signifier A=A and everything it implies or condenses. Ferreira (1997) indicates the reluctance of Brazilian Indians to make themselves represented by such tautologies.

> What the white men actually think is more important than adding or subtracting. (Ferreira, 1997, p. 135)

How might our students 'avoid' the anxiety of making their social self dependent on such a narrow basis? Accepting as natural the results of the short circuit introduced in natural speech by asserting that A=A is by no means a trivial educational operation. This very assertion generates anxiety. We have found students, some of them rather bright, who have refused to accept it. When stimulated by 'if A is B then B is...' they do not conclude that B is A and continue searching for a possible meaning of B in the problem where the situation emerged. Even when we insist and their friends collaborate, it still takes some weeks until they accept 'naturally' that 'if A is B then B is A'. But it seems that they cannot avoid smiling. According to Lacanian theory the obsessive subjects are always trying to find a hidden meaning underneath the signifiers: B has to mean something else... They refuse the idea of being represented themselves by A=A.

Embarking on an irreversible process provokes anxiety, but in this case, embarking on A=A produces an additional element; it is a fear, the fear of being wrong, a fear well known to mathematicians. What if I make a mistake and my claim does not hold? Fingers will point at me! Fear has a specific object. Anxiety's object is more difficult to discern. It is what Lacan calls the object-a. Loving maths anxiety means that we do not want to avoid anxiety. Rather we shall use anxiety itself to rebuild the subjects' relation to the Other's desire, to help them in finding their way towards their always receding and never reachable object of desire.

The fear of being wrong became manifest in a very dramatic fashion at the beginning of last Century in the form of the philosophical paradoxes, the most famous of which is Russell's. After Russell presented his paradox 'the set of all sets that do not belong to themselves', mathematicians made efforts to mend their science by introducing language conventions that led to the elaboration of several set theories, but they retained the hope that a paradox-free system could be found. In 1934 Gödel, however, showed that this hope was vain and that, once self-reference of the signifier was admitted, one could not be sure that paradoxes would not emerge, even in arithmetic statements.

The emergence of such paradoxes was no accident. This formula, A=A had already been considered by Hegel in 1816. In a score of splendid dialectical pages he showed that whoever argues that 'A=A is the first law of thinking', necessarily contradicts him/herself. He shows that in the enunciation, the statement reverses its meaning and denies itself. He concludes that 'these laws contain more than it is meant by them, namely, this opposite – Absolute Difference itself'. (Hegel, 1929, II, p. 43) People who are used to the logic of simple understanding might think that the dialectical inversion proved by Hegel implies that A=A ceases to be a basic law of thinking. Not at all, what dialectics shows us is that thinking has, for its basis, a contradictory law or, at least, a law that cannot be sustained without incurring in contradiction. We infer that mathematics contains built-in contradictions and if Bertrand Russell had not found his paradox in Frege's work it would have emerged sooner or later elsewhere.

The implications that this view of mathematics may have for mathematics education, and specially to issues of maths anxiety, may become clearer now. The identity A=A is an expression of the identity of beginning and end, of birth and death that we indicated above as the fundamentally dangerous situation that sounds the anxiety alarm in life.

In order to do justice to Lacan we feel obliged to locate the spot where we went to sample such ideas. Thus the rest of this section will be rather technical and may

I LOVE MATHS ANXIETY

be skipped, unless the reader is interested in a short introduction to Lacanian signifier theory.

So, pursuing our question 'what is mathematics?' we consider Lacan himself who says:

> Mathematics can only be constituted from the fact that the signifier is capable of signifying itself. The A that you have once written may be signified by its repetition of A. This position is strictly unsustainable, it constitutes a violation to the rule of the function of the signifier that may signify anything, except, certainly, itself. One must free oneself from this initial postulate so that mathematical discourse can inaugurate itself'. (Lacan, 1991, p.103)

Briefly, the formula of the simple identity A=A is the first hallmark of mathematics. Signifier is a central concept for Lacan: 'The signifier is distinguished from the sign by the fact that sign is what represents something for someone, but the signifier represents a subject for another signifier'. (Lacan, 2004, p. 77) In order to make this statement clear we stress that it should be read as: 'the signifier represents a subject for another signifier which represents a subject for another signifier, which...' A signifier only exists in the presence of at least another one: S_1 represents the subject to S_2. The very word 'signifier' only has a meaning when a subject is in the action of representing him/herself. Through this act of representation the 'subject' becomes, or can be recognised as, a human subject. Signifier is a concept of language, understood in all its aspects, starting with spoken language and including a language of the body. Any word of this text is a signifier in so far as it represents its authors to the code of signifiers known as Twentieth-First-Century-English-Mathematics-Education, which, in this case, is what Lacan calls the big Other.

The identity A=A expels the subject: no meaning can be derived from a representation of A before A. 'God is God' does not add any meaning to what one understands by 'God'. However, to make oneself represented by the identity 'A=A', to proclaim that 'obviously A is A', to declare that A=A is a basic law of thinking or still, to sustain that 'God is God' is by no means meaningless. To take 'A=A' or 'God is God' as S_1 and to make oneself represented by this new signifier, implies the subject in the field of mathematics in the first case and of religion in the second.

Thus we have provided one answer to the terrible question: what is mathematics? *Mathematics is the discourse in which A=A functions as signifier* S_1 and the mathematician is the subject who makes him/herself represented by this new inaugural signifier. This fabrication of new signifiers from old ones through 'definitions' is characteristic of twentieth-century mathematics. All the history of mathematical discoveries shows that it has not always been so. Hence, Mathematics and religion may be said to have a common root in language.

One has to get rid of this initial postulate of the signifier in order that the mathematical discourse may be inaugurated. The most severe consequence of such violation is that it leads directly into the several forms of the paradox of self-reference. The most famous is Russell's paradox that destroyed Frege's hope of

75

having found a complete language for mathematics. One of the most popular versions is that of the barber who shaves everyman who does not shave himself. [1]

As a consequence, there are two basic ways of dealing with anxiety once it is installed through A=A, that is, two ways of passing into action, of 'losing oneself into life' as Diaphany said. One of the ways is to assume A=A as a new signifier and try to avoid consequent paradoxes. This way leads to mathematics and science, it is the route of metonymic definitions of 20th Century Mathematics inaugurated by Cauchy's 'on dit que…' (one says that…). The other way is to systematically refuse A=A as a signifier and to avoid the attachment of signifier to meaning through endless metaphoric chains. This is the route to literature, poetry and art.

THE CLASSROOM ORGANIZATION

To the reader who has followed us thus far it has become evident that we are not going to propose a therapy consisting of diagnosis, treatment and evaluation. If overcoming the effects of maths anxiety requires a repeated back and forth movement from the normal polysemic everyday use of words into the narrow realm of self-referential signifiers, diagnosis, treatment and evaluation have to occur simultaneously in direct contact with the student. So we proceed to describe how we set up the classroom situation so as to allow this contact.

In Baldino (1997) and Baldino & Cabral (1998a, 1998b, 1999) we have justified the organization of our college-level classrooms into a form of pedagogy that we call *solidarity assimilation groups* (SAG) as an alternative to current traditional teaching (CTT). In CTT as well as in SAG the class starts when the teacher rests his/her briefcase on the table. Already in this initial moment the school institution has determined teacher and student positions. The teacher certainly occupies the position of what Lacan calls the *subject* (who is) *supposed to know* (*sujet supposé savoir*). The teacher is supposed to know, not only the subject matter, but also how to lead the course to its final moment, when a verdict has to be made on each student regarding the fulfilment of the institutional requirements. Lacan says that wherever there is a subject supposed to know, transference has already started. Transference is a demand for/an offer of love. Here we are dealing only with pedagogical transference since we are bound by the ethics of our position as teachers. (Wilson explores such boundaries later on in this book.) Pedagogical transference is the attempt that the student makes to convince the teacher that he or she has exactly what the student misses in terms of knowledge of the syllabus. From the side of the teacher pedagogical transference means to supply the students lack of knowledge by climbing the platform and providing a clear explanation. Love is to give what one does not have, says Lacan. The student gives the teacher his/her attention and the teacher gives his/her knowledge back. None have either. Lacan says that love is a specular mirage that is essentially deceiving. Pedagogical transference is not different; very soon the teacher will be required to 'control' the class and will be made responsible for 'motivating' the students. So, pedagogical transference has to be dealt with.

In this first moment, in both, CTT and SAG, the teacher is just an empty figure supported by his/her relative lack of resources, subjected to the students' demand of filling their knowledge gaps. Both, teacher and students, are supposed to sustain a situation where mathematics appears as an object of desire. Lacan calls this situation the *discourse of the master.* Here CTT and SAG start moving in different directions.

In the next step the CTT teacher responding to students' demands, starts talking and makes the students his/her object of desire. He/ she is supported by his/her precarious authority granted by the institution. Students and teacher are supposed to produce a kind of unsatisfiable desire for knowledge. This situation is the *university discourse.* In the third step mathematics, as an object of desire produced in the first step, is called for the unsatisfiable desire for knowledge supposedly produced in the second step. Mathematics is well grounded on knowledge previously produced and the joint enterprise is supposed to produce a verdict of right or wrong and correct answers to the exercises that have carried out. This situation is the *discourse of the analyst,* or, in our case, the discourse of the teacher. Finally in CTT's fourth step the unlimited desire for knowledge of the student supposedly produced in the university's discourse, is subjected to an anguishing demand: what do you know? This is the moment when one confronts the prospect of final exams. The student is supported by mathematics, supposedly his/her object of desire, while the whole enterprise is centred to produce a subject supposed to know, made as an image based on similarity to the teacher. This is the *discourse of the hysterics.* This name alludes to some of the students' productions in their final exams, such as Iskios' that we will report below. In one word, through these four steps, the discourses of the master, the university, the analyst and the hysterics, CTT seeks the identification of the student to the teacher by sustaining pedagogical transference as a love relation.

In SAG we reverse the order of these speeches. The second step is the discourse of the hysterics, but now the classroom is organised in groups, the teacher circulates among them sustaining the questions made in a worksheet. The teacher does not explain, he/she poses questions and deals with pedagogical transference from the beginning. When the students ask: 'May I do it this way?' the teacher simply answers: 'If it is correct yes, if it is wrong, no; check it'. The students thus lose their habitual grounds within transference relations and are directed to their peers for support. They are pressed to find support for mathematics as their object of desire and the whole enterprise is aimed at producing collective knowledge. The students only go to the front of the class when the subject has already been sufficiently worked out by the groups and they make very short expositions.

In the third step the discourse of the analyst is installed, so that the students having supposedly developed a desire for knowledge that cannot be satisfied, check their previous mathematical knowledge, seek to support it in the textbook and produce a verdict of right or wrong. This is done during the semester, in weekly tests.

Finally, in the fourth step the university discourse is installed, with the difference that now the students are the ones who speak. Groups on the platform tell their findings to their peers. What this activity is supposed to produce is precisely the unsatisfiable curious subject that CTT failed to produce in its second step.

We are not saying that SAG turns the classroom into a paradise on Earth. There are difficulties, the whole process has to be introduced slowly through negotiations but some principles cannot be negotiated, the working rules have to be clear to the groups and penalties hit whole groups or the whole class, never individuals. Oppositions have to be democratically defeated in plenary meetings occurring at the end of each class where everybody has the right to speak freely, though during a limited time. We could not dispense with written finals, however, as our classroom organisation has not yet produced a sufficient level of mutual commitment among students so as to naturally exclude students copying from each other. If our classroom organisation were strong enough, with sufficient mutual commitment, the students would control each other so as to be sure that no one left the room without an adequate understanding. They would not tolerate a peer who is just sitting back and copying. They would eliminate corporative tendencies among them and take learning as their honour. In this case we would be sure that the classroom environment would have led them to the best possible level of learning. In this case it would be useless to establish further control and exams could be dropped.

The whole SAG process rests on an aphorism driven from Lacanian psychoanalysis: *it is by listening that one teaches and it is by talking that one learns*. Listening means to let oneself be hypnotized by what the student says, to follow his/her reasoning up to the point where we can say: Aha! Now I understand what you are saying. Only at this moment can we make an intervention, make a question or suggest a way out. This can also be understood through the work of Carl Rogers, except that we are not, like him, participating in a general educational or developmental process. Rather we *select* what we hear from the student so as to keep it within the bounds of the mathematics classroom and to constantly rebuild the insertion of the mathematical object between student and teacher.

> If the transference is that which separates demand from drive, the analyst's desire is that which brings it back. And in this way it isolates the *a*, places it at the largest possible distance from the I that he, the analyst, is called upon by the subject to embody. It is from this idealization that the analyst has to fall in order to be the support of the separating *a*, in so far as his desire allows him, in an upside-down hypnosis, to embody, himself, the hypnotized one. (Lacan, 1973, p. 245)

SAG classroom organization has provided the framework and data for several research reports (Baldino & Cabral, 2002, 2004, 2005, 2006; Cabral, 2004; Carvalho & Cabral, 2003; Walshaw & Cabral, 2005). Recently we have adopted an additional strategy to deal with classes of repeat students. Since these classes occur in sixty 50-minutes meetings we organise the teacher input so as to cover the whole syllabus in the first 15 meetings, ending with a written examination. Those who pass do not need to continue. The process is then repeated in the next three sets of 15-meetings. In this way, at the end the only remaining students are those that: 1) have severe difficulties with the subject and 2) persevere!

This was the situation from which we extract the reports that follow. They refer to mathematics classes within an engineering program on digital systems provided by a multi-campus public university founded in 2002 whose establishment and functioning remains somewhat precarious. The first report, Maria, was written up immediately after the class (November, 16, 2006) and only slightly modified her. The second report, Iskios, is reproduced from memory shortly after the encounters between January 15 and 31, 2007 in a special course for repeaters. The first report deals with spoken, the second with written students' productions.

MARIA

Maria had to laugh ... and when she laughed her grey-green eyes sparkled with disappointed shyness and the tip of her nose nearly met the tip of her chin. (Joyce, 2000, p. 83)

We commence by focusing on a class on analytical geometry for repeaters on November 16. Maria asks to have another attempt at the drawing of conics. We suggest. She looks dismayed and somewhat upset, realizing that she had been through this several times in previous classes, but she still does not know how to complete the squares.

1. Teacher: There is not much I can do about this. You have to find your way out.

After some attempts she had written:

$3(x-3)^2 - 27 + (y+2.5)^2 - 6.25 = 60$. She then reached for her pocket calculator.

2. Teacher: No calculators please; use only ordinary fractions. How did you get these decimals? Replace them with fractions.

3. After a while she had written:

$3(x-3)^2 + (y+2.5)^2 = 60 + 27 + \dfrac{25}{4} = 87 + \dfrac{25}{4}$ and got stuck.

4. Teacher: This is your old trouble isn't it?
5. Maria: Yes.

Now she makes a face that clearly indicates stress. We try to encourage her to face the problem but she seems more and more distressed.

6. Teacher: Well, let us see... how many quarters are there in: 87?
7. Maria: (No answer.)
8. Teacher: How many quarters are there in 5?
9. This takes her one or two minutes, but she comes out with 20. She was cheered a little and looked less unhappy.

10. Teacher: And how many quarters are there in 87?

11. After a while she writes $\dfrac{348}{4}$ and continues her calculation:

12. $$3(x-3)^2 + (y+2.5)^2 = \dfrac{373}{4}$$

13. Teacher: Well, what do you have to do now to put this under the form $\dfrac{(x-x_0)^2}{a^2} + \dfrac{(y-y_0)^2}{b^2} = 1$ and make this 1 appear here on the right handside.

14. Maria: I have to divide by this... on both sides.

15. She indicates the operations and writes: $\dfrac{3(x-3)^2}{\dfrac{373}{4}} + \dfrac{(y+2.5)^2}{\dfrac{373}{4}} = 1$

16. Maria: What now? I should have squares here.
Her voice and face indicate more of a meditation than simple dismay.

17. Teacher: (Immediately, writing the question down:) Three is the square of what?

18. She looks surprised; a peer asks her:

19. Peer: Don't you know?

20. Maria: (Smiles) No...

21. Teacher: (To the other student:) Psst. (Always writing the question down:) Twelve is the double of what?

22. Maria: (Almost immediately) Of 6.

23. Teacher: Seven is the double of what?

24. Maria: (Timidly:) Of three and a half.

25. Teacher: Thirteen is the triple of what?

26. Maria: (She thinks for a while and talks more to herself:) I have to divide by three. (And to all:) Thirteen over three.

27. Teacher: 'a' is the triple of what?

28. Maria: (Writes) $\dfrac{a}{3}$ (She seems sure and looks happy.)

29. Teacher: (Points at the initial question) Three is the square of what?

30. Maria: (She looks surprised as she answers:) Square root of three!!!

31. And she starts laughing. She laughs and laughs as her whole tiny body shakes. Then she stops laughing for a second.

32. Teacher: Why do you laugh?

33. Maria: (Looks surprised at the question and restarts laughing convulsively; finally:) How come we did not realize...
Of course, everybody had realized, except her.

I LOVE MATHS ANXIETY

34.   Teacher: Do you drive?
35.   Maria: I used to, sometime ago...
36.   Teacher: Did you do well in backing up?
37.   Maria: (Smiles) No!
38.   Teacher: Who is the father of John's son?
39.   She looks thoughtful.
40.   Peer: Don't you know who is the father of John's son?
41.   Teacher: Psst.
42.   Maria: It is John!
43.   And she laughs again, but no so much. She looks thoughtful.

Comments on Maria

Reading a previous version of this chapter one reader exclaimed: 'When I came to this point, I had a very strong reaction. Until now, the discussion has been radically challenging. Now I see standard mathematics, exactly like what I did at school 50 years ago. What is learning stuff like this for? In other words, I see a mismatch between the deconstruction (if that's the right word) of the interpersonal relations in teaching/learning and the apparent acceptance of the status quo in what is being taught/learnt'.

Aha! In spite of all our warnings and all the introduction to Lacan that we provided, this reader kept the secret hope that Lacanian theory would serve his cherished purpose of freeing students from the harsh mathematical situations that he experienced as a youngster. He seemingly did not take it seriously when we told him that it is a theory about him: it could indicate why his private enjoyment (*jouissance*) is thinking of it in terms of 'deconstruction'. Besides, we are not reporting an off-class experience or interview situation. We are describing a real maths class within a real engineering program, constrained by a syllabus, by an adopted textbook and by the vigilance of colleagues who teach the subsequent courses. Furthermore, the fact that we are dealing with 'standard mathematics' is irrelevant in order to make our point about anxiety as we shall see.

Line 1 is a typical Lacanian cut technique. It is the moment when the psychoanalytical session is broken and the subject is left alone to think about his/her production. Here this moment occurs at the beginning of the class.

In line 2 we used our previous knowledge of Maria's strategy to deal with these problems and for the first time we insisted that she did something differently. We pushed her directly into her zone of conflict. She could not refuse, once she had implicitly admitted that her old strategy of avoiding fractions by substituting them by their decimal representation had not worked thus far.

In line 14 she shows that she is finally using the method that we had urged her to learn for dealing with algebraic equations, operating simultaneously on both sides instead of 'passing' from one member to the other.

In lines 3 to 5 the anguish is recovered. We imagine that she recalled childhood scenes where she was required to pass from numbers to letters or, at least, speak about the operations she was carrying out with numbers in order to reach higher levels of abstraction. As she faced difficulties, she was allowed to reinforce her calculating abilities with decimals as an alternative way of solving the problems aimed at pedagogical instruction. Indeed, it is a well-established 'culture' in upper class Brazilian schools where personal creative solutions are appreciated so that students can boast: I passed without having to learn all of that. Maria was probably a victim of this sort of 'culture'. The teaching of methods is not enforced so that she ended up with no fractional and, consequently, with poor algebraic abilities. Besides, her gesture to reach the calculator seemed symptomatic in character, perhaps indicating that some material had already been repressed. However, she apparently kept longing for a way of carrying out calculations whose existence she knew but which she never understood. So, the question 'This is your old trouble isn't it?' led her to the edge of a toboggan run at the end of which her small-a object waited for her under disguise. Affect is never repressed, it just moves elsewhere. This is why she asked to go back to the question of drawing conics, where this calculation intervenes crucially.

All these are conjectures. We are in a regular classroom, which has limits that we cannot change readily. If it were in a psycho-pedagogic clinic such conjectures would be called *interpretations*. Freud used to suggest them to his patients. Some of his conjectures became accepted, others were discarded by the patient as the treatment went on. In Lacanian clinic this practice is abandoned and substituted by the cut technique. The patient is led to elaborate his/her own conclusions under adequate marks inserted by the analyst into his/her speech. What we do from lines 6 to 30 is to follow a stepwise path from question to question. Each question is like a cut where Maria has to elaborate something by herself and produce it. The process is guided by a pre-established endpoint, and here it completely breaks apart from the model of the psychoanalytic clinic.

The way that we treated the apparent anxiety in line 5 should be emphasised. We acted like Diaphany's other in the dark room: Maria was never left alone. The teacher and, in most cases, her peers, knew the answers of the questions that were being posed. At each question, however, she was given time to recover her balance and she knew that if she could not find the answer, an 'easier' question would be posed, rather akin to the funnelling process described by various researchers (e.g. Brousseau & Otte, 1991). That is, a question would be forthcoming that could be answered within the domain of decimal notation where she felt more comfortable. It was as if she was asked to recognise familiar objects in a dark room, namely, numbers. She could multiply 87 by 4 to find out how many quarters there were, she mentally divided 12 and 7 by 2 and 13 by 3 to find out the double or the triple of what they were. At this point she was able to name the number without calculating it 'thirteen over three' and this was accepted as an answer by the Other. Next, the $a/3$ that answered the question 'a is the triple of what?' made her sure that the names of the numbers could just as well serve as an answer instead of their decimal expressions. Finally, she realised that the question '3 is the square root of what?' could be answered by the name of the number square-root of three, not necessarily by 1.73205... which she had been seeking to locate through trial and error. But, why did she laugh so much? We will consider this laughing a little more closely as we feel it confirms the success of our teaching method.

First, for a naïve understanding of Maria's laughing we can rely on our metaphor of walking through a dark room. Maria was recognising numerical objects: 348/4, 6, 3.5, ... Then these objects started to become less familiar: 13/3, a/3. Secondly, instead of an object she grabbed the *name of an object*: 'square-root-three'. ... Then a short-circuit seemingly occurred between arithmetic and common language. A signifier was mixed together with things. Indeed this should be most hilarious...

But we can also rely on Freud's *Jokes and their relation to the unconscious* for a more precise remark. Freud says that a joke always requires three people, the teller, the personage about whom the joke is told and who may be absent, and the receiver, who laughs. He says that nobody can laugh alone. Likewise there is no self-psychoanalysis. In this case, how could we refer to him if Maria apparently laughed alone? However, Freud contradicts such understanding in the following excerpt.

> Thought returns for a moment to childhood stage so as to get hold of the infantile source of pleasure once more... The strange unconscious revision is just the kind of infantile activity of thought... whose peculiarities stay repressed in the adult's unconscious. This way of thinking is rectified as if it were in *statu nascendi.* ... Many of my neurotic patients under psychoanalytical treatment, regularly show the habit of confirming a fact through laughing, when I manage to provide them a truthful picture of their unconscious, hidden by conscious perception. (Freud, 1938, p. VI)

Apparently, just as Maria did, Freud's patients also laughed alone. Who is the person about whom the joke is told if only the patient is concerned in Freud's comments? He provides us the answer in the last line: he shows the patients a 'picture of their unconscious'. At the time Freud wrote this paper (1905) he was still based on the first topology, the opposition of conscious and unconscious and this short circuit between them was the insight. Laughing indicated insight. Now it is clear why Maria laughed. We did not present her with a picture of her unconscious but she was led to it through our teaching method. She elaborated the picture herself, just like in a Lacanian clinic. Her conscious perception was on numeric decimals and all the connections to everyday language had been repressed, repressed as drives, we should say, since she kept the desire of recovering them when she asked once more about the drawing of conics.

At this point the reader could ask: 'Why is Maria in this class, given that the teacher has to do so much work to reach solid ground and build up again?' Maria is in this class because there are no alternaitves for her. The engineering program is the only one on this campus. This mathematics class is the only one for repeaters and we are the only mathematics teachers. Besides, we do not think that the teacher's mission includes discouraging students and telling them to look for something else to do. Our university reserves 50% of freshmen places to low income students and 10% to physically handicapped ones. It is our obligation to deal with students like Maria. The reader could ask further: 'Won't the same process have to be gone through every time? I had a reaction here that the teacher is having to go too far down to reach solid ground. Can this work, except locally?' Worse than that, this generally *does not work*, even locally. We never managed to recover more than ten per cent of the students who lack the adequate basis. Maria, for instance, has failed a 2007 calculus course for seven repeaters taught on the same basis. A reader who makes such a question reveals that he keeps the secret hope that Lacan would provide a solution for the afflictive problem of student failure. Indeed, we are also looking for a solution but... may be there is none; if there is one we would like to start it today.

ISKIOS

Iskios entered the University in the first semester of 2006; he passed the first course on calculus and failed the second one. The data for the present report were collected during the special course for repeaters during the summer, in January 2007, taught according to the strategy referred to above. Iskios takes the university in an extremely serious way; he never misses classes and works hard during them. He acquired the nickname 'The Shadow' from his peers, after the 1940s US-radio series character of W. B. Gibson. In the plenary meetings at the end of each class he seriously outlines the doubts that he has encountered. He does this in a spontaneous, almost naïve way that makes everybody laugh. This does not seem to disturb him. He keeps a thick copybook that was almost full at the end of two semesters. He copies the problem statements leaving a delimited blank space and fills them with the solutions as the course goes on. This copybook is apparently somewhat haphazard yet he can quickly relocate specific earlier jottings.

On one occasion we presented him a Möbius' strip and asked him how many sides the surface had. 'Certainly two', he answered, and indicated them with the pen. Then we made him follow the line along the strip until he ran into contradiction. 'I can't believe!' he exclaimed. He had to follow the path several times and was fascinated. 'I never thought that such a thing could exist!' During group work he is obstinate at his own doubts and asks many questions that his peers cannot answer. This hinders the group harmony a little and the teacher's assistance sometimes becomes necessary. He expresses dissatisfaction with female assistance and asks for male support. Once, we casually asked whether he had a job; he explained: 'Yes' and added: 'I live with my mother'. We could not probe further without trespassing our boundaries as teachers. We can only guess that we are dealing with a strongly obsessive character.

The summer calculus course was designed in three daily 50-minutes class periods during four weeks, each week ending by a written final exam. He failed in the first week's final. In the second week, someone confused him with a homonym and informed him that he had passed. He came Monday morning to check and was very disturbed in seeing the actual grading list. We sat down find out what he had done wrong. We pointed to his first mistake, a classical one: $\dfrac{1}{a+b} = \dfrac{1}{a} + \dfrac{1}{b}$ (Figure 1).

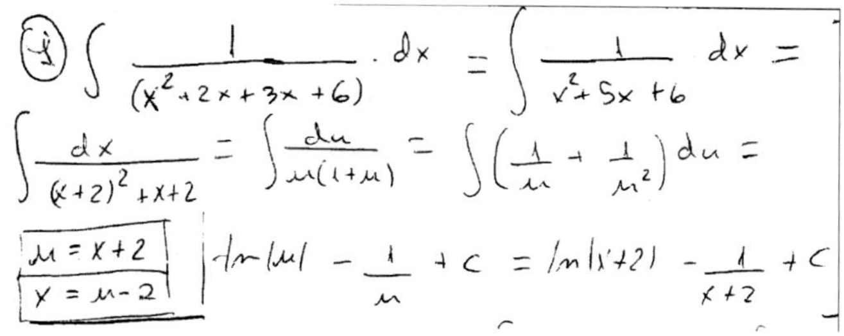

$$\text{①} \int \frac{1}{(x^2+2x+3x+6)} \cdot dx = \int \frac{1}{x^2+5x+6} \, dx =$$

$$\int \frac{dx}{(x+2)^2 + x + 2} = \int \frac{du}{u(1+u)} = \int \left(\frac{1}{u} + \frac{1}{u^2} \right) du =$$

$$\boxed{\begin{array}{c} u = x+2 \\ x = u-2 \end{array}} \quad \ln|u| - \frac{1}{u} + c = \ln|x+2| - \frac{1}{x+2} + c$$

Figure 1. A classical mistake in algebra

The second mistake, although in a more complex situation, was essentially due to his writing

$$\frac{\dfrac{2}{3}}{4}$$

without observing the level of the fraction bars so he got

$$\frac{\dfrac{2}{3}}{4} = \frac{1}{6}$$

instead of

$$\frac{2}{\dfrac{3}{4}} = \frac{8}{3}$$

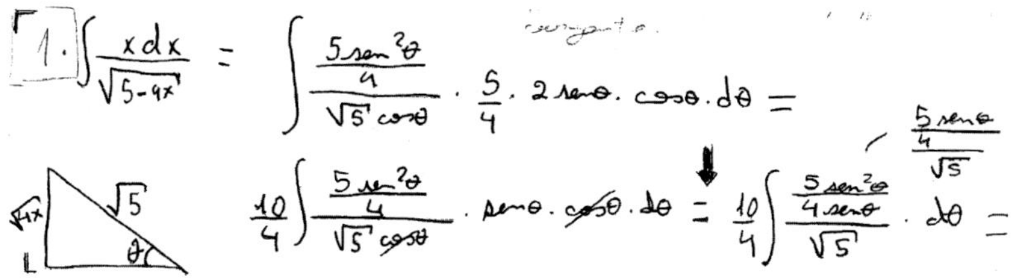

$$\boxed{1.} \int \frac{x \, dx}{\sqrt{5-4x^2}} = \int \frac{\frac{5 \sin^2 \theta}{4}}{\sqrt{5}\cos\theta} \cdot \frac{5}{4} \cdot 2\sin\theta \cdot \cos\theta \cdot d\theta =$$

$$\frac{10}{4} \int \frac{\frac{5 u^2 \theta}{4}}{\sqrt{5}\cos\theta} \cdot \sin\theta \cdot \cos\theta \cdot d\theta = \frac{10}{4} \int \frac{\frac{5 \sin^2 \theta}{4 \sin\theta}}{\sqrt{5}} \cdot d\theta =$$

Figure 2. The level of fraction bars

Iskios: But the development is correct?
Teacher: Yes, your mistake was here. (arrow in Figure 2)
Iskios: This means that if I had not made this mistake the question would be correct:

R.R. BALDINO AND T.C.B. CABRAL

Teacher. Yes. And you would have (checking the scores) almost passed.
In an instance Iskios asked for 'mercy' as freshmen often do. He showed no trait revealing any feeling of injustice. He was visibly stressed, leaning forward, elbows on the table, legs bent back under the chair. He considered his paper gravely and finally said, on the verge of crying:

Iskios: I do not know... This sort of thing has been happening since the first semester... I have tried hard ... what do I have to do? ...

Teacher: It is about your notation. These are elementary questions. As I have been telling you, you will need to redo some of your high school mathematics. Based on our classroom contact I see that you can do more than many students who have already passed...

Iskios: (Very serious) I know.

Teacher: ...but I cannot simply say 'you pass' as this would be unfair to the others. We have to judge everybody on the same footing. You have to produce a written document, an exam as everybody else. This course is not just to support the next ones; it concerns your mathematical development as an engineer and I cannot let you proceed while you are making mistakes like these.

Iskios: (Nod in agreement.)

Teacher: There is no other way out. You still have two weeks to go. You can get more assistance now, since there are fewer students in class.

Our first comment is that we did not ask Iskios if he felt anxiety. We did not ask him to express his feelings of anxiety. We deduced that he was anxious from his bodily expression and we sought to open the valve a little. That is, we showed some vacillation in our desire, saying something like: there is still time for you to do what we are suggesting. We did not follow the path of love, saying something like: don't worry, things will work out, we will help you. The anxiety was preserved. We emphasise that the anxiety arose, was observed and dealt with in a regular classroom situation.

It is clear that for Iskios it was the perspective of failing the course again that generated the anxiety. Courses have a ritual of enrolment and a moment of decision of pass/fail. Enrolling in a course is to enter a process that has a predetermined end and which one cannot abandon after a certain date. The institution naturally provides a miniature of what Diaphany called her 'life-span'. Anxiety is framed, says Lacan.

Someone might ask whether this is maths anxiety of a general nature or merely anxiety specific to the course or teacher. We could reply with another question. Is there maths anxiety without mathematics? Is there maths anxiety in without mathematics courses, teachers, and the attendant institutional dispositions pushing the students towards mathematics? According to MARS, Iskios would probably be classified as not being especially anxious in mathematics. He did not go as far as repressing scopic and vocalic drives, so maths anxiety did not emerge as a symptom. He speaks of mathematics in public and does not hide himself during group work. If Iskios had already reached the stage of symptomatic maths anxiety, we simply would have to be more careful in controlling our own desire.

Comment on Iskios: pas à lire (what cannot be read)

Over a two-week period Roberto worked closely with Iskios one to one. We will discuss his solution to an exam problem at the end the third week, endeavouring to present the discussion in such a way that can be followed by readers unfamiliar with integral calculus. We first stress that we are not dealing with a log resulting from an interview or application of a research questionnaire. We are dealing with a genuine student response in an exam situation within a genuine university course. According to the work contract we face as teachers, we have to assign a grade, which will certainly affect the student's life. Inevitably ethical issues emerge. From the assessment we are also expected to guide the student.

The question is not in a multiple-choice format and there is no doubt that Iskios *wrote* something on his exam sheet. We scanned his work electronically. This is presented in Figure 3. We are expected to grade it, that is, to assign it a number that will represent Iskios chance of passing. In order to do this we must *read* it, interpret it somehow so that it makes some sense to us, say X, then compare this X with what we expected, say X', and translate this comparison into a number from zero to one, say X/X'.

This first difficulty that arises is as to where we should start our reading. Should we commence at the first line? Or should we wait until the final result? Or should we analyse the formula that appears as central in the development? If we start reading from the first line, it seems not to make sense. If we start at the final answer, it is wrong. If we start reading at the formula that looks as though it might be central in the reasoning, we may interpret it as being correct. Since this work was in the context of an open-book exam, Iskios had adapted the solution of a problem that had been worked out in class just as we expected but, in the subsequent calculation, he apparently made a mistake and came out with a wrong result. If he had not written anything else we would not have elements to either confirm or disrupt our interpretation. A closer look, however, shows that this interpretation cannot find support in the surrounding elements. We would say that much of what is written does not make sense.

How did Iskios articulate all this? Should we have required him to write the mathematical statements in a more linear fashion so that it could be unfolded more readily and perhaps read aloud? Or what if we had not, assuming that this is not crucial at the student's apparent developmental stage? Could we call the student in, and ask him to explain what he meant or what he thought when he wrote this all down? We could tape-record whatever he says, decode the tape and *read* it. But this is not what we mean by *reading*. We are supposed to make some sense of what is written, to assign a meaning to it. Calling the student in, we suggest, would only transport the problem elsewhere or even add further difficulties to it.

Questão 2

Determine o campo elétrico produzido no ponto $P(0, y, 0)$ por um anel plano de raio interno a e raio externo b situado no plano xz com centro na origem e carregado com ρ coulombs por metro quadrado.

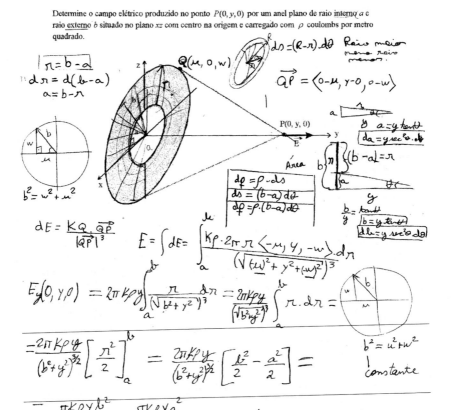

Figure 3. Where should we start our reading?

Our plunge into the apparent non-sense of the student's work has led us to a feeling of vertigo. We encounter what seems to be a rather curious 'logic'. Proceeding along this path we risk not being able to find our way back. At the end of this path our old small *a* object expects us. Anxiety is produced. Trying to make sense of Iskios' writing we conclude that it is more like the product of delirium; or perhaps, a *dream*. Perhaps Freud could help us to recover our balance. His terminology in *Interpretation of Dreams* (Freud, 1932) is perfectly adequate here. If we call Iskios' writing the 'manifest content' and the classroom situation the

I LOVE MATHS ANXIETY

'latent content', our interpretation becomes an attempt to decipher the 'work of the dream' that transformed latent into manifest content. Freud would ask whether this interpretation is true. We suggested it to Iskios and he confirmed it: 'This is the way I thought.' he said. He sustained this view and it took us a great effort until he recognised that something did not work. We would say that it took us a great effort to wake him up.

But now we face a new question. If what the student writes is like the manifest content of a dream, how do we grade it? Can we be just with regard to other students in comparing what Iskios has written to what should have been written? No, whatever the comparison it will be and arbitrary. We would like an assessment method that we could defend publicly, in our classroom plenary sessions. This objectivity cannot be obtained if we stick to X/X'. Indeed, how could we publicly justify the number that we assign to the relation of our personal feeling of understanding to the expected answer? However, if we assume that this relation is given for one student, the question of how we are fair to the others is made easier. We do not have to justify each X/X', we only have to justify the comparison X/X' with Y/Y', from one student to the other. That is, our criterion to assign a number to X/X' may be arbitrary. In fact it depends on how high or low we want the average grade to be, according to the ability that the program finds adequate for further development of the students. What we have to justify is the comparison for different students: applying the criterion uniformly to students, is the highest level of justice that we can attain. Of course, this paragraph concerns our own level of anxiety.

APPENDIX FOR CALCULUS TEACHERS

If, instead of passing over the difficulty, we persist in our efforts to interpret the student's work, we may wonder how he reached the seemingly strange results? It is clearly not a random scattering of marks on paper. It has some 'logic' to it. For instance, there were two concentric circles with radius a and b forming an annulus in the region between them. Iskios called r the difference: $r = b - a$. Nothing is wrong with that. But subsequently he wrote $ds = (R - r)\, d\theta$, a notation that is typical of the expression of the length of an arch subtended by an angle of $d\theta$ radians on a circumference of radius $R - r$. Indeed, he adds that R is the bigger radius and r the smaller one $ds = (b - a)\, d\theta$. Where did he get this from? Our interpretation is that he tried to apply the result of a problem worked out in class, just as we expected him to do; this problem contained the situation $ds = r\, d\theta$ (second part o Figure 4). A radius r has to appear in the exam question so that the connection to a supposedly known result can be established. If two radiuses a and b are given, it seems 'logical' to take their difference $b - a$ as the new required radius. Mathematically, there is nothing wrong with this, except that the result obtained following the calculation will have nothing to do with the original problem. The expected radius *r* should be a variable running from *a* to *b*, which is not the case of the fixed number $b - a$.

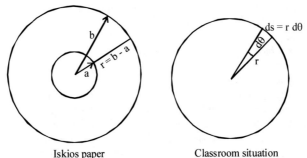

Figure 4. Connecting with a supposedly known result

The question asked the determination of the electric field produced by a uniformly loaded plane ring with radius *a* and *b* at a point situated on the ring axis and distant *y* from its centre.

We expected the student to decompose the thick ring into an infinity of thin infinitesimal rings of thickness *dr* and radius *r* varying from *a* to *b*, and to apply the formula for the field of the thin ring already developed in class, readily available since the exam was open-book (Figure 5).

He only had to consider the second component of the vector $<-u, y, -w>$, because by reasons of symmetry, the other components of the field would be zero. Taking the formula he wrote as the central point was:

$$\int_a^b \frac{K \rho\, 2\pi r <-u, y, -w> dr}{\left(\sqrt{(-u)^2 + y^2 + (-w)^2}\right)}$$

Suppressing the first and third components:

$$\int_a^b \frac{K \rho\, 2\pi r\, y\, dr}{\left(\sqrt{(-u)^2 + y^2 + (-w)^2}\right)}$$

Assuming that $u^2 + w^2 = r^2$, we get

$$\int_{r=a}^b \frac{K \rho\, 2\pi r\, y\, dr}{\sqrt{r^2 + a^2}}$$

This is the formula that we would obtain considering a thin ring of infinitesimal thickness *dr*. Iskios is apparently correct, it is enough to calculate the integral.

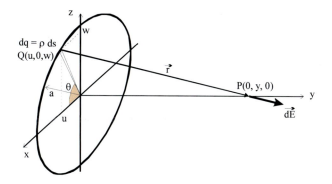

Figure 5. The classroom situation

However this interpretation is not confirmed by the continuation of Iskios' calculations. He actually considered $u^2 + w^2$ as the exterior radius b, the denominator became constant, he pulled it out of the integral. In the first class after the exam we discovered that the word 'decomposition' had no meaning to Iskios or, at least, it did not mean what we expected. We handed him a sheet of paper and asked him to 'decompose' it. He cut off a tiny piece from a corner and handed it to us: 'This is the decomposition'. We worked hard with him, recovering integral calculus from the area concept. In the final exam he achieved the maximum grade and passed.

NOTES

[1] Gödel's second theorem is basically a translation of the barber paradox into an arithmetic proposition.

REFERENCES

Baldino, R. R. (1997). Student strategies in solidarity assimilation groups. In V. Zack, J. Mouseley, & C. Breen (Eds.), *Developing practice: Teachers' inquiry and educational change*. Geelong, Australia: Deakin University.

Baldino, R. R., & Cabral, T. C. B. (2004). Formal inclusion and real diversity in an engineering program of a new public university. In *PME 28* (Vol. 2, pp. 175–182). Bergen: Bergen University College.

Baldino, R. R., & Cabral, T. C. B. (1998a). Lacan's four discourses and mathematics educational credit system. *Chreods*, *13*, 45–59. Retrieved from http://s13a.math.aca.mmu.ac.uk

Baldino, R. R., & Cabral, T. C. B. (1998b). Lacan and the school's credit system. In *PME 22* (Vol. 2, pp. 56–63). Stellenbosch: Bellvillle.

Baldino, R. R., & Cabral, T. C. B. (1999). Lacan's four discourses and mathematics education. In *PME 23* (Vol. 2, pp. 56–63). Haifa: Technion Institute.

Baldino, R. R., & Cabral, T. C. B. (2002). Lacanian psychoanalysis and pedagogical transfer: Affect and cognition. In *PME 26* (Vol. 2, pp. 169–176). Norwich: University of East Anglia-UK.

Baldino, R. R., & Cabral, T. C. B. (2005). Situations of psychological cognitive no-growth. In *PME 29* (Vol. 2, pp. 105–112). Melbourne: University of Melbourne.

Baldino, R. R., & Cabral, T. C. B. (2006). Inclusion and diversity from Hegel and Lacan point of view: Do we desire our desire for change? *International Journal of Science and Mathematics Education*, *4*, 19–43.

Breen, C. (2000). Becoming more aware: Psychoanalytical insights concerning fear and relationship in the mathematics classroom. In *PME 24* (Vol. 2, pp. 105–112). Hiroshima: Hiroshima University.

Brousseau, G., & Otte, M. (1991). The fragility of knowledge. In A. Bishop, S. Mellin-Olsen, & J. van Dormolen (Eds.), *Mathematical knowledge: Its growth through teaching* (pp. 13–36). Dordrecht: Kluwer.

Brown, T., Atkinson, D., & England, J. (2006). *Regulatory discourses in education, a Lacanian perspective*. Oxford: Peter Lang.

Cabral, T. C. B. (2004). Affect and cognition in pedagogical transference: A Lacanian perspective. In M. Walshaw. (Ed.), *Mathematics education within the postmodern*. Greenwich, CT: Information Age Publishing Inc.

Carvalho, A. M. F. T. de, & Cabral, T. C. B. (2003). Teacher and students: Setting up the transference. *For the Learning of Mathematics*, *23*(2), 11–15.

Evans, J. (2000). *Adult mathematical thinking and emotions*. London: Routledge.

Ferreira, M. K. L. (1997). When $1 + 1 \neq 2$: Making mathematics in central Brazil. *American Ethnologist*, *24*(1), 137–147.

Freud, S. (1932). *Interpretation of dreams*. London: Allen & Unwin.

Freud, S. (1933). *New introductory lectures on psychoanalysis, 1933*. London: Hogarth Press.

Freud, S. (1936). *Inhibitions symptoms and anxiety, 1926*. London: Hogarth Press.

Freud, S. (1938). *Wit and its relation to the Unconscious, 1905*. New York: Random House.

Freud, S. (1950). *Beyond the Pleasure Principle, 1920*. London: Hogarth Press.

Hegel, G, W. F. (1929). *Science of logic*. London: Allen & Unwin.

INSERM. (2004). *Psychotérapie. Trois approaches évalués*. Paris: INSERM.

Joyce, J. (2000). *Dubliners*. London: Penguin Books.

Lacan, J. (1973). *Le Séminaire, Livre XI, Les quatre concepts fondamentaux de la psychanalyse, 1964*. Paris: Ed. du Seuil.

Lacan, J. (1991). *Le Séminaire, Livre XVII, L'envers da la Psychanalyse, 1969–1970*. Paris: Ed. du Seuil.

Lacan, J. (2004). *Le Séminaire, Livre X, L'angoisse, 1962–1963*. Paris: Ed. du Seuil.

Laplanche, J., & Pontalis, J.-B. (1973). *The language of psychoanalysis*. London: Norton.

Miller, J.-A. (2005). Introduction to reading Jacques Lacan's seminar on anxiety. *Lacanian Ink*, *26*, 8–67.

Miller, J.-A. (2006). Reading Jacques Lacan's seminar on anxiety II. *Lacanian Ink*, *27*, 8–63.

Restivo, S. P. (1992). *Mathematics in society and history: Sociological inquiries*. Dordrecht: Kluwer Academic Publishers.

Walshaw, M., & Cabral, T. C. B. (2005). Reviewing and thinking the affect/cognition relation. In: *PME 29* (Vol. 4, pp. 297–303). Melbourne: University of Melbourne.

Roberto Ribeiro Baldino
Tânia Cristina Baptista Cabral
Digital Systems Engineering
State University of Rio Grande do Sul (UERGS)
Brazil

PART THREE

BECOMING A TEACHER

TONY BROWN (BRISTOL)

4. BECOMING A TEACHER

INTRODUCTION

This chapter examines the process of becoming a teacher through a focus on professional identity and its important connection with emotions (Saltzberger-Wittenberg, 1983; Ball & Goodson, 1985; Greenhalgh, 1994; Nias, 1996; Noddings, 1996; Hargreaves, 1998; Damascio, 2000; Day 2004, 2006). Much of the literature challenges the received view that emotion interferes with wise decision-making. Saltzberger-Wittenberg's work was an important attempt at providing a pathway between psychoanalytic thinking and education. Greenhalgh provides many examples of psycho-dynamically informed interventions by teachers working in a range of school settings. Damascio's work as a leading neuroscience specialist shows emotion as a crucial component of cognition. Damascio argues that primary emotions are intrinsic states of being; internal processes triggered by events. Secondary emotions are an amalgam of primary emotions and socially learned behaviours.

The process of learning how to work effectively in the classroom – how to do the right things and how to do things right – is a complex example of the need to integrate primary and socially acquired secondary emotions. This learning process inevitably engages us in explorations of self-development and identity. Because emotions are integral to learning we must understand our emotions and their origins as we go about learning how to work as classroom teachers. And because the process of learning to work professionally in classrooms is so important to student teachers' self-esteem, it is inevitable that the learning process engages the emotions deeply, as students work at becoming teachers.

Teacher identity seen from an interventionist-managerial perspective is something to be shaped primarily by training. Identity, if it is considered at all, becomes synonymous with professional competence achieved by adhering to the instructions of development programmes based on performativity, where technicist approaches are seen as enhancing professionalism by increasing teachers' ability to follow externally imposed procedures. There is much evidence from the literature referred to above, that teachers' notions of identity transcend the technicist approach that has come to dominate some views of training.

In sharp contrast to imposed technicist approaches to teacher development is the critical pedagogy espoused by writers like Giroux (2005, p. 99):

T. Brown (ed.), The Psychology of Mathematics Education: A Psychoanalytic Displacement, 95–117.
© 2008 Sense Publishers. All rights reserved.

> Part of the legacy of critical pedagogy is to make clear that pedagogy is a moral and political practice rather than merely a technique or method. ... pedagogy is the outcome of particular conflicts and struggles and cannot be approached as an a priori method or technique. Pedagogy is directive and is, in part, about the struggle over identities, values, and the future. It articulates and shapes the connection between knowledge and morality, how we get to know and what we know, and it alerts us to how power shapes and is reinvented in the interaction among texts, teachers, and students.

Schools and teachers are pressed by neo-liberal policies that celebrate a free market approach whilst regulating at every opportunity. They are encouraged by government policies to teach 'emotional literacy' whilst scant recognition is paid to what such as project means for teachers and students if it is to succeed. Whilst policies acknowledge emotional factors such as teacher stress and the need for children to be taught about emotions as part of a health and well-being curriculum, there has been little sign of interest in looking more closely at the origins of stress or the connections between teachers' emotional well-being and its impact on their professional decision-making skills. Rather than following Descartes' duality of mind and body, it is Spinoza's argument that reason is shot through with emotion, which needs to be central to discussions of teacher development. This artificial separation of modes of thinking and being, discourages professional exploration of the underlying affective repertoire necessary for improving effectiveness in the classroom. Being sensitive to opportunities for promoting creativity, and being creatively persuasive with school students who are troublesome in classroom settings, requires emotional work on behalf of the teacher. How that emotional work shapes decision-making should be central to the development of teaching and learning: especially for those teachers and student-teachers whose ways of responding to classroom encounters exacerbate the problems they encounter.

It is important to recognise that student teachers can experience strong emotional disturbance during transition to a professional role. Recent work by Day, Kington, Stobart & Sammons (2006, p. 601) has re-emphasised that:

> identities are neither intrinsically stable nor intrinsically fragmented, as earlier literature suggests. Rather, teacher identities may be more, or less, stable and more or less fragmented at different times and in different ways according to a number of life, career and situational factors.

Day summarises teacher identity as comprising 'the interactions between professional, situated and personal dimensions. There is a close association between teachers' sense of positive, stable professional identity and their perceived effectiveness.' (Day, Stobart, Sammons, Kington, Gu, Smees & Mujtaba, 2006, p. xiii) Emerging professional identity can be experienced either positively or negatively with variations and fluctuations over time. Student teachers' professional identity is shaped by notions of *who I am, who I am becoming,* and *who I (don't) want to be.* The experience of being a student teacher disturbs the sense of *who I am,* in complex and often unanticipated ways, around the fluctuating integrity of an emergent professional self.

Many individuals engage productively with unanticipated primary and secondary emotions, although there is little recognition of these challenges to identity in some professional training programmes forcing students to manage these disturbances outside the programme. Some students are disturbed by their training to such an extent that they withdraw from their course.

EDUCATION, DISTURBANCE AND IDENTITY

Bachelard, the philosopher of psychoanalytic ideas, reminds us that 'rather than the will, ... Imagination is the true source of psychic production. Psychically, we are created by our reverie... Imagination works at the summit of the mind like a flame'. (Bachelard, 1987, p. 110) Professional identity is a dynamic and often contradictory interaction of affective and behavioural responses, of imagination tempered by daily necessity. Identity emerges from within the psyche through a dynamic of engagement between an inner world and the real and imagined challenges of practical training.

Education is a potential source of profound disturbance because it demands change. Professional development requires new insights and practices. Change demands giving up, letting go of old positions. Because education threatens the status quo, by offering new opportunities and horizons, we are often ambivalent to education: we can both seek and fear the change it offers. When the change that education demands is experienced as a challenge to the security of the now-self, the effects of education are often resisted, denied or rejected. Identity becomes a contested field accompanied by feelings of excitement at new possibilities, by desires to abandon old positions, by hopes for renewal, by anxieties and resistance to new demands and the expectations of self and other. We often invest a great deal of ourselves in education as the transformative vehicle that will turn us into someone new[1]. This same transformative process and its consequences can then profoundly disturb us.

Learning is a relational process both at the human level and at the level of facts and ideas. Over-emphasis on the individual learner is a gross simplification and at times thoroughly unhelpful to a study of the learning process, particularly the shaping of professional identity. Bion (1961) offers a challenging but valuable psychoanalytical perspective on the individual's experience of learning with and from others in groups. Bion presents the group as challenging for both the individual group members and for the survival of the group itself.

The experience of relating is particularly imposing on student teachers when they make their initial visits to schools as part of their university programmes. They often find themselves in ambiguous situations in schools where they are neither the designated *teacher* (the adult with authority) nor the *pupil* (the child/ adolescent who must defer to school authority). Teachers in school too can find these situations unclear, treating student teachers like they do pupils. The ambivalence affects pupils too: some pupils ignore students or fail to respect them. Whilst some relate positively to student teachers and confide in them more readily than they do their teachers, others resent or fear the absence of their regular teacher. Some students enjoy the idea of the teacher as a source of knowledge but are uncomfortable with the disciplining roles that teachers must adopt. Some students find the *not-teacher-and-not-pupil* bubble a seductive and comfortable haven from which they are reluctant to leave.

The role and context ambiguities that student teachers experience can be useful in allowing relationships to develop, but for some the lack of clarity is disturbing. The ambiguous roles in which students find themselves in the different spaces that schools generate for them can be difficult to interpret and in sharp contrast to behaviourist role model demanded by the precise and lengthy list of 'professional standards' that students need to acquire and demonstrate as they refine their performance in school.

Simplistic behavioural models around which performative assessment is built are to large extent detached from students' personal values, beliefs and emotional engagement with the world. They are partial, highly selective, linear models of performance designed to measure a narrow range of interactions with the immediate physical world to the exclusion of one's inner life. Variable levels of role clarity and the requirement to be assessed in public can cause identificatory confusion. These diverse and often contradictory demands create powerful conditions for what Freud (1916) calls an *after-education.*

> Two dynamic actions allow after-education its diphasic qualities. After-education refers us back to an original flaw made from education: something within its very nature has led it to fail. But it also refers to the work yet to be accomplished, directing us toward new constructions. … Freud suggests that if education incites pleasure, and if it also attempts to move pleasure closer to reality, then this very trajectory requires that we think about education after the experience of education. (Britzman, 2003, pp. 4-5)

After-education becomes a possibility when we experience something that carries a strong emotional charge and challenges the now-self. Sometimes the emotional charge that accompanies an event is even stronger because we make an unexpected association with an earlier experience that has been held in memory (though perhaps not very accessibly). The richness of the student learning experience and its strange contrasts of highly and loosely defined roles is a potent trigger that can create unexpected associations with earlier critical incidents (Tripp, 1993). A student teacher observing a mathematics lesson, or preparing for their first practical lesson may suddenly recall an experience that they have not thought about for many years. Many such memories carry a heavy emotional charge. It could be a previous occasion as a child or adolescent when they performed publicly, or where they were assessed in a positive or a negative way. Preparing for work in schools provides considerable opportunity for unexpected associations.

Although the time and location of many associated experiences are recalled, it is not usually the activity or location that holds the greatest significance. More often it is the emotional energy associated with the earlier experience that is strongly felt *again* (elation, embarrassment, guilt, pride, fear) and linked with the current experience, giving it an even stronger emotional charge. 'What does have a lasting effect? Anything that stimulates, mobilizes, creates feelings belonging to the love-hate spectrum'. (Bion, 1991, p. 362)

After-education in the Freudian sense is the education we construct for ourselves from the re-working of earlier experiences, or from the unexpected associations made between a recent experience and a much earlier one. After-education can begin when we work creatively on recent and remembered experiences in ways that lead to new and different constructions: seeing ourselves and possibilities for ourselves in ways that we could not imagine previously. We can see ourselves as successful instead of failing; we can transform feelings of paralysing guilt into anger that enables us to act. Instead of numbing embarrassment, we push ourselves to 'walk the talk'. We learn to transmute feelings of anger and disappointment with ourselves when we find mathematics difficult, and instead learn how to construct our 'teacher' self and our behaviour as an object of study that has the potential to enhance or impede learning. After-education brings the possibility of re-working, and re-educating the self in ways that bring us closer to psychic wellbeing.

The demands of teacher education are such that inevitably they provoke recollections of childhood learning in students who are becoming teachers. The objects of study of the student-teacher include:
— *me* as teacher (with its echoes of the parental role of disciplinarian);
— *me* as no-longer-pupil (with its sacrifice of the child dependent role)
— *me* as adult (becoming a skilled observer of the impact I have on pupils and colleagues.

Inevitably these processes disturb the now-self. They place students in varied and ambiguous roles, and they tend to produce resonance with earlier experiences of power relations between child/adolescent and adult. The process of becoming a teacher creates conditions for the re-membering of one's previous education, for the recalling of previous responses to education and to the awakening of old desires and phantasies about the direction one's education and therefore - one's life - could have taken.

Identificatory Confusion

One possible consequence of an after-education is that we see ourselves in a new light. But not everything we see is pleasing – either to us or to those who know us. We may be painfully reminded that we haven't learned from experience – and find ourselves in the same old cycle of behaviour that we hoped we had transcended. We may of course feel a strong sense of having moved on, of having developed, of having gained new strength and resolve.

The move to a professional status through an undergraduate or postgraduate programme prompts us to set up expectations about how we might present ourselves vis-à-vis the cultural landscape of formal education – not just in relation to sex, drugs and rock and roll, but also our stance on smoking, alcohol, religion, abortion, green issues, social justice and broader political issues. For young student teachers in their twenties the fluidity and transitional nature of professional training and the emergence of a new persona is brought into awareness sharply by unexpected interactions: being asked by a parent for advice on how to bring up a teenager, or being asked out on a date by a school student. Our public persona, if we are to remain employable in our new milieu, may need a major overhaul. The need to appear publicly as something other than we are is nothing new nor exclusive to teaching, however society projects powerful, ambivalent and often contradictory views of the professional teacher. Anxiety about social breakdown can be violently expelled and projected into professional groups, with strong condemnation of those who fail to adjust to what is deemed appropriate to their professional roles, for example in the case of Shelley White[2] in 2005.

For the majority of students however, the transformation to a professional identity is a rite of passage that brings enjoyment and a sense of success. It is worth exploring the process in depth, not least because it provides valuable insights into self-other relations – a fundamental part of the work of the teacher, but as argued above, the separation of emotional and rational processes is artificial. Emotions are at the heart of decision-making and understanding our emotional make-up enhances the quality of professional decision-making.

The process of after-education, the interaction between our psychic work of building a professional identity out of new experiences and the unexpected associations with earlier encounters, can lead to a state of identificatory confusion, putting our identity under threat or under notice to change. We may suddenly notice aspects of our self in sharper detail (bossiness, compliance, shyness, over-confidence) and begin to feel more or less comfortable with these qualities and behaviours.

Barry, a very successful student trained to work with 5-7 year-olds. He concealed his earlier experience as a nightclub bouncer during his training, only to discover after he qualified that members of staff at his new school relished the idea of going to a nightclub with someone who was very familiar with clubbing. He felt relieved at being able to present a more accurate, rounded persona to his colleagues.

Roseanne, elected to go with a small group of peers to an island away from mainland UK for an extended teaching practice lasting ten weeks. The students made preliminary visits to their practice schools to make preparations for the practice and to meet the staff they would be lodging with. Roseanne settled into the practice and was surprised a few weeks later by an intense and unexpected feeling of being abandoned. She reverted to self-destructive anorexic episodes that undermined her health and disrupted the opportunity to learn what was happening to her in this setting. It is possible to view the return of anorexic episodes as a reversion to earlier dispositions whilst under pressure, or as a way of defending against the need to tackle the challenges of working in a new school and anxiety brought about by the absence of friends and family.

DEVELOPING THE ROLES OF CONTAINER AND CONTAINED

The student teacher has to take increasing professional responsibility for managing the teacher-pupil relation. To do this effectively the student teacher has to engage reflexively with the effects of moving *from* student *to* teacher, and with what is brought into consciousness by this re-engagement with schools and pedagogy. Earlier experiences of being a child/adolescent/student in various relationships with teachers/ adults, will have influenced the potential for self-other relations needed in the new role of *student as teacher*. This is not to imply a causal relationship. Education is also about becoming new, different, un-dreamt-of. But container and contained is a dynamic that teachers cannot avoid, even though they can resist and deny them.

Bion sought to avoid definitional language and he is a challenging read. He employs the symbols ♀ ♂ partly to avoid being trapped by the language. The symbols are intended to represent container-contained in a non-gendered way where ♀ represents the capacity to contain and ♂ the need to be contained. Although the earliest construction is the relationship between the mother's breast and the infant, Bion argues that ♀ ♂ is a continuing feature of life. The transformation from layperson to professional places the teacher in settings where container-contained roles are carried out in public spaces. Just as the infant can experience strong emotions, which are not-yet-thoughts, the student of mathematics can have uncomfortable or intolerable sensations around the ability to learn and the possible consequences of learning. The teacher's capacity to be a container for learners' incomplete anxious thoughts and ideas, emotions and emerging but fragmentary knowledge, has a direct influence on learners' capacity to learn. The teacher's incapacity to tolerate the learners' anxiety and frustration (which is often projected onto them by the teacher: 'I can't stand teaching Year 9', ... 'Year 8 girls are a pain'... 'First year undergraduates know nothing'...and so on) is felt as a disruptive experience by all those involved, whether the educational context is the school, college or university.

Bion argues that personality is created out of dual elements of ♀ ♂ in a dynamic, changing state and that the container actively seeks the (to be) contained, both within the individual and between individuals. To be effective, the container must be neither too rigid nor too porous and unlike Winnicott's notion of *holding,* containing/contained is always a dynamic state, never passive.

To (re)turn not-yet-thoughts into thoughts and images which can be worked on by the learner requires the teacher to be available to function as a container when needed. Holding the material of not-yet-thoughts for learners, may free them from feelings of being overwhelmed. Returning the not-yet-thoughts at a later stage and in forms that offer descriptions, labels and names, permits the learner to construct images and thoughts around what could previously only be felt as dangerous, exciting, important or incoherent.

This is demanding enough in a dynamic setting where learner and teacher are positive about the process. When we consider the anger of a learner who feels exposed or betrayed by peers, or a teacher angry with students' resistance to taking responsibility for their studies, their behaviour or their responsibility to peers, then

TONY BROWN (BRISTOL)

the dynamics are not simply based on mutual positive regard for the processes of container/contained.

In typical conversations in a lecture or classroom lesson for example, it is possible for the speakers and listeners to generate visual and other sensory images that capture the essence, not just of the content of the discussion, but also the whole emotional frame of experience. When this process fails, as for example with a highly articulate student who was rendered speechless in a job interview and then again the following week during a group activity when she reported the experience to the group, there is an opportunity for work around container/contained. The group activity provided an opportunity to review and rehearse for job interviews[3]. The teacher and student's peers functioned as *container* helping the student resist a desire for flight into panic and denial. This is not to imply working with the student against her wishes, but rather an invitation to her to stay with the difficulty and try to resist the desire for flight from job applications and interviews.

By acting as container we draw on our capacity for taking inside the mind and tolerating, processing and eventually giving back the poorly formed notions of self, self-and-other, self-as-learner, and pieces of subject knowledge that learners can sometimes disgorge into the teaching and learning space. The act of healthy containing returns the content in forms, which are sufficiently coherent and tolerable for the learner to work on. Giroux's demands for a critical pedagogy that studies the power play of education are important in this context because the process of ♀ ♂ play out within power relationships that should not be ignored.

Clare displayed considerable ambivalence in lectures and seminars, sometimes enthusiastic, sometimes withdrawn, sometimes failing to attend. She was often late for appointments and often only presented scribbled drafts of assignments for discussion with her tutor. Clare's conversation in tutorials was frequently dominated by her fears for her horse, which was ill, and her injured pet dog. Earlier in seminars she had referred to the death of her mother and her boyfriend.

The tutor sustained conversations with Clare in one-to-one tutorials by using the student's worries for her injured and needy animals, whilst at the same time talking about what is needed in terms of attendance, punctuality and proper caring if a good owner is to look after an animal in a way that leads them back to health. In this example of tutor as container, the student was offered the opportunity to remain engaged with the academic content of the tutorial through the tutor's extended use of metaphors for caring for sick animals. Clare learned over time to relate more appropriately to the tutor and to tolerate her own anxiety about being a useless (sick) student. Their conversations retained a strong metaphorical element that proved useful for establishing an effective professional relationship. The challenge for the tutor was to keep Clare engaged, provide some respite by containing her overwhelming fears of failure (presented through anxieties about sick animals and death), but without allowing Clare to evade the anxieties.

The most crucial decision on which mental growth depends is whether frustration is evaded or faced. Encountering a painful state of mind, does the individual immediately engage in one or more of the numerous defence mechanisms readily available for the purpose of getting rid of the awareness of the frustration... (Symington & Symington, 1996, p. 67)

Some student teachers beginning to work in schools, do not automatically have the capacity to be containers for adolescents, younger children or teacher colleagues, nor may they immediately be able to access others as containers to help them work on their own feelings, thoughts, and images provoked by frustration, anxiety and anger when learning how to teach. When working in classrooms, some student teachers display great rapport from the start, able to take up positions within either part of the ♀ ♂ dynamic showing a considerable capacity to be available to others during the earliest part of their training.

Mathematics is an interesting site for the production of excitement, fear and anxiety for students (and teachers) as reported in depth by Buxton (1981). It is also a powerful vehicle for representation of human relations. It is used often unconsciously to explore, represent and symbolise internalised notions of human situations. In phantasy we make links with numbers and procedures. Zero can come to represent absence; nothing. Zero and infinity can represent birth and death. 2 is the symbol for parents and parental relations. 3 stands for triangulation, mother, father child. Subtraction is synonymous with removal, departure. An absent father, a dead sister; that is subtraction at its most tangible. Multiplication suggests pregnancy and birth; go forth and multiply. A child abandoned by a parent may well struggle to understand the purpose of their birth and the facts of multiplication. Divorce and remarriage create multiple families, and the child who suffers during these changes, may well represent that suffering through mathematical symbols. Division is sharing – the Oedipal conflict. A child who finds it difficult to share one parent with another or with a sibling can make unconscious connections between division and their human situation.

Nimier (2006, pp. 67-68) reports a conversation with an eighteen-year-old female student at the end of the science programme in a French high school. She loves maths and is good at it, but in an interview demonstrates a resistance to using it to describe human situations. She finds it bizarre to count years for example, even though she has no conceptual difficulties in doing this. She works as a baby sitter at weekends and reports that when she started babysitting, the little girl was three-years-old. Two years later, the child has grown up and the student herself has changed. Human development takes place in important little steps she argues. Counting the years, 1, 2, 3, disregards this important process and destroys the humanness of the experience. For this able maths student, counting the years since her birth erodes her being and her experience.

Especially for the beginning teacher, managing one's own capacity for staying with the complexity of personal learning is a difficult challenge. The fast moving and challenging process of training has relatively few mechanisms for supporting identity development. Performative models of competence demonstrate a low regard for personal health and development and place a heavy emphasis on behaviourism through the adoption of tick box competencies. The result is that beginning teachers are susceptible to being overwhelmed by their own anxieties

TONY BROWN (BRISTOL)

about becoming a teacher. A coherent professional identity is also challenged by the need to defend against the desires and fears that school students and staff project onto them.

School students can experience great excitement and anxiety following the arrival of this unknown authority into their teaching and learning space. Student teachers often overlook the shift in relations between school students and the displaced teacher who has to be increasingly sidelined as the student's practice becomes established. This can produce feelings of loss for the displaced teacher and for some pupils.

Bion's work on the application of thought to emotional experience led him to claim, 'an emotional experience cannot be conceived of in isolation from a relationship'. (1962, p. 42) Bion reduced the links between humans to three components Love (L), Hate (H), and Knowledge (K) and their negatives, (-L), (-H) and (-K) as referred to in Tamara Bibby's chapter above. Bion's point is that whilst some knowledge leads to understanding, some knowledge can lead to a loss of understanding. Student teachers can experience –K when required to perform in classrooms in ways that are antithetical to their value systems and beliefs. They end up confused and unable to work effectively in the classroom.

READING CLASSROOM SPACES

Unexpected associations with earlier experiences can draw attention to how we perceive intuitively what psychoanalysis calls subject-subject relations – how we countenance relationships between teacher and learner at a most fundamental level. The ways in which we see these relations often reflect both our earliest experiences of learning in formal settings and our early familial experiences.

For learners to make use of what is returned from the teacher (and from each other), the classroom has to be experienced as a space in which growth is possible – though this will be felt largely at an unconscious level and accessed only through associations. Drawing on the work of Winnicott (1988) the transitional object (a teddy or piece of blanket) becomes the mechanism by which the infant sustains and develops the notion of the coexistence of subjective and objective reality.

The classroom becomes a creative space when we can draw on these earliest experiences and use them to explore the coexistence of self and other engaging with the discipline of mathematics. Our effectiveness in using the classroom space as a potential or transitional space is derived in part by the quality of the learning we achieved in our earliest subject-object relations. The physical attributes of the classroom space are relevant but not paramount, though the effective teaching of mathematics appears to be supported by certain forms of classroom organisation.

Rather, the effective mathematics classroom is a space that creates a sense of a *third position* – an affective experience rather than a physical arrangement, recognised unconsciously as not me, not you, not us. It functions as a Winnicottian potential space and comes into being when we are able to construct mathematics as an object of study with which we as subjects engage in relation to the discipline. This is quite different from Yackel and Cobb's (1996) notions of socio-

BECOMING A TEACHER

mathematical classroom norms, which equate more to the teacher's construction of classroom rules and protocols of interaction intended to influence learners' behaviours in ways thought to support the public exploration of mathematical thinking.

The third position is more closely related to Ogden's psychoanalytic third, a deep and lasting change in the learners' and teacher's relation to self, other and the discipline: a change lying in between them that leads to a repositioning in relation to mathematics in the deepest sense. My learning of maths depends on more than my ability to construct mathematical knowledge; it also depends on how I use maths to construct myself, the teacher and our relating. Debussy sensed something similar when he commented that 'music is the space between the notes'.

The development of the potential space depends on the teacher's capacity to relate to learners and to take the learner into mind.

> If the patient (learner) does not feel safely taken into the analyst's (teacher's) mind, the observing position of the third is experienced as a barrier to getting in, leading to compliance, hopeless dejection, or hurt anger. (Benjamin, 2004, p. 28)

STUDENT-TEACHER TRANSITIONS

Most students make their transition to teaching without very much difficulty and manage to balance studies, employment and care responsibilities remarkably well. Some students do experience considerable disturbance from the moment they are accepted on a course, through the first year of teaching and beyond. The disturbance can be totally unexpected, adding to its impact on student learning. Student teachers, tutors and school mentors would benefit from greater attention being paid to the experience of developing a professional identity. At the very least it might ease retention problems if staff and students recognised and were helped to articulate the disturbances that students are sometimes expected to manage entirely alone. At best, a psychoanalytically informed view of the transitional process from student to teacher (and no less from teacher to teacher educator) will provide a basis for studies of effective teaching of mathematics that goes beyond didactics and a constructivist pedagogy, studies which generally exclude consideration of the love-hate spectrum.

Some tutors and mentors have a strong desire or need for students to follow their advice, which means they do not always work effectively on the student-teacher's behalf. Their desire can infantalise students, leaving them with restricted opportunities for making decisions. Josie, a student teacher who had been highly successful in her first secondary school placement, was told insistently by her male teacher-mentor in her second school, how to manage students. She should adopt his tactic of standing very close to pupils who annoyed him and literally shout at them from inches away. Her distress was not just the experience of being told to perform in a way that was ethically unacceptable to her. What caused her the

105

greatest distress were the associations with the way she had been treated at home and her earlier experiences as a pupil with a teacher who behaved in a similar way. Her mentor's insistence that she follow his advice brought back strong memories of unpleasant power relations at home and school. In all three situations she had experienced her agency as limited and frustrating. It took a while for Josie to establish a secure relation with her mentor, as she worked to overcome the confusion resulting from what Bion would call –K (destructive knowledge that leads to incoherence). She was able to move to a position where she was not being dominated and had greater agency.

Sally

Students can begin to feel different as soon as they are accepted on a course. For Sally, the gap between the mathematics teacher she could imagine herself to be and the reality of the early part of the training course was irreconcilable. In answer to the question about how she was settling in after one term, she replied:

> I'm still not sure to be perfectly frank with you. A couple of weeks ago I did think, 'Why am I putting us all through this?' to be honest. Because, I thought at my age and at my, with my experience, it would be like coming and doing a job of work. And I knew there would be work to do at home, but I didn't think it would be as emotionally draining as my A levels[4] were. But it is.

Sally had a long and successful career in building societies and banks. She was highly motivated, able and keen to succeed with what she saw as her one opportunity to be a student. The greatest disturbance for her was around the guilt she felt about disrupting the family routine and provoking changes to childcare and housekeeping. Any problem at home, with her husband, with the children and their school, or a backlog of ironing waiting to be done, became associated in Sally's mind with the guilt of her student role, the luxury of having time to study, of indulging her desire to be a teacher.

> I want to be ... a useful working member of society I suppose. I want a really useful role. It's not having a degree. If ... if it wasn't vocational I don't think I'd do it because ... I think it would be too selfish, you know, on the family. I did say to my husband, actually, 'Oh! apparently if you don't get on very well with the teaching side of it, which actually isn't a problem for me at the moment, I feel very comfortable with that side, but if you don't, you can change to a BA. He said, 'What would be the point of that at your age?' ... OK his support will only go so far.

For Sally, the move to her new student role brought unanticipated feelings of guilt, which undermined her. She knew she had the skills, ability and motivation to be a mathematics teacher, but her earlier identity appeared to have been more strongly bound up in her fulltime work, running the household routines, managing childcare and relationships with school, than she had realised. Adjusting to life as a student was experienced as a loss of self. She was unable to represent her new identity in terms of growth or achievement, of being mother, wife *and* student. The additional role of student created a sense of (-K) confusion and guilt, and included a vulnerability to identity change that had not been at all evident to her during the application and interview stages.

Nicola

For Nicola, a great tension arose as she moved into the role of student teacher on a four-year undergraduate degree. Nicola was married with two children. She saw studying at degree level as offering a big opportunity for personal development and her initial motives could best be summed up as self-improvement.

> Although I didn't originally set out with the idea of being a teacher, I didn't particularly want to, I've never wanted to teach. I wanted to do some kind of education, Further Education and I can't remember if I told you this, I was going to do radiography.

Nicola became disillusioned when she explored the role of the radiographer. She saw becoming a professional as a route out of menial work that carried low status, poor pay and little responsibility, but shadowing a radiographer in the work place made her realise that responsibility was limited and the level of access to the patients was minimal. She realised she was searching for a professional role that brought her into direct contact with the patient, or client. *Who am I becoming?* and *What do I want to become?* are important themes for many students, sometimes difficult to work on until the life of student has begun. Students want to explore possible futures in terms of power and other relations, levels of responsibility and decision-making, not necessarily in terms of precise occupations. Some choose higher education (unconsciously) in order to work through these and similar questions. Thus higher education can be chosen as a vehicle for producing disturbance - although is often mistakenly identified as the cause of disturbance (based on constructivist notions of learning that perceive challenges to success only in terms of developing academic understanding or tackling difficult conceptual knowledge.

In her first year of study, Nicola's husband effectively studied the course with her. He read her lecture notes and helped her with assignments. By the second year animosity had developed between them. She felt he did not want to understand the more complex ideas. He felt she had become an intellectual snob – too big for her boots. The situation precipitated a split. She left home and rented a flat. During the third and fourth years of study the relationship with her husband remained strained and problematic. It was later when she successfully completed the course as a highly talented teacher and began full time work that they became reconciled and Nicola returned to the family home.

During her time as a student Nicola remained ambivalent about whether there is space for theory in a course for teachers: perhaps echoing social perspectives on how teachers should behave. In some ways the single Nicola came to represent the

TONY BROWN (BRISTOL)

theoretically informed teacher whilst her husband's position was presented in discussions with me as an apprenticeship model of teaching, with the theoretical components of a course on teaching and learning implicitly viewed as irrelevant.

> The second year, um, perhaps a few doubts started to creep in. Mostly about the theory and the practice of it. I felt there were differences there about what (the college was) saying and what it was actually like. There were obvious problems there but not just for me I think even for people that had come in desperately wanting to teach.

We might be forgiven for hoping that the process of *becoming* can be relatively smooth, during which time a relatively stable psyche can be maintained. Both Nicola and Sally were strong, confident, intelligent and successful. Both were looking for a course to provide a vehicle for change, but as their experience shows, managing personal change is highly problematic when the sought-after effects are to become other. Nicola's slip of the tongue is a powerful reminder of the challenges faced in adjusting to the changes:

> But um, the third year, I've got doubts that are more personal to me. Um, because I think that Mrs. W. and the maths lectures that we've had with you have been particularly interesting to me because I do think that now I'm starting to question whether or not I can actually go out of here, still with a bit of me left, that's not going to be infected, or affected. I mean, you know, you could use either of those words really.

Merryn

Endings can provoke separation anxiety. Some very capable students fail crucial parts of the course near the point of completion, requiring them to return and re-take the failed components thus prolonging their studentship. For some, endings seem to provoke a sharper realisation that the direction and consequence of change remains unclear – that there is work still to be done. For some anxiety may be less about separation and more about *who* is the separating subject.

Merryn had proved herself an able mathematician, a successful teacher and a well-integrated member of a cohort that had studied together for four years of undergraduate education. During the final few weeks of her course she felt overwhelmed by anxiety and disappointment. I didn't know her very well, having taught the cohort only briefly two years previously. At the end of a teaching session when I was substituting for another tutor, she asked if she could remain behind when the mathematics session finished. As the other students left, she burst into tears and reported several crises with her friendships. Her boyfriend was angry because she was too absorbed in other things. Her immediate group of friends had dropped her because she was too serious, too bossy, unwilling to socialise. She reported feeling confused, alone, isolated and rejected. I paraphrase Merryn's[5] remarks following the teaching session:

108

BECOMING A TEACHER

I hate who I am. It's horrible, I don't like being like a teacher. But I have to be like a teacher or I won't pass an interview or get a job. I've spent four years, doing this. I don't want to waste it, but I can't be the person I need to be without losing my friends.

The inner world of the student is where the adjustment to the new identity has to begin.

Trevor

Trevor completed a postgraduate course and began work in a secondary school mathematics department but resigned during the first year. For Trevor the school experience both as a student teacher and as a qualified teacher raised anxieties that he defended against by splitting. He split the various attributes of schools and teaching into good and bad. The good bits were his relationships with pupils, which he retained as a positive personal quality, whilst the bad bits he projected onto schooling, and onto teacher colleagues. He thought pupils' psyches suffered though he failed to see that in fact this was what he experienced. School was a place where it was impossible to be oneself. He described pupils as forced into playing games where they had to present a certain type of persona whilst hiding another. These were his own problems but his need to protect himself made it difficult for him to recognise this. Instead he projected his anxieties onto others, the school and the education system – these were to blame for the intolerable nature of schooling. He gave the impression of being both under attack and seeing himself as part of education's attack on pupils. Schooling was a fight from beginning to end.

I was always on their backs, nothing to do with maths but other stuff that I didn't believe in, doing the school bit, uniform, being on time, that sort of thing. I could keep them busy. I liked them but I didn't see the real them. I was playing at teacher and they played at being a certain kind of kid. I learned what to do on the course but what I had to do wasn't me. Sure it was noisy some times and I wasn't always organised enough.

In an earlier paper (Brown, 2006) I describe Trevor's position as *unbearable identificatory compromise.* The identification that was available to Trevor as a professional teacher did not nurture or sustain him. Confusion over identity is reported by Alsup (2005, p.182) in a study of identity of student teachers.

One of the problems faced by some students in this study is that although their personal identities were multiple and diverse, their perceptions of the identity of the teacher were not.

Splitting may lead to temporary protection of the psyche from feelings of persecution but in the long term according to Klein, the fragmented and partial nature of relations and perceptions of self and others needs to give way to a more rounded view of people as neither perfectly good or irredeemably bad – what Klein

109

referred to as the *depressive position*. Overcoming the need for defensive behaviours and relaxing one's guard has the dual consequences of leaving the psyche less protected and therefore more vulnerable, but also more open to experience of other, with the potential for growth, development and greater rapport that comes from self-other interactions. Learning to live with less defensive positions gives rise to experiencing self and others as multi-dimensional, complex and capable of a greater range of relational possibilities.

Secure Attachment

Attachment theory (Bowlby, 1999)[6] provides valuable insights into the range of relations that staff and students experience in higher education settings. For the most part, relationships between student and tutor reflect shared interest, pleasure, mutual recognition and the ability to enjoy the difference of the other - where the relationship develops as 'being and being with' rather than 'doing and being done to'. (Winnicott, 1988)

We can identify several distinct tendencies in the formation of attachments - *secure, anxious, ambivalent* and *avoidant*. Secure attachments rest on a sophisticated sense of self with other that is borne out of the successful primary relation with the principal carer and the successful management of anxiety during periods of separation. The growth of independence comes from successful adjustment to separation and fear of loss and the recognition that personal growth and development is only achieved by overcoming the use of defensive strategies to protect against anxiety.

The ability to form secure attachments in adolescence and adulthood is built from the childhood experience of realising that the mother/ principal carer holds the infant in mind during periods of absence. Students and tutors who achieved secure attachments in childhood are more likely to develop and sustain them in adolescence and adulthood. Secure attachments are essential for effective functioning in higher education settings but changes in the way higher education is organised make this more difficult to achieve.

QUALITY OF THE STUDENT LEARNING EXPERIENCE

'One of the central questions in education is: who are we studying for, and who are we attempting to educate? It is not always clear.' (Coren, 1997, p. 33) Establishing secure relations for the first time away from home is an important activity for many university students. For many students in recent years, the most common experience in *academic settings* in UK universities is of relating to tutors within large group settings, such as lectures, where it is more difficult to establish a personal connection. The healthy development of the student-tutor relation requires that students are aware of being noticed as an individual, sensing they have been noticed and are being held in mind during intervening periods between meetings. This natural way of human relating is disrupted when teaching is predominantly through large impersonal groups. It presents problems too for new staff who require the same symmetry of being known and regarded by students if they are to relate successfully to them.

If our personal history is of secure attachment we can more easily tolerate a level of poor quality tutor-student relating. Many students and staff are likely to find satisfying friendships with peers and mixed groups in social settings such as sport, music, religious and other meetings. However, this still leaves the academic side of life in a degraded state where the quality of learning and teaching has been weakened by structural features that limit the opportunity for relationships to develop. The dominant paradigm, which constructs learning primarily as an individual intellectual exercise, has allowed the political desire for massification and efficiency to be achieved without regard to the quality of learning in its proper sense. If tutors can learn to apply entertaining teaching techniques to larger and larger groups, then all will be well in a world where learning has been reinvented as the intellectual pursuit of individuals devoid of any affective component.

ANXIOUS ATTACHMENT

Sometimes students do not operate from a secure base. Many teachers in higher education have had to respond to a student whose contribution in seminars and student presentations is to repeat what the tutor has provided earlier, or who seeks numerous opportunities for contact but whose academic ideas fail to develop. In tutorials such students are often enthusiastic, sometimes over-familiar and sometimes fearful of independent thought and action. These can be thought of as *anxious attachments*, with varying degrees of over-dependency. The student finds it difficult to establish or risk a personal viewpoint for fear of the imagined consequence. The student who uses the tutor mainly for discharging feelings of anxiety may fail to benefit from normal levels of guidance, advice and support. The help they receive fails to alleviate the students' anxiety and reduce their dependence. Although they are constantly looking for food they remain hungry, unable to obtain sufficient nourishment to thrive. Tutors and peers can feel at a loss when they have provided as much as they can, only to find it insufficient and the student perhaps even critical of the help that was offered.

AMBIVALENT, DESTRUCTIVE DEPENDENCY

A student may submit work for assessment that is clearly plagiarised, despite having received the same guidance as other students about how to avoid this situation. A student may frequently miss lectures, seminars or planning meetings with peers who are working towards a group presentation. The student may be very demanding; highly vocal perhaps and even angry about these missed opportunities and may offer very elaborate explanations as to why things have not worked out.

Tutors and peers can experience these incidents as a repetitive cycle that the student doesn't seem to recognise, and may feel persecuted by the student who is never satisfied. The tutor and the student's peers may feel under attack and prevented somehow from taking any really effective remedial action, leaving everyone feeling frustrated and the student feeling abandoned and let down. The student's feelings may appear to swing from wanting to create attachments, to anger and dismissal when help or friendship is made available.

It can be useful to think of this behaviour as ambivalent or destructive dependency, with the student 'needing to take things out' on others when things don't go right, and unable to tolerate the necessary degree of independence. Relations feel like 'being done to' rather than 'being and being with'. In the case of tutors operating from this position, students may find the tutor uncomfortably familiar and also at times distant and overly critical of their work.

AVOIDANT RELATING

In a third type of relating which can be seen in tutors' and students' behaviour, crises emanate from real or imagined relations with disembodied groups, committees or the university as a generalised 'them'. Difficulties experienced with these relationships are associated with uncontrollable regulations, mindless bureaucracy, a non-defined *they* who make life difficult or impossible. For students, this can lead to self-destructive behaviour, such as non-attendance at a crucial exam because they didn't read the timetable, or failing to apply for an extension for a piece of work because there was no-one to provide the form that they needed. In these situations there is an absence of relating to any particular individual, behaviour is self-destructive and non-relating. The student fails to make use of good relationships with tutors that have been built up over time and instead of using good relations that already exist, follows a self-destructive path.

The challenge for staff and students is to realise that we all move between these various forms of relating when stressed and under pressure. Those with experience of secure attachments will more easily be able to return to more effective ways of relating, whilst those whose earlier attachment experiences were predominately insecure may find it difficult and may need some support.

Roseanne hid the return of her anorexic episodes until she began to faint in public during her work based training at her primary school. She was unable to use the good relations established with the class teacher and head teacher to help with her anxiety about being away from familiar surroundings and friends.

Clare managed a fragile anxious attachment to her tutor through conversations that revolved around her pets' dependence on her as their carer. The tutor managed Clare's anxiety with skill. She avoided offering to rescue her thus avoiding the risk of creating greater dependency by taking over the student's worrying for her. Instead she managed to support Clare by using and extending the needy animal dialogue to help Clare assess her performance at university in realistic terms and manage her anxieties.

Josie needed to manage her feelings of being dominated by a teacher-mentor and worked hard to establish a relationship in which she felt secure. She achieved it, within a small mathematics department where relational dynamics were very public. The working relationship that Josie and her mentor achieved is a good example of the non-symmetrical mentor-mentee role that needs to be professionally effective and personally appropriate, but which cannot be equal in terms of power.

Sally's experience of guilt as a strong feature of the transition to studentship became unbearable and disrupted her relationships both within the university and at home, so much so that she withdrew a few months after beginning her course. Becoming a student exposed the anxious attachments on which parts of Sally's home life was based. She couldn't be the parent who delegated collecting the children – for fear of what people would think of her. She couldn't leave the ironing for her husband to do despite the agreement they had made.

For Nicola, the disturbance to family relationships lasted for over three years and was very stressful for all concerned. At our last meeting, she had qualified and was working successfully as a teacher, enjoying her professional role, feeling respected and valued at work and at home, having returned to the family. Nicola used a network of friendship and study groups within the university to develop secure attachments that enabled her to cope with the painful and risky process of becoming an independent professional woman.

Merryn's case was interesting in that her anxiety overwhelmed her quickly and briefly at the end of a long and successful training period. Even at the point where all formalities had been completed and she knew she had passed, there were strong emotional forces in play that provoked anxious questions about her developing identity as the mathematics teacher she was becoming, and how she would accommodate both the professional and the private person. As with Nicola, there is a sense of Merryn's self having become infected/affected by the experience of training to be a teacher.

In Trevor's case the training seems to have been a reminder of an earlier infection, which prevented him from forming relationships with colleagues in school. When he talked to me, he gave no sense of belonging. He hardly mentioned any professional relationships with colleagues. All his relationships were described in the language of fighting, struggling, contesting, of 'doing and being done to', rather than 'being and being with'.

The extent to which student teachers are able to make secure attachments during their study period is an important determinant of the extent to which they can make use of and create the conditions for their own effective learning.

THE NEED FOR A PARADIGM SHIFT

In many current models of learning and teaching in higher education, student desire is taken for granted. This perspective focuses student motivation in and on the individual. The student either has what it takes to benefit from higher education or is deficient in some way. Having constructed *learning* as essentially an individual process involving cognitive judgments related to intrinsic and extrinsic factors that determine motivation, the paradigm points to the conclusion that poorly performing student are in deficit. They lack something; study skills, academic development in the discipline, access to 'academic English', ... and so on.

Whilst many contemporary learning paradigms limit student motivation primarily to cognitive and affective processes exclusively within the individual, it is difficult to explore key areas of learning that a psychoanalytic paradigm can open up and illuminate. A psychoanalytically oriented view emphasises the relationships between all those engaged in learning-teaching interactions. The introduction of a psychoanalytic viewpoint has the effect of moving from a pathology of student strengths and weaknesses to a study of the relationship between teacher and learner and the impact this has on the learning process. Inevitably, it follows that in this model disruption of the student's learning will raise questions about the quality of tutor-student and group relationships. This position directly challenges the current utilitarian perspective of individual cognition that political discourse emphasises in order to reinforce the view that rapid expansion of provision has been at no cost to student learning.

FROM RELATIONAL PSYCHOANALYSIS TO RELATIONAL EDUCATION

Relational psychoanalysis has sought to move away from the classical psychoanalytic model that emphasised client/ patient subjectivity whilst avoiding exploration of the analyst's subjectivity. The intention of relational psychoanalysis has been to create a greater mutuality in client-therapist interactions through the disclosure of subjectivity and the exploration of mutuality. In parallel with the education context, relationships are recognised as non-symmetrical, with mutual respect for the otherness of the other as an essential basis.

Respect and understanding of otherness develops from disclosures that reveal subjectivity in positive ways that are appropriate to professional contexts. In education as well as in therapeutic settings, appropriate disclosure helps foster mutual respect, sustains and supports the teaching-learning dynamic, and creates the opportunity for an educational equivalent of the 'third subject', (Ogden, 1999) which in education's case can be experienced as a love of the subject and pursuit of understanding of the discipline. Mutual interest in deepening one's understanding of the discipline can serve as a vehicle that brings tutor and student together in non-symmetrical but mutual alliance. Mutuality is enhanced through the use made by students and tutors of the natural third subject – the academic discipline that higher education offers, but it does so in ways that shape subjective and objective relating.

The massification of education, without regard for student-tutor relating, and the tendency in some discourses to position employability and skills acquisition as polar opposites to scholarly activity, has had the effect of devaluing scholarship in higher education and reduced the opportunities for students to locate themselves in relation to a body of academic knowledge.

The response in many institutions has been a failure to engage with a critical pedagogy that examines power relations within society and the political desire to subjugate education to the influence of the workplace. Solutions are often thought to reside mainly in developing teaching strategies for working with large groups, implying that all the problems of large group work can be addressed if tutors ensure that students' cognitive processes are engaged. Whilst this is important, effective student learning will not necessarily follow if the psychodynamic processes of relating are overlooked or left for the students to sort out alone.

The students' narratives referred to in this chapter testify to a duality in university life comprising engagement with the discipline and high quality relationships with tutors, experienced as 'being and being with' rather than 'being done to' by agents working for an impersonal organisation geared to processing information through bureaucratic procedures. Higher education at its most effective remains a relational enterprise where students and tutors have opportunities for mutual disclosure so that subjectivities can enter and enrich the learning process. It is perhaps self-evident that since this chapter argues that mathematics is a special case, there is a particular challenge facing teachers of the discipline. The structure, rules, procedures, generalisability and abstraction of the discipline provide it with the potential to be used at a symbolic level by teachers and students to explore and represent personal experience, relationships and phantasies. It is hardly surprising that students of mathematics remember episodes where they can recall difficulties; the power of mathematics to (re)present offers us endless possibilities. The nature of unconscious processes suggests that not all stories about wicked teachers and humiliating experiences should be revisited as literally true. The great challenge for those becoming teachers of maths is that they have three inter-related challenges: to know oneself as a becoming teacher, to understand the pedagogy and acquire sufficient skills of teaching to survive and continue learning and to know the didactics of mathematics from a psychodynamic perspective, which is to know it in a deeper sense than is usually implied by didactical studies.

NOTES

[1] *Educating Rita* by Willy Russell (1983), and *Oleanna* by David Mamet (1992) capture the desire and motivation as well as the resistance, ambiguity and risk that education projects present.

[2] A geography teacher was told today she would not be jailed after being found guilty of "snogging" a 15-year-old male pupil on three occasions. ...During the seven-day trial, the jury was told that she became attracted to the teenager and found him easy to talk to. She said she felt more and more isolated at the west Yorkshire school and felt stressed as a relatively inexperienced teacher. (Guardian, 20 October 2005), http://education.guardian.co.uk/schools/story/0,5500,1596881,00.html accessed 15.07.07)

[3] The tutor chose a strategy that tends to provoke anxiety, which is to ask students to offer the group their favourite interview question and the one they most fear. This helps the group get quickly to the tensions experienced in many job interviews. Students may oversimplify their 'favourite' question and others in the group can often help them develop their answer even further. Because they are working from a claimed position of confidence, building a better interview response is usually quick. Interestingly, their proffered 'worst' question is often rather a favourite of someone else. Being made aware of this difference often helps to turn a question around - the confident student

TONY BROWN (BRISTOL)

sees more clearly why it is a good question for them, as well as helping the anxious student what they need to do in order to grow to like it.

[4] A levels (Advanced) are post compulsory public examinations taken in parts of the UK by school students typically aged 18-19 years, prior to university entrance.

[5] For a detailed discussion of this study, see Brown (2006).

[6] See Inge Bretherton (1992) for a full discussion of John Bowlby's psychoanalytic background as a psychiatrist and Head of the Children's Department at the Tavistock Clinic, London and the development of attachment theory.

REFERENCES

Alsup, J. (2005). *Teacher identity discourses: Negotiating personal and professional spaces*. Mahwah, NJ: Lawrence Erlbaum Associates.

Bachelard, G. (1987). *The psychoanalysis of fire*. London: Quartet.

Ball, S. J., & Goodson, I. (1985). *Teachers' lives and careers*. Lewes: Falmer Press.

Benjamin, J. (2004). Beyond doer and done to: An intersubjective view of thirdness. *Psychoanalytic Quarterly, 73*(1), 5–46.

Bion, W. (1961). *Experiences in groups*. London: Tavistock Publications.

Bion, W. (1962). *Learning from experience*. London: Heinemann.

Bion, W. (1991). *A memoir of the future*. London: Karnac Books.

Bowlby, J. (1999). *Attachment* (2nd ed.). New York: Basic Books.

Bretherton, I. (1992). Origins of attachment theory: John Bowlby and Mary Ainsworth. *Developmental Psychology, 28*, 759–775.

Britzman, D. (2003). *After-education: Anna Freud, Melanie Klein and psychoanalytic histories of learning*. Albany, NY: State University of New York Press.

Brown, T. (2006). Negotiating psychological disturbance in pre-service teacher education courses. *Teaching and Teacher Education, 22*, 675–689.

Buxton, L. (1981). *Do you panic about maths? Coping with maths anxiety*. London: Heinemann.

Coren, A. (1997). *A psychodynamic approach to education*. London: Sheldon Press.

Damascio, (2000). *The feeling of what happens: Body and emotion in the making of consciousness*. Fort Washington, PA: Harvest Books.

Day, C. (2004). *A passion for teaching*. London: Routledge Falmer.

Day, C., Kington, A., Stobart, G., & Sammons, P. (2006). Personal and professional selves of teachers: Stable and unstable identities. *British Educational Research Journal, 32*(4), 601–616.

Day, C., Stobart, G., Sammons, P., Kington, A., Gu, Q., Smees, R., et al. (2006). *Variations in teachers' work, lives and effectiveness. Final Project Report RR743*, DfES.

Freud, S. (1916). *Introductory lectures in psychoanalysis Part III* Standard Edition 16.

Giroux, H (2005). Henry Giroux and the politics of higher education under George W. Bush: An interview. *The Review of Education, Pedagogy, and Cultural Studies, 27*, 95–107.

Greenhalgh, P. (1994). *Emotional growth and learning*. London: Routledge.

Hargreaves, A. (1998). The emotional practice of teaching. *Teaching and Teacher Education, 14*(8), 835–854.

Nias, J (1996). Thinking about feeling: The emotions in teaching. *Cambridge Journal of Education 26*(3), 293–306.

Nimier, J (2006). *Camille a la haine et... Leo adore les maths: l'imaginaire dans l'enseignment*. Lyon: Aleas.

Noddings, N. (1996). Stories and affect in teacher education. *Cambridge Journal of Education, 26*(3), 435–447.

Ogden, T. H. (1999). The analytic third: An overview. In S. Mitchell & L. Aron (Eds.), *Relational psychoanalysis: The emergence of a tradition* (pp. 487–492). Hillsdale, NJ: Analytic Press.

BECOMING A TEACHER

Saltzberger-Wittenberg, I. (1983). *The emotional experience of learning and teaching*. London: Routledge.

Symington, J., & Symington, N. (1996). *The clinical thinking of Wilfred Bion*. Brunner-Routledge.

Tripp, D. (1993). *Critical incidents in teaching: Developing professional judgment*. London: Routledge.

Winnicott, D. (1988). *Playing and reality*. London: Pelican.

Yackel, E., & Cobb, J. (1996). Sociomathematical norms, argumentation, and autonomy in mathematics. *Journal for Research in Mathematics Education*, *27*(4), 458–477.

Tony Brown
Escalate
Graduate School of Education
University of Bristol

MARGARET WALSHAW

5. DEVELOPING THEORY TO EXPLAIN LEARNING TO TEACH

INTRODUCTION

What does it mean to create an identity as a teacher? I address that question by offering a theoretical grounding as well as empirical evidence for the part identities play in learning to teach. The discussion parallels an important moment for education, when the theoretical resources available for explaining participation in and engagement with teaching practice are considerably more expansive than at any previous time and the chapter seeks to engage with some of these resources. There are some important guideposts in the theoretical development at hand. For example, we learn from Wenger (1998) that 'the experience of identity in practice is a way of being in the world' (p. 151); it is an experience that is rendered meaningful by particular groups and institution. We know, too, from the insights provided by Gee (2001), and others, that an individual participates differently between and within social groups, cultures and institutions and that this differential participation occurs in relation to the individual's role and position within each social practice.

Understandings like these, developed from Vygotsky's work (see, for example, Valsiner, 1987; Lave, 1988; Rogoff, 1990; Lave & Wenger, 1991; Wertsch, 1991; Gee, 1997, 2001; Wenger, 1998; Roth, 2004), have acquired pre-eminent status within education. Granted, the theory adds a compelling layer to our understanding of how and why people identify with the contexts within which they are positioned. The assertion that what people say and do contributes to the development of their identity at a given time and place, also implies that a change in social practices has a direct bearing on learning. Put succinctly, 'learning is change in a socially situated identity'. (Gee, 2004, p. 38) Lave & Wenger (1991) go so far as to say that changes in identity brought about through changes in social participation, represent 'an epistemological principle of learning'. (p. 98) And for Gee (2004), learning is 'a type of social interaction in which knowledge is distributed across people and their tools and technologies, dispersed at various sites, and stored in links among people, their minds and bodies, and specific affinity groups'. (p. 33)

Cutting edge work like this emphasises socially constituted identities, and these, in turn, have allowed us to problematise conditions as 'holding good' for all, irrespective of one's history, interests and circumstances. However, such insights have recently come under scrutiny. Brown (2008b) maintains that proposals

T. Brown (ed.), The Psychology of Mathematics Education: A Psychoanalytic Displacement, 119–137.
© *2008 Sense Publishers. All rights reserved.*

MARGARET WALSHAW

advanced by neo-Vygotskians are based on 'reductive conceptions of the human subject' and deny readers adequate conceptual preparation to figure out subjectivity in an adequate fashion. Pointing to shortcomings in, for example, the intent of Cole (1996), Brown maintains that such efforts offer only a limited perspective of activity, and hence do not tell us the full story about identity. Bibby makes a similar observation about the deficiencies of neo-Vygotskian insights in her chapter in this volume. With its orientation towards a practical social organisation, Vygotskian inspired work tends to 'understate the productivity of the gap between social tools and the individual's apprehensions of them.' In the view of Sfard and Prusak (2005), 'the notion of identity cannot become truly useful unless it is provided with an operational definition'. (p. 15) It is possible to provide an operational definition built around a 'psychoanalytic displacement' to enhance our understanding of how pre-service teachers learn to teach.

Contemporary insights into the development of a teaching identity can be gauged in the literature from a variety of standpoints, all of which reveal a commitment to teacher empowerment. Cooney (2001) and others have developed their analyses around the constructs of beliefs and knowledge. They sketch out what teachers believe and know, often before and after their involvement in professional development or curriculum reform. On the other hand, Sherin, Mendez, and Louis (2004) maintain that effective learning is dependent on activity, reflection collaboration, and community. Reporting on their work with teachers implementing pedagogical reform, they conclude that teachers must be active and reflective agents in the learning process and must be given the opportunities to work together in ways that support and nurture each other's learning. Other researchers work long-term with individual teachers (e.g. Franke, Carpenter, Levi, Jacobs & Empson, 2001; Simon, Tzur, Heinz, Kinzel & Smith, 2001; Shulman & Shulman, 2004). Each of these approaches has given teachers a personal voice and each has made it possible for teachers to assess as well as improve their public practice.

If there is no consensus about how one learns to teach effectively, there has at least been common agreement over the overwhelming complexity of teachers' work. This claim is most clearly expressed in the findings from the Third International Mathematics and Science Study (TIMSS) 1999 Video Study (Hiebert, Galimore, Garnier, Givvin, Hollingsworth, Jacob, Chui, Wearne, Smith, Kersting, Manaster, Tseng, Etterbeek, Manaster, Gonzales & Stigler, 2003). The Video Study involved seven countries—Australia, the Czech Republic, Hong Kong, Japan, the Netherlands, Switzerland, and the United States—and was undertaken as an adjunct to their participation in the comparative study of student achievement across systems of education in 50 countries. In all, 638 mathematics lessons were collected from Year 8 classrooms. One thing that became clear is that there is no general teaching method for generating high performance amongst students (Hiebert et al., 2003). What works for one teacher and one group of students will not necessarily work for another teacher with a different group of students. The 'concepts, beliefs, and actions in one context and those in another...are qualitatively different by virtue of those contexts'. (Lerman, 2001, p. 36)

DEVELOPING THEORY TO EXPLAIN LEARNING TO TEACH

I wondered if it might be possible to identify what contributes to the creation of an identity as teacher, whilst simultaneously capturing the fluidity and complexity of identity constitution. Is it possible to account for the tentative and shifting balance between theory and classroom experience and the recurring tension between curriculum and the emergent personal relationships and meanings? In an attempt to do this I have chosen an approach that focuses on power and the emotive and unconscious aspects of identity construction. Specifically it offers insights from Foucault's (1977) work and from Lacan's (1977a, 1977b) psychoanalytic horizon.

I offer a theoretical account and an analysis of identity for one teacher - whom I name here as Helen - and I do this through the representation of what I have classified as three sites in the discourse of teaching. These instances of narration investigate how teaching identity is produced and reproduced through social interaction, daily negotiations, and within particular contexts. Brown, Jones, and Bibby (2004) have shown how personal accounts are construed from past, present and future experiences in a multiplicity of sites. All of these aspects weave through Helen's story. Like the trainee teachers in Brown's (2008a) study, Helen's account spells out the constant tension of confronting normative visions of what it means to be a teacher while negotiating visions yet to come. The story she tells cannot escape her contradictory experiences; nor can it escape the effects of her own desire to relate a coherent and compelling account that allows me, the listener, to close the gap between my 'outside' and her 'inside' knowing.

The data were collected from the transcript of my extended interview with her at the end of her year. The intent in the interview was to understand how Helen understood her own process of learning to teach and, in the process, the discussion became a significant space for her own theorising. In the telling I have tried to move from the relatively unknown-to-her researcher, with a position of authority, to one in which boundaries between the personal and public are blurred. But in this I am acutely aware that researcher/researched relations of power have informed and politicised what she says. To that end, I have tried to negotiate between a desire to understand and a strong commitment to thinking of research data as a site of political struggle over meanings. My interpretation of the story is not about getting it right, but, rather, it is about recognising that hidden forms of social relations lie behind what Helen tells me.

TOOLS FOR CONCEPTUALISING IDENTITY

Conceptual Tools from Foucault

Foucault's work is part of a wider intervention concerning debates in which issues of agency, reflexivity and identity formation are paramount. Foucault (1984) does not engage the common quest of uncovering one's true identity or self. In fact he explicitly asks that we give up thinking about the self as a centre of coherence. His notion of identity places into question the very idea of authenticity. In *Discipline and Punish* (1977) he develops the theme of the governmentality of individuals in which processes of identification are explored as they are lived by individuals in relation to both structural processes and lived experiences. To capture this more nuanced understanding of an on-going changing relationship between the individual and that to which he or she identifies, the word 'identity' is often replaced by the term 'subjectivity'. For him, identity is historical and situationally produced; it exceeds singular definition precisely because it is always contingent and precarious. This is what Butler (1997) means when she claims that there is no originary moment establishing pure identity, which can be rationally unpacked.

For Foucault, politics enter into any discussion of subjectivity. Social institutions like universities and schools have particular modes of operating, particular knowledges, and particular positionings. Particularities that relate to the school, the classroom, the associate/ supervising teacher, the university course, previous classroom experiences, personal biography, and so forth, all have their place in constituting the pre-service teacher as 'teacher'. Systems of power both produce and sustain the meanings that pre-service teachers make of themselves and it is through these systems that identities and subjectivities are strategically fashioned and contested in the dynamics of everyday life. Thus, integral to the construction of subjectivity and identity formation, is an *a priori* set of rules of formation governing beliefs and practices in such a way as to produce a certain network of material and embodied relations: they 'do not merely reflect or represent social entities and relations: they actively constitute them'. (Walshaw, 2001, p. 480-1) For the pre-service teacher this means that he or she *is* the production of the practices through which he or she becomes subjected. Britzman (1991) and Davies (2000) speak of this as the discursive constitution of pedagogical subjectivity. This idea is important because it suggests practices of disciplining and regulation that are, simultaneously, practices for the formation of a pre-service teacher.

Pre-service teachers need interaction with others and their discourses in order to form a self-concept. Indeed, the very possibility of forming and articulating concepts of one's self (e.g. as a teacher in the classroom) is ultimately dependent on language and the meanings of other people (Blake, Smeyers, Smith, and Standish, 1998). Others define what is normal, and full engagement by a pre-service teacher in those normalised practices would reveal that he or she has learned to perform and enact not only the genres that constitute the knowledges, modes of operating and theories and practices of the classroom, but also the particular positionings and embodied practices that construct mathematics teaching in a particular site. Individual pre-service teachers become 'successful' when their engagement is self-actualised and no longer requires regulation.

In attempting to understand how this process operates Butler (1997) asks: 'What is the psychic form that power takes?' (p. 2) Understanding how the psyche contributes to learning to teach requires a language for the unconscious, psychical representations and the processes involved in the pre-service teacher's subjection. A theory of the psyche will allow us to explore the trajectory of the unconscious and the part it plays in the constitution of the identity of the pre-service teacher.

Conceptual Tools from Lacan

Psychoanalytic theories, in general, and those of Lacan and of Žižek, in particular, provide us with a conceptual apparatus for understanding the constitution of identity (Felman, 1987; Ellsworth, 1997; Walkerdine, 1997; Britzman, 1998; Jagodzinski, 2002). Methodologically, Lacan's (1977a, 1977b) focus on identity explores the *gap* between potentiality and actuality - the *gap* that divides the Cartesian subject from the self-transparent ego. What interests Lacan most are the subject's unconscious levels of awareness.

Lacan conceptualises identity as double-edged. For him, identity is not 'the autonomous source of spontaneous, self-originating activity'. (Žižek, 1998, p. 5) In Žižek's view, '(t)he Cartesian ego, the self-transparent subject of Reason, is an illusion; its truth is the decentred, split, finite subject thrown into a contingent, nontransparent context'. (p. 2) We become caught up within a context and social network through language and communication. Therefore, the role of language is primordial, and not a mere instrument for communication.

Lacan grounds his development in what he calls the Symbolic and the Imaginary registers. The Symbolic identification (constitutive identification) allows the subject to assume the place from where she is being observed, from where she looks at herself as likeable, and worthy of being liked (Žižek, 1989). In particular, the subject's cultural determinants foreground a particular subjective position and, as a consequence, the narratives that one is led to endorse are often not chosen through rational deliberation. For all their power in guiding actions and thinking, designated identities are merely the product of discursive dissemination – they are simply stories that exist in social spaces.

Lacan (1977a, 1977b) maintains that it is through the unconscious that we come to understand these stories and the network of symbolic social relations that structures what we can and cannot do. Through the notion of the unconscious as the discourse of the Other, we can explain how we are positioned in a cultural network of the Big Other in which some relations are sanctioned and other relations are prohibited. If the Symbolic represents the *constitutive* identification, the Imaginary represents the *constituted* identification through which the subject identifies herself with the image that represents what she would like to be. Arguably, the Imaginary and the Symbolic registers of subjectivity are responsible for processing different sets of 'data' – the Symbolic (words, laws, numbers and letters), and the Imaginary (visual-spatial images as well as illusions of self and world) – yet both function interdependently, working together to inform the subject's experience of self and sense of perception. The Imaginary does not deal with 'the actual state of affairs'. (p. 18) Its focus is on images with which we choose to identify.

What needs to be emphasised here is that between the identifications we, and others, have of ourselves, there will always be a divide. There is always a trace of mis-recognition that arises from the difference between how one party perceives itself and how the other party perceives it. Pre-service teachers want their practice to be effective. They 'dream up' characteristics that designate the ideal teacher.

MARGARET WALSHAW

They make assumptions about what is good and what is not good. Yet between their understanding of good teaching and the meaning of good teaching presupposed by Others lies a fundamental mismatch. Žižek (1989) puts it this way: The subject 'put(s) his identity outside himself, so to speak, into the image of his double'. (p. 104)

The subject's very existence consists of closing the gap towards a secure identity. And, for pre-service teachers, closing the identity gap is what learning to teach is all about. In the Lacanian tradition, learning consists of engaging, confronting, making decisions, and resolving conflicts between Symbolic and Imaginary images. However, learning implies a choice of *being*, and that choice of being, in turn, indicates that something has been discarded; something has been repressed. Žižek (1989) contends that the repression is the subject's ontological condition. It is in this way that we can understand the ways in which language plays a key role because it is the '*reality* of the unconscious'. (Grosz, 1995, p. 67) And it is in this way that we can understand Lacan's claim that the subject is an effect of language.

In putting these Lacanian theoretical tools alongside those discussed earlier from Foucault, we have a framework and a language for looking at identity construction. Taken together, the theoretical resources provide a productive approach to the issue of learning to teach.

THREE SITES OF IDENTITY IN ACTION

It is impossible to discuss learning to teach in Lacan's terms as closing the *gap* between potentiality and actuality without taking into account participation in the social practices of schooling. For the pre-service teacher, learning to teach is a culturally shaped activity. It is an evolutionary process, necessarily involving what I have identified as three distinct sites. Each context is chronologically and geographically distinct one from the other; each presents a different set of assumptions and demands; and each makes available a different range of voices and discursive practices.

Pre-service teachers entering the course bring with them their first over-familiar context, constructed through their own educational biography and through common sense ideas about the roles and functions of teachers in school. The second context is composed of personal student experiences in the university degree course and the postgraduate teacher education programme during which they become privy to aspects of the teaching profession. The third context is given definition from teaching practice. During the practicum, new aspects of the teacher's world and departmental and school politics are laid bare, and new relationships with teachers, administrators and students are made possible (Britzman, 1991). Precisely because each of the three contexts (prior educational biography, tertiary studentship, and teaching in schools) carves out its own borders, each represents different and competing relations of power, knowledge, dependency, commitment, and negotiation. More importantly, each institutionalises mandates for conformity, authorising particular frames of reference that effectuate certain ways of doing and being in teaching. As neither wholly 'student' nor 'teacher' in the classroom, the pre-service teacher brings all three contexts to bear as she attends to the task of educating others.

Constructing a sense of self as a teacher presupposes and constitutes a power relation. In a way that we cannot adequately imagine, the school, the classroom, the associate/ supervising teacher, the teacher education course, previous classroom experiences, personal biography, and so forth, all have their place in constituting the pre-service teacher as 'teacher'. They all bring with them, to the construction of teacher, particular modes of operating, particular knowledges, and particular positionings. According to Foucault, *systems* of power both produce and sustain the meanings that people make of themselves. By any measure, this is a remarkable idea because it suggests that identities and subjectivities are strategically fashioned and contested through systems of power in the dynamics of everyday life.

For Foucault, it is the discursive constitution of pedagogical subjectivity that is important. It is important because it suggests that identities are always relational: we can only be teachers in relation to the meanings of others. The reason for this is that other people, as well as systems in place, define what is normal. And what is not normal generates the need for normalisation, through procedures that are made both explicit and implicit. Institutionalised practices exercise control over the meaning of teaching by normalising and providing surveillance practices to keep such meanings in check.

The Context of Biography

Teachers 'take up' their identities through processes of classification and division. Practices that Foucault calls 'dividing practices' are fundamental to the way in which we differentiate teaching from other workplace practices. In all societies, and particularly in highly structured democracies, we make distinctions between people; and we make judgments based on the categories and differentiations that we have established. Pre-service teachers, in their involvement in a wide range of social practices, experience the effects of 'dividing practices' impact in ways that lead to the creation of a different sense of self. 'Dividing practices' that are at odds with each other are most keenly felt by pre-service teachers as they move from one disciplinary institutional site to another.

For as long as she can remember Helen has wanted to be a teacher and she entered the secondary teaching course with the encouragement from her (now retired) teaching parents. Early school experiences create specific conditions and forms of control that have shaped her behaviour, her attitudes and her expectations of pedagogical practice. It is not an especially obvious procedure on the part of her early schooling but, nevertheless, in its subtlety, it is extremely powerful in establishing the parameters along which future pedagogical practice will be defined.

Her undergraduate double major in mathematics and in statistics at a New Zealand university provided a way to put her knowledge of mathematics and her enjoyment in helping other people to use. Like many of her peers, she felt she could make a difference in the lives of students by helping them, and for her, at this point of time, that meant more in the manner of the teachers she encountered for her final three years of formal schooling in middle and upper secondary school classrooms of around thirty students in New Zealand classrooms than the teachers inscribed in her first nine years of schooling within Chinese classrooms. She spoke of those earlier experiences in China as more formal, 'being there to learn', and 'being silent', 'sitting in rows' and of 'one teacher to fifty students'. Yet while Helen believed there were certain limitations to her early experiences of teaching practice, her latter secondary education produced its own set of constraints:

> The teacher can pay more attention to individuals. I think teachers have more time to talk to you and also to give you individual help. One to thirty is really different from one to fifty...You can sit on a group or in pairs. So there is a really big difference. And I feel that the maths class is more relaxing. But sometimes I don't feel that I learnt much in one lesson.

Foucault explicitly asks that we give up thinking about disciplinary (or pedagogical) knowledge as something in peoples' heads, and instead consider the political, economic institutional regime' central to the production of that knowledge (Foucault, 1980). Helen's view of her educational history is constructed from two opposing national perspectives on the teaching and learning of mathematics both of which dictated unique conditions and circumstances for schools and for teachers and students. Such differing circumstances release a tension between an internally persuasive discourse from Chinese classrooms precisely because she is trying to sustain her first Chinese image of self, in which student learning and classroom control are paramount, at the same time as she recognises the benefits of nurturing learning community. As a compromise she worked at constructing an identity which could both celebrate individuality whilst simultaneously pressing for control and curriculum coverage. She gave expression to Lacan's claim that 'identification is always identification on behalf of a certain gaze in the Other' (Žižek, 1989, p. 106), in the image of self that she produces. In order to continue as a pre-service teacher within New Zealand, Helen had to learn to value those differences and find new sources of validation. She had to negotiate her own space, ever mindful of the definitions of schooling mapped out by her own diverse classroom experiences as a learner.

> There were lots of teachers in my past who I thought I'd really like to be like, many of them and all in different ways. And there was one lecturer – his teaching style, like, to me, was excellent because he introduced a really difficult concept. Because it was like he was telling you a story. It's not a story really but the way he said it was like he was telling a story. I thought this could be a really good model for me.

Helen's talk evokes traces of other events and other interpersonal relations from her university mathematics and statistics undergraduate course that create a rationale and a sense of cohesion to her sense of self as mathematics teacher. Her relatively recent experience as a student of mathematics opens up important aspects of her subjectification in relation to being a mathematics teacher. Whilst Helen desires recognition from her peers and from her course lecturer, her early experiences as a mathematics student has the capacity to undermine her sense of self in the course. New mathematical experiences have the effect of constructing a particular mathematical identity for her - one to which she may not necessarily relate. Put simply, her 'true' sense of self at this moment is betrayed. It is alienated from itself and has developed in relation to the vagaries of the symbolic order of, and social interchange within, this classroom. It is in this sense that we can understand the psychoanalytic claim that the 'core' inner self is nothing more than a sense of self constructed through language and intersubjective images projected onto us by others (teachers, students, lecturers, and so forth) of how they would 'see' us within a set of given social relations (Laclau & Mouffe, 2001). Social relations are, however, never exacting; they are always just out of grasp. Butler (2004) puts it like this:

> If I have any agency, it is opened up by the fact that I am constituted by a social world I never chose. That my agency is riven with paradox does not mean it is impossible. It means only that paradox is the condition of its possibility. (p. 3)

It is not simply the present that factors into identity construction: past as well as anticipated experiences, in a wider range of sites, also play their part in how Helen lives her subjectivity. Thus, her identity is produced through the convergence of a number of discourses and practices, experienced at different times, all positioning and designating her in some way as a becoming teacher of mathematics.

The Context of the Teacher Education Mathematics Course

The teacher education course is a powerful factor in identity construction. An ideological construction of a teacher is advanced within the course and mechanisms are produced with the view to shaping, monitoring, and disciplining the knowledges, modes of operating, and positionings of pre-service teachers. Those who enact those ideologies into being, and write about them in assignments, are duly accredited. In New Zealand teacher education institutions, very few pre-service teachers fail to do so. Furthermore, the attrition rate is small. Hence, the university operates as a disciplinary technology that, without really being aware of it, attempts to control, classify and delimit the work that new teachers do. In a very real sense, disciplinary institutions create the conditions for certain discourses and not others, in relation to categories of being, acting and thinking, to be entertained. Foucault notes:

> Every educational system is a political means of maintaining or modifying the appropriateness of discourses with the knowledge and power they bring with them. (Foucault, 1972, p. 46)

Institutions like the university perform the function of a technology of power, 'determin(ing) the conduct of individuals and submit(ting) them to certain ends or

MARGARET WALSHAW

domination, an objectivising of the subject' (Foucault, 1988, p. 18), without, of course, resorting to physical restraint. They train people towards acceptable behaviour, providing '(1) technologies of production which permit us to produce, transform or manipulate things; (and) (2) technologies of sign systems, which permit us to use signs, meanings, symbols, or signification'. (p. 18) Those within these institutions guarantee their compliance through 'technologies of the self, which permit individuals to effect by their own means or with the help of others a certain number of operations on their own bodies and souls, thoughts, conduct, and ways of being, so as to transform themselves'. (Foucault, 1988, p. 18)

If, as in Foucault's understanding, teaching identities are constituted and negotiated within contexts of ongoing participation, then those identities are constantly on the move. Within and between different contexts pre-service teacher identifications are marked by competing meanings of experience, circumscribed by differences in time, place, events, and commitment. It makes little sense then to reduce the complexity of pedagogical activity to a technical solution. Yet prospective teachers want and expect to receive practical ideas, automatic and generic methods for immediate classroom application. They bring to their mathematics teaching course a search for recipes for putting across the mathematics content. Such a process sits comfortably within the tradition 'institutionalised in Western schooling, in which teaching/transmission is considered to be primary and prior to learning/internalising culture'. (Lave, 1997, p.10)

> I expected that the teachers' college course (in New Zealand) would teach me how to teach maths. I didn't know in what way. Maybe the best thing is to give them ten questions to do and then warm up to the main work, like copying down into notebooks, or like how you organise your lesson. Like what's the first thing that you want the students to do and next, how do you set up your notes on the board, and the way you get students to do the exercises. The organisation is really important. Sometimes I feel that students are slack during the period. The teacher might not have the control to deal with that because the whole class won't do any work. So I also wanted to know how to handle the classroom.

Two expectations are collapsed into one: knowing how to teach and knowing how to gain and sustain classroom control. Helen looked to the course as the source rather than the effect of pedagogy. She expected to acquire 'tricks of the trade'. She sought methods for classroom discipline presumably in order to put across the mathematics content and ultimately to gain respect as a competent member of the teaching profession. The central issue here is that mechanistic applications present knowledge as an accomplished fact, separate from discursive practices and the relations of power it presupposes. Becoming knowledgeable in a practice, in Lacan's understanding, entails more than learning *from* talk about techniques for immediate classroom application; it involves learning *to* talk within and about the practice. Technical approaches seriously limit the pre-service teacher's understanding of the relationship between pedagogical practice and theory to one unencumbered by the specificity and political commitments of the pedagogical act.

Helen's course work did not provide her with the methods she desired.

Helen: I didn't think we would learn so much about creative thinking.

MW: Did you think that the course might tell you that this is the best way to do things; that you start with this and then move onto that?

Helen: Yes, that's right. And, like, give you a couple of ways to work through a problem, instead of so many ways.

MW: Have you found that confusing?

Helen: No, not at all. It's really interesting. And I think that it's important because, like, if you can stimulate your brain then you can also stimulate your students. That's really important. I think the teacher has to be all the time thinking and being creative about maths.

There is a hint here that Helen is providing the kind of response she thought I expected to hear. However, I have no additional evidence to support this claim. What we do know is that in the course Helen was learning powerful lessons from teaching training discourses that provided her with cultural meaning systems about teaching mathematics. In the weeks she had been in this class, she had learned what does and does not count as performance. She did this by looking for an image of a teacher with which she felt comfortable and hoped to be liked by others (the Imaginary realm). These images - ones that alienate her from her position and fix her in the Others' view - are governed to a significant degree by the course lecturer's own pedagogic practices and the possibilities made available through them for pre-service teachers in the course. Precisely because it is the lecturer who is the subject-supposed-to-know in the classroom, it is the lecturer to whom pre-service teachers look for *closing the gaps* in their knowledge about how to 'perform' in mathematics classrooms.

Important issues of pedagogic governance and surveillance are at stake. Like the others in her course, Helen worked hard to gain recognition from the lecturer. This she did by attempting to embody the expected signifiers, continuously reflecting upon whether or not the signifiers are present or absent within themselves. Specifically, in the course, these signifiers included the more messy questions of what to teach and why particular methods are suitable. It required students to discuss and debate the main terms of the prescribed curriculum and their theoretical underpinnings, and work through the types of practice born out of such theorising. It also focused on the technologies of lesson preparation, computer software evaluation and the critique of the microteaching of peers. In Helen's estimation, those approaches did provide pre-service teachers with an opportunity to unmask their own relationship to mathematics. In the process it offered a set of landmarks rather than specific procedures for pre-service teachers. It endeavoured to shape opportunities for the activity of teaching and hence the process of learning to teach.

One classmate in the course introduced Pythagoras with the areas, you know, the squares - the little squares that add up to the big one. And I thought that was a great idea and most of the students would like that idea as well. I thought that if I didn't introduce the idea properly, then I'm going to have a heap of trouble for the following two or three weeks.

The significance of micro-teaching events such as these within the course becomes evident when we understand that it is through these experiences that specific identities are constructed for pre-service teachers. This is not to suggest that other social practices are not involved in developing in pre-service teachers a sense of self as teacher, but it is to point out that the course is tremendously influential in controlling the sorts of practices and teaching images that pre-service come to create. Knowledge about appropriate behaviour and practice is developed through these dividing practices - they are instrumental in shaping the way pre-service teachers come to think about teaching.

The Context of Teaching in Schools.

During three blocked weeks of the course year the pre-service teachers worked in schools under the supervision of their assigned associate teacher. The practicum is the time when a sustained structure of support is made available to pre-service teachers. It is founded on the presupposition that school life is the authentic moment for knowing, thinking, and understanding about teaching. Like others in apprentice situations student teachers observe 'experts' and others at work and they evaluate for themselves the 'products' of the experts' labour. Pre-service teachers value the 'practicum' experience as an opportunity to think, act and interact with knowledgeable others. In most schools, the teaching practice phase is carried out with one-off lessons at first, and builds to a much longer set of consecutive and sequenced lessons. A reasonable execution of the various constituencies such as questioning, and facilitation of student engagement is important but it is the overall pedagogical encounter which the pre-service teacher will be developing.

In Foucault's terms, we can speak of classroom teaching as positioned in relation to the discourses and practices levels operating within the classroom and school community. Those newly inserted into such practices, such as pre-service teachers, attempt to engage with those discourses. Pre-service teachers seeking membership to the category, teacher, attempt to mobilise the discourses of the school community and, in doing that, they mark out distinctions between practices about teaching as established from other relevant and meaningful systems and practices. More authoritative others in schools offer persuasive ways of doing things.

In practicum arrangements, the importance of learning to teach depends a great deal on collegiality and the opportunity to construct and reflect on new understandings. However, the complex and constantly shifting experience of teaching in schools places them in a vulnerable and dependent position, receptive to advice, support and guidance. Generally speaking, they make the best of things, even when what they understand by the category 'teacher' is challenged by the school. In seeking to resolve ambiguous and contradictory meanings, the pre-service teacher may well modify and adapt the school's ideas, language and practices of teaching. Often a new or hybrid discourse about what it means to be a teacher eventuates and, to that extent, the creation of teacher identity is derived in part and negotiated from the identity and discursive practices of others. Thus the pre-service teacher's membership in the category teacher is contingent, provisional, and in process.

It is within the classroom that a wide range of practices are at play to create distinctions between the associate and the pre-service teacher. In Foucault's understanding, pre-service teachers are objectified and classified according to the associate's standards, organisation of physical space and time in order to support particular kinds of pedagogical approaches, to create particular kinds of provision for students, and to nurture particular kinds of relationships between teachers and students as well as between students themselves. Helen talks of the ways in which the practices of the school, in general, and the mathematics department, in particular - their inclusive practices, and the 'inner workings' of their deliberations as a community - were made transparent for her:

> There were about 1100 students and there are about seven maths teachers, including the junior teachers…In the maths teachers' meeting I felt like I'd come to a classroom, because there was one speaker and I sat at one table and they were looking at assessment and it felt like being in the classroom. But then, after a while, I felt it's great to work with a team. They made me feel part of the group though they didn't talk to me but I knew that they saw me as another maths teacher. Those teachers were really sharing, and my associate maths teacher gave me a lot of help as well. They talked about what they had done in class all the time. So that's really helpful for other teachers to know and try out. They just talked about it as normal talk.

Like others in her course, Helen is constantly trying to close the gap between how she sees herself and how she thinks good teaching should be. She is always attempting to reconcile what she is with what she might become. In this school, she has found instances or episodes, or what Lacan calls a 'quilting point', that will provide her with a marker, a strategic place from where she will make her choices about how to close the gap between her own and others' views of her as a good mathematics teacher. In schools, the quilting point can be triggered, as Britzman (1998) has argued, by, among other things, an encouraging or supportive comment, a kindly word, or even the tone or modulation of another's voice. In Helen's case, it is triggered by the practices of inclusion and support operating within the mathematics department, and, importantly, other teachers' acknowledgment of Helen's status as a teacher. Having secured that marker, Helen began to act upon her 'imagined transformation of status'. (Walkerdine, 2003, p. 254)

The anticipation of future classroom experiences also plays a part in how Helen lives her subjectivity. She wants to become an expert and effective teacher. From her standpoint, the 'expert teacher' knows the mathematics content. This

MARGARET WALSHAW

compelling idea developed from the early yet influential work of Shulman and his associates at Stanford University (e.g., Shulman, 1986, 1987; Grossman, Wilson & Shulman, 1989), which presupposed a close association between teachers' knowledge and student gains. Others (e.g. Hill, Rowan & Ball, 2005) have substantiated the claim more recently. In addition to knowing the content, Helen, like many other pre-service teachers, has developed in her mind a check list of behaviours of practice that need to be learned and which are integral to the process of becoming a good mathematics teacher. Theorising about such connections for the pre-service teacher allows a double insight into the meanings of their relationships to individuals, institutions, cultural values and events, and how these relationships constitute his or her own identity, values, and ideological orientations. This kind of insight is helpful to the new teacher who can, in turn, participate in shaping and responding to the special forces, which impinge and construct teaching identity. Helen described a teacher she had observed during the practicum:

> The teacher is a really caring person. He showed a great interest in his students in the way he explains... Like the way he speaks. I can't think of any examples. He sort of talked to each of them, although he was talking to the whole class but you felt that he was talking to you - only talking to you so that's really good. And he also moved to the centre of the students, or quite close to the students so that the students won't think, oh, he's just so far away from us, so far away. And also he moved around the classroom. When he was introducing a new topic he'd use some activity and he used to involve his students. Once he bought a box of ice cream to share with everyone. They were doing the Poisson Distribution. He had the little lollies in the ice cream - Hokey Pokey. He used this to chat a little bit with the students...I think that another thing is that he tried to make things easy and clear. Say, like, he introduced 'exponential'. He just said it's a special number because he didn't need the students to know exactly so he just made it simple for students.

Normative notions of teaching style tend to ignore the social basis of pedagogy. In Lacan's understanding, however, every pedagogy is influenced by the complex social relations between teachers, students, school culture, and the larger social world. Within this compulsory relationship teaching style cannot be construed as an extension of one's personality. Rather, contradictions and social dependency are inevitable dynamics, and teaching style becomes subject to social negotiation. As Britzman (1991) has noted, teaching style then turns out not so much an individual determined product as a dialogic movement between the teacher, the students, the curriculum, the knowledge produced in exchange, and the social practices that make pedagogy intelligible.

> Another teacher was a really old teacher – he was due to retire in two or three years. The way he taught is that he knew whatever things the student knew, you know. Like say, for example, in (the local town) he used the highway that everyone knows. He knows the road names and all that. All the students

132

DEVELOPING THEORY TO EXPLAIN LEARNING TO TEACH

know where he was talking about and he used this to kind of apply a really difficult formula. The topic was 'making x the subject', and he used this formula. He introduced this by telling them how the highway is built and all the students were focused on it. I'd like to be like this teacher, this older teacher.

What I am at pains to stress is that a teaching identity is not constructed at the exclusion of the desires, interests, and investments of others. Theories that expand on Vygotsky's ideas tend to overlook the part that psychic processes play in the production of mathematical identity. For all their emphases on social practices, such theoretical treatments of identity constitution tend to downplay the importance of unconscious interference – interference from forms of reciprocity and obligation that are integral to classroom, familial and other social relationships. Such theories fall short of theorising how obligation, and so forth, are enacted into being.

Creating a teacher identity is a complex phenomenon. In psychoanalytic understanding, it has nothing to do with a pre-service teacher's nature or 'inner' mental capacity in relation to learn teaching methods, but, rather, it is about complex social relations within a mobile space. In the psychoanalytic tradition, identity does not presuppose a subject whose ontological status is necessarily coherent. It is, rather, 'necessarily *not* coherent' (Rose, 2005, p. 31), continually subverted within a kind of *metaphorical space between people.* The identities we have of our selves are made in and through the activities, desires, interests, and investments of others. For Helen this older teacher became one who could provide her with entry into the community of teaching practice. At first these steps were tentative and constituted an intellectual and emotional activity:

> I don't think I managed classroom control until the last about two weeks of my third teaching experience. I suddenly got some idea of how to control students. It's very slow, but at last I know that. At the beginning of the course I didn't expect that teaching would be so hard. And now although I think it's still a hard job I still think I'm capable. I mean I'm quite happy about it. I feel it's still difficult but I think I can do it.

What sense of identity will Helen now construct to legitimate her efforts to become a mathematics teacher? What images of teaching work through her narrative? How do those images match the Big Other with respect to her assessment of her own practices? Helen's narrative can be read as an effort to 'deconstruct old patterns and speak into existence new ones'. (Davies, 1997, p. 12) Within her practice there will 'inevitably point to a gap between how one is and how one might be'. (Brown & England, 2004, p. 72) Her sense-of-self is 'caught in a never-ending attempt to capture an understanding of...her relation to the world in which...she lives'. (Brown & England, p. 72) In Žižek's (1989) terms, Helen is 'hungering for new and better destinations, but never actually arriving'. (p. 14) In other words, there will never be complete reconciliation between what is demanded of her as a teacher and how she responds.

133

The fantasy functions as a construction…by giving us a definite answer to the question 'What does the Other want?', it enables us to evade the unbearable deadlock in which the Other wants something from us, but we are at the same time incapable of translating this desire of the Other into a positive interpellation, into a mandate with which to identify. (Žižek, 1989, p. 114)

CONCLUSION

In drawing attention to the creation of a teaching identity, I have put a 'psychoanalytic displacement' to use by combining Foucauldian and Lacanian treatments for exploring power and the intra-psychic processes that operate in the constitution of identity. In the discussion the concepts of dividing practices and registers of identifications were introduced. Neither of these theoretical tools is commonly employed within mathematics education. In advocating for their use, the overarching aim has been to stimulate reflection and discussion that will act as a catalyst to expand the scope of our analyses, and will spark the introduction of new questions and renewed engagement with theory.

Both Foucault and Lacan provide us with the theoretical resources to develop a new attitude towards systems, processes and people with mathematics education. Foucault's conceptualisations of power, discourse, and knowledge make a significant contribution to our analysis. His signature statement – that power and knowledge directly imply one another – has allowed us to think of the way power infuses itself in our very beings. In this analysis on learning to teach, we used the idea to show how pre-service teachers depend on it for their very existence, as they create their identities as teachers. It became apparent how systems of power classify and divide, producing and sustaining the sometimes contradictory meanings pre-service teachers have of themselves.

In particular, Foucault is able to theorise how identity is produced. Lacan, on the other hand, is able to theorise how identity is enacted into being. Whereas Foucault is able to show how a pre-service teacher is produced and regulated in discourses involving relations of power, Lacan provides us with the tools to track the way in which power insinuates itself to make a pre-service teacher *want* to be a specific kind of teacher. Both approaches are helpful to the analysis, but in my view, as a complement, the two together give us the tools and the language to get to the core of what learning to teach is all about.

Using the two approaches to develop a kind of conjoint framework, I tried to come to terms with biography, initial teacher education, as well as the practicum experience, and the discursive practices of all three. Meanings of a teaching identity have been constructed in relation to a number of significant others involving significant Others – previous school teachers and current lecturers, other pre-service teachers, and mathematics teachers in schools. The interrogation examined the 'simultaneous articulations of a dispersed and localised shifting nexus of social power' (Haywood & Mac an Ghaill, 1997, p. 268), surrounding the world of mathematics teaching. The three sites were chosen because the university and the school are social institutions that, like many others, are populated with viewpoints, identifications, images and choices, all of which shape the motivation to become a teacher.

In the telling of the teaching accounts we have seen how the construction of an identity is spoken into existence and lived in relation to processes and relationships operating in social spaces; how it is continually evolving, and structured through language and inter-subjective negotiations. In Helen we have seen traces of a secure identity. We have witnessed how she subscribes to 'intellectual package deals laid on' (Brown, 2008b) her in her university course. We have noted how when alternative versions of 'good' teaching become intelligible to her, dilemmas and contradictions came to the fore. Through them, we have become aware of the choices that Helen has to make. The work of Helen, like all other pre-service teachers, is formed in the gaps, the silences, and the contradictions within and amongst social practices and the images they have of them. And it is only when contradictions are worked through that one is able to sustain the illusion of a coherent and cohesive self.

REFERENCES

Blake, N., Smeyers, P., Smith, R., & Standish, P. (1998). *Thinking again: Education after postmodernism*. Westport, CT: Bergin & Garvey.

Britzman, D. (1991). *Practice makes practice: A critical study of learning to teach*. Albany, NY: State University of New York Press.

Britzman, D. (1998). *Lost subjects, contested objects: Toward a psychoanalytic inquiry of learning*. New York: State University of New York Press.

Brown, T. (2008). Comforting narratives of compliance: Psychoanalytic perspectives on new teacher responses to mathematics policy reform. In E. de Freitas & K. Nolan (Eds.), *Opening the research text: Critical insights and in(ter)ventions into mathematics education* (pp. 97–110). Dordrecht: Springer.

Brown, T. (2008b). Lacan, subjectivity and the task of mathematics education research. *Educational Studies in Mathematics*.

Brown, T., & England, J. (2004). Revisiting emancipatory teacher research: A psychoanalytic perspective. *British Journal of Sociology of Education, 25*(1), 67–80.

Brown, T., Jones, L., & Bibby, T. (2004). Identifying with mathematics in initial teacher training. In M. Walshaw (Ed.), *Mathematics education within the postmodern* (pp. 161–180). Greenwich, CT: Information Age.

Butler, J. (1997). *The psychic life of power: Theories in subjection*. Stanford, CA: Stanford University Press.

Butler, J. (2004). *Undoing gender*. New York: Routledge.

Cole, M. (1996). *Cultural psychology: A once and future discipline*. Cambridge, MA: Belknap Press.

Cooney, T. J. (2001). Considering the paradoxes, perils, and purposes of conceptualizing teacher development. In F.-L. Lin & T. J. Cooney (Eds.), *Making sense of mathematics teacher education* (pp. 9–31). Dordrecht: Kluwer Academic Publishers.

Davies, B. (1997). Constructing and deconstructing masculinities through critical literacy. *Gender and Education, 9*(1), 9–30.

Davies, B. (2000). *A body of writing 1990–1999*. Walnut Creek, CA: AltaMira Press.

Ellsworth, E. (1997). *Teaching positions*. New York: Teachers College Press.

Felman, S. (1987). *Jacques Lacan and the adventure into insight: Psychoanalysis in contemporary culture*. Cambridge, MA: Harvard University Press.

MARGARET WALSHAW

Foucault, M. (1972). *The archaeology of knowledge and the discourse of language* (A. Sheridan Smith, Trans.). London: Pantheon.

Foucault, M. (1977). *Discipline and punish*. Harmondsworth: Penguin Books.

Foucault, M. (1980). *Power knowledge: Selected interviews and other writings by Michel Foucault 1972–77* (C. Gordon, Ed. and Trans.). New York: Pantheon.

Foucault, M. (1984). *The care of the self* (R. Hurley, Trans., 1986). Harmondsworth: Penguin.

Foucault, M. (1988). *The ethic of care for the self as a practice of freedom*. Cambridge: The Massachusetts Institute of Technology Press.

Franke, M. L., Carpenter, T. P., Levi, L., Jacobs, V. R., & Empson, S. B. (2001). Capturing teachers' generative change: A follow-up study of professional development in mathematics. *American Educational Research Journal, 38*, 653–689.

Gee, J. P. (1997). Thinking, learning, and reading: The situated sociocultural mind. In D. Kirshner & J. A. Whitson (Eds.), *Situated cognition: Social, semiotic, and psychological perspectives* (pp. 235–259). Mahwah, NJ: Lawrence Erlbaum.

Gee, J. P. (2001). Identity as an analytic lens for research in education. *Review of Research in Education, 25*, 99–125.

Gee, J. P. (2004). Discourse analysis: What makes it critical? In R. Rogers (Ed.), *An introduction to critical discourse analysis in education* (pp. 19–59). Mahwah, NJ: Lawrence Erlbaum.

Grossman, P., Wilson, S., & Shulman, L. (1989). Teachers of substance: Subject matter knowledge for teaching. In M. C. Reynolds (Ed.), *Knowledge base for the beginning teacher* (pp. 23–36). New York: Pergamon.

Grosz, E. (1995). *Jacques Lacan: A feminist introduction*. London: Routledge.

Haywood, C., & Mac an Ghaill, M. (1997). Materialism and deconstructivism: Education and the epistemology of identity. *Cambridge Journal of Education, 27*(2), 261–272.

Hiebert, J., Gallimore, R., Garnier, H., Givvin, K., Hollingsworth, H., Jacob, J., et al. (2003). *Teaching mathematics in seven countries: Results from the TIMMS 1999 video study*. Washington, DC: U.S. Department of Education National Center for Educational Statistics.

Hill, H., Rowan, B., & Ball, D. (2005). Effects of teachers' mathematical knowledge for teaching on student achievement. *American Educational Research Journal, 42*(2), 371–406.

Jagodzinski, J. (Ed.). (2002). *Pedagogical desire: Authority, seduction, transference, and the question of ethics*. Westport, CT: Bergin & Garvey.

Lacan, J. (1977a). *Ecrits: A selection*. London: Tavistock.

Lacan, J. (1977b). *The four fundamental concepts of psycho-analysis*. London: The Hogarth Press.

Laclau, W., & Mouffe, C. (2001). *Hegemony and socialist strategy*. London: Verso.

Lave, J. (1988). *Cognition in practice: Mind, mathematics and culture in everyday life*. Cambridge: Cambridge University Press.

Lave, J. (1997). The culture of acquisition and the practice of understanding. In D. Kirshner & J. A. Whitson (Eds.), *Situated cognition: Social, semiotic, and psychological perspectives* (pp. 17–35). Mahwah, NJ: Lawrence Erlbaum Associates.

Lave, J., & Wenger, E. (1991). *Situated learning: Legitimate peripheral participation*. Cambridge: Cambridge University Press.

Lerman, S. (2001). A review of research perspectives on mathematics teacher education. In F.-L. Lin & T. J. Cooney (Eds.), *Making sense of mathematics teacher education* (pp. 33–51). Dordrecht: Kluwer Academic Publishers.

Rogoff, B. (1990). *Apprenticeship in thinking: Cognitive development in social contexts*. New York: Oxford University Press.

Rose, J. (2005). Femininity and its discontents. *Feminist Review, 80*, 24–43.

Roth, W.-M. (2004). Identity as dialectic: Re/making self in urban school. *Mind, Culture, and Activity, 11*(1), 48–60.

Sfard, A., & Prusak, A. (2005). Telling identities: In search of an analytic tool for investigating learning as a culturally shaped activity. *Educational Researcher, 34*(4), 14–22.

Sherin, M. G., Mendez, E. P., & Louis, D. A. (2004). A discipline apart: The challenges of 'Fostering a Community of Learners' in a mathematics classroom. *Journal of Curriculum Studies*, *36*(2), 207–232.

Shulman, L. S. (1986). Those who understand: Knowledge growth in teaching. *Educational Researcher*, *15*(2), 4–14.

Shulman, L. S. (1987). Knowledge and teaching: Foundations of the new reform. *Harvard Educational Review*, *57*(1), 1–22.

Shulman, L., & Shulman, J. (2004). How and what teachers learn: A shifting perspective. *Journal of Curriculum Studies*, *36*(2), 257–271.

Simon, M. A., Tzur, R., Heinz, M., & Smith, M. A. (2001). Characterising a perspective underlying the practice of mathematics teachers in transition. *Journal for Research in Mathematics Education*, *31*(5), 579–601.

Valsiner, J. (1987). *Culture and the development of children's action: A cultural-historical theory of developmental psychology*. Chichester: John Wiley and Sons.

Walkerdine, V. (1997). Redefining the subject in situated cognition theory. In D. Kirshner & J. A. Whitson (Eds.), *Situated cognition: Social, semiotic, and psychological perspectives* (pp. 57–70). Mahwah, NJ: Lawrence Erlbaum Associates.

Walkerdine, V. (2003). Reclassifying upward mobility: Femininity and the neo-liberal subject. *Gender and Education*, *15*(3), 237–248.

Walshaw, M. (2001). A Foucauldian gaze on gender research: What do you do when confronted with the tunnel at the end of the light? *Journal for Research in Mathematics Education*, *32*(5), 471–492.

Wenger, E. (1998). *Communities of practice: Learning, meaning and identity*. Cambridge: Cambridge University Press.

Wertsch, J. V. (1991). *Voices of the mind: A sociocultural approach to mediated action*. Cambridge: Cambridge University Press.

Žižek, S. (1989). *The sublime object of ideology*. London: Verso.

Žižek, S. (Ed.). (1998). *Cogito and the unconscious*. Durham: Duke University Press.

Margaret Walshaw
College of Education
Massey University
New Zealand

ELIZABETH DE FREITAS

6. ENACTING IDENTITY THROUGH NARRATIVE: INTERRUPTING THE PROCEDURAL DISCOURSE IN MATHEMATICS CLASSROOMS

INTRODUCTION: MATHEMATICS TEACHER IDENTITY

This chapter emerges from a research project designed to explore the complexities of mathematics teacher identity. Four mathematics teachers were studied in their classrooms during one semester. Notes and transcripts from the class observations were analysed using a discourse analysis framework. The discourse was treated as cultural data regarding identity in the mathematics classroom. Analysis focused on the use of the narrative register in classroom discourse, and on how this register was contextualised within the dominant procedural discourse.

Teacher identity is sutured onto and through the socio-political framing of mathematics education – that is to say, in teaching mathematics, teachers negotiate a provisional identity through the enactment of various social positions. Teachers perform in/through discursive patterns of instruction and curriculum while also enacting (often unconsciously) power differentials across the larger structural formations of sexuality, ethnicity, and economic status. This complex discursive performance points to the multiple ways in which teachers 'teach' both content and identity.

Identity is not simply 'situated' in particular discursive practices; identity is both subjected to dominant normative discourse and also constituted and enabled through such compliance (Butler, 1997). Our discursive enactment of identity involves a contradictory mix of *submission* to the cultural norms inscribed in the discourse, and *empowerment* through this act of re-inscription. Teachers perform through a professional discourse of curriculum and instruction – they submit to the power relations that are embedded in this discourse – but they are also constituted by these power relations. They are hailed as subjects in an institutional discourse. Teacher agency emerges through this contradictory mix. My focus in this chapter is on how teachers enact identity in classroom discourse. I analyze teacher talk for evidence of this 'paradox of subjectification (Butler, 1997) by which subject positions are simultaneously constituted and enabled by the very discourse that also inhibits their agency.

Butler (1997) offers a theory of partial agency by pointing to the ways in which resistance and transformation are possible through the construction of 'critical capacities' that allow identities to re-define their position within particular

T. Brown (ed.), The Psychology of Mathematics Education: A Psychoanalytic Displacement, 139–155.
© *2008 Sense Publishers. All rights reserved.*

ELIZABETH DE FREITAS

discursive practices. She is careful to insist that these moments of resistance or agency are not simply a matter of freely determined choice, but rather 'performative' in the sense of being discursive enactments of contingent cultural norms. Each enactment involves some form of modification of the cultural norm, but is simultaneously constrained by the rules of the discourse. My goal is to understand how these 'critical capacities' might emerge in school mathematics where the classroom culture continues to be dominated by procedural tasks. Despite 'best practices' that celebrate diverse problem solving processes, and despite attempts by the reform movement to disrupt teacher-centred instruction, mathematics classroom discourse is still overwhelmingly governed by procedural discourse, and mathematics classrooms are still communities of consensus that disallow divergent positions (Malloy, 2004).

A classroom culture where procedural discourse dominates - where teacher talk is machine talk – has oppressive impact on identity. The place of identity construction becomes a 'place of splitting' (Bhabha, 1994, p. 44) precisely because of the erasure of difference and the silencing of dissent. This is a site in which 'the invitation to a wholeness of identity carries with it the implicit requirement that I disconnect from myself, or, more specifically, that I speak from only one position as the totality of my subjectivity.' (Sasaki, 2003, p. 41) The consensus model of mathematics education, in which procedural tasks govern classroom discourse, erases all contingent, provisional, conflicting subject positions, leaving room for only one legitimate 'identity of mastery'. Many mathematics teachers, however, disrupt this seamless identity by performing *against* mastery in both deliberate and unanticipated ways. Teacher narratives, for instance, often erupt unbidden in classroom discourse, disrupt the procedural sequence of blackboard instruction, and function as embodied performances of socio-historical identity. Personal narratives that are grounded in the embodied experiences of the teacher often constitute teacher identity in terms of vulnerability and contingency.

When teachers shift back and forth between procedural discourse and personal narrative they enact radically different identities (Adler, 2001). The procedural discourse enacts a mastery identity ('I' as machine) while the personal narrative enacts a vulnerable identity ('I' as embodied self). At the same time, each discourse is inscribed with normative messages about the legitimacy of particular subject positions in the classroom; the procedural discourse positions the teacher as expert ('I' as authority) and the personal narrative positions the teacher according to race, gender, ethnicity and class ('I' as member of the community). Although the procedural discourse also locates the speaker within these social constructs – because procedural discourse is never neutral – I am focusing here on the functions of personal narratives. For instance, stories about events seen as one drove to work that day communicate messages about one's socio-economic position within the community. If one accepts that these personal narratives also 'teach' students about socio-cultural positioning within mathematics classrooms, often without teacher awareness that they are doing so, then the need to study the role of personal narratives in relation to the dominant procedural discourse becomes essential.

ENACTING IDENTITY THROUGH NARRATIVE

In this chapter I examine when, how and why mathematics teachers shift between the procedural and the personal narrative registers. The shift between procedural and personal narrative register is almost always awkward because of the radically different subject positions constituted through the two discourses. Indeed, the two discourses are so radically displaced from each other, it is difficult to imagine the bridging or blending that might create a cohesive discourse that includes them both. It is this apparent incomprehensibility, which is the focus of this chapter. My aim is to show how the personal narratives are actually used to enforce the legitimacy of procedural discourse.

Four high school mathematics teachers were studied in their classrooms during one semester. Notes and transcripts from the class observations were analyzed using a discourse analysis framework. The discourse was treated as cultural data regarding identity and community in the math classroom. Analysis focused on the use of the narrative register in classroom discourse, and on how this register was contextualized within the dominant procedural discourse.

PATTERNS OF DISCOURSE

A discourse analysis framework (Fairclough, 2003) was used to examine the transcripts from the classroom observations. The data was first coded for shifts between three kinds of discourse: mathematical (inquiry, procedural, conceptual), administrative (assessment, management, school issues), and contextual (personal narrative, anecdote, metaphor, application). These were then subdivided into eight registers: (1) procedural (2) conceptual (3) inquiry questions (4) personal narrative (5) anecdotal (6) metaphoric (7) classroom management (8) school business. The transcripts were analyzed for occurrences of and transitions between these registers. I use the term *register* to refer to a subset of the many genres that characterize conventions of spoken language. As Fairclough suggests, the term *genre* – which some might prefer - is extremely vague in discourse analysis because it can refer to everything from the meta-level generic structures of discourse to the communicative strategies of particular forms of writing (Fairclough, 2003, p. 68). The term genre functions effectively in reference to the field of possible sources of generic structure in discourse, but it seems to lose its capacity for specificity in doing so. Texts or interactions 'are not 'in' a particular genre, they do not instantiate a particular genre – rather they draw upon the socially available resource of genres in potentially quite complex and creative ways'. (Fairclough, 2003, p. 69)

In this chapter, the term *register* refers to different modes of address in spoken language. A register enacts rules or conventionalized practices of language use. The different registers listed above are usually found in classroom discourse, and in some cases are blended or mixed. The first data coding revealed the patterns of discourse over the entire period of observation (20 occasions in total). With each of the four participants, the procedural register dominated the classroom discourse. Observation notes from all of the twenty observed classes recorded teacher-directed pedagogy (whole class instruction and teacher transmission) and an overwhelming emphasis on mastery of procedure (in contrast to inquiry instruction

141

ELIZABETH DE FREITAS

or conceptual investigations). These teachers were not 'exemplary' teachers in terms of reform or other criteria. They represent the vast majority of mathematics teachers who continue to invest in transmission pedagogy and continue to emphasize procedural mastery. They were selected for that reason. Because of my focus on procedure and narrative, I will define only these two registers and leave the others alone.

The procedural register is highly abstract and depersonalized. It contains almost no traces of personal presence – or rather, procedural discourse enacts the absence of the personal. Personal narrative, on the other hand, positions the speaker and explicitly constructs a social identity. My analysis focused on the juxtaposition between procedural and personal narrative registers. This chapter examines the relationship between these two registers, focusing on the way that teachers blend or join the registers. Narrative embodiments within the realm of procedural discourse can be seen as an attempt to introduce a sense of self or identity. The personal narrative register presents the speaker as a situated body in a socio-cultural and physical world. The discourse within the narrative is understood to be of a different ontological status than the discourse within the procedural register. Each register seems to interrupt the other because they seem so mutually incomprehensible. I argue, however, that the two function alongside each other in co-constituting the subject position of the teacher. I argue that the process of suturing an identity across these two radically different registers must be read in terms of the dominant procedural discourse.

In other research areas, studies of patients' use of personal narrative during medical examinations have suggested that the storying of the self creates a safe enclave for identity, while the body is subjected to the disarticulating experience of the medical discourse (Young, 1999). In Young's study, patients' stories were tokens of a life history, invoked on the occasion of a medical examination, as evidence of personhood and presence. Young examines the social function of stories in particular contexts, like that of the medical examination, as a way of understanding how individuals construe their lives. The embodied self is enacted through stories, but a different self is enacted in medical procedural talk, although many might contend that no self at all is enacted in procedural talk. Young argues that the storied self is presented or enacted as a proprietary act within a discourse that threatens the self. But she sees each discourse as an enactment of identity, each enactment involves a 'modulation from embodied to disembodied performances'. (Young, 1999, p. 430)

Shifting registers or frames is a complex linguistic capacity. When a speaker moves abruptly from one form of address to another, they often enact two radically different and sometimes mutually incomprehensible forms of subjectivity. The shift involves more than two specialized sets of vocabulary in two different discourses. Each register has its own social grammar, and each thereby interpellates a distinct subject or identity. Both the speaker and listener are constituted through the form of address. The meaning of an utterance is constructed within the social grammar and the implied power relations of the register. In order to comprehend an utterance, the learner and speaker must locate

142

ENACTING IDENTITY THROUGH NARRATIVE

the utterance within a particular register, and simultaneously, the learner and speaker must also recognize themselves as constituted as subjects through the register. When speaker and listener use a narrative register about personal experience, for instance, they are hailing each other as personal acquaintances. The personal narrative register often enacts power relations of intimacy, exposure and vulnerability. The listener is addressed as a confidant. Refusal to be recognised as personal acquaintance would disrupt the power relation conveyed within the register. The act of personal narrative is one of vulnerability but it is also an act of centering. The story-teller offers personal anecdote and seemingly 'exposes' a private world, but she or he also demands that the listener recognize (by listening) her status as a person with a life history, and, in some cases, her status as an agent of change or action. The following are a few facets of subjectivity that are constituted through the personal narrative register: (1) vulnerability (2) agency (3) social position/ presence, and (4) temporality. In contrast, the procedural register is characterized by rigorous rule following and the imperative mode, and thereby constitutes facets of subjectivity that are radically different. In the procedural register, both speaker and listener are addressed in terms of: (1) proficiency (2) compliance (3) abstraction/absence (4) atemporality.

WHY TELL A STORY?

One can characterise registers in terms of purpose, but one has to be careful to not overemphasise purpose. While it is possible to read registers in terms of purpose, and it seems as though most discourse occurs for a purpose, it is essential that we recognise the difference between overtly purposeful discourse – like that found in the procedural register – and what is often apparently non-instrumental discourse – like that found in personal narrative discourse. Although both registers in the classroom can be read through the lens of strategy, as can the 'informal chattiness' of employees in other work environments (Fairclough, 2003, p. 72), the personal narrative can also appear entirely without purpose. Overemphasis on purpose privileges the rationality and intention of the speaker, and fails to recognize the complex ways in which the speaker remains unknown to him/herself. Speakers often spontaneously erupt into story, without any premeditation. Although one could argue that stories are told when a speaker deems it fortuitous or appropriate, it is important to recognise the apparent spontaneity of story in particular instances, and to note that this perceived spontaneity marks the narrative as a kind of psychoanalytic trace. We are not thoroughly rational creatures enacting our rational intentions. Narratives often erupt unbidden, disrupt our attempts to present ourselves in a professional or other way, and thereby indicate facets of our subject position, which we enact without conscious intention.

Whether it be the narrative or procedural register, the speaker is subjected by the generic structure of the register – is made compliant to the rules of the discourse – but is never completely inscribed by this discourse. There is always a strong measure of misrecognition. Processes of subjection are never entirely perfect, mechanisms of social reproduction are definitively incomplete, which is precisely

ELIZABETH DE FREITAS

how variation and resistance arise. If the subject were perfectly constituted through the purpose of the speech act, then there would be no possibility of dissent, difference, resistance, and some might argue, no possibility of learning. Resistance relies on the imperfection of social control, difference relies on the unpredictability of action, and dissent relies on there being an unanticipated alteration in the act of communication. Mis-readings are crucial in learning and individuation.

Labov & Waletzky (1967) developed a framework for understanding narrative structure in terms of temporal junctures. They analyzed adult narratives of personal experience in terms of a linear sequence of six moments: 'abstract, orientation, an evaluation section embedded in the complicating action, a resolution and a coda'. (Labov, 2006, p. 37) This common structure of narrative (although not universal) helps us recognize the narrative register, but Labov points out that the essential first step in story telling is the decision to report an event (Labov, 2006). These decisions to relay a particular story are crucial in understanding how and why individuals invest in certain subject positions or identities. One can envision identity as a temporary attachment to a subject position constructed through the discursive practices of the narrative (Hall, 1996, p. 6). Attending to the personal narratives enacted in classroom teacher talk points to both the socio-cultural and the psychological aspects of the self. Careful attention to that which is storied speaks to the social positioning of the teller, and attention to the structuring of the narrative and its relation to the other discursive registers speaks to the psychic work of narrative. Attention to these two aspects of narrative discourse offers a heuristic for analysis. In this project, the narratives were not invited in an interview, but simply emerged spontaneously in the classroom. This research method allowed for a more accurate study of how narrative functioned in the classroom discourse. The approach allowed me to focus on what stories are *doing* for the participants, and on what stories are designed to do in this context. In contrast to a more deliberate collection of stories through interviews, this approach examined how narratives function ethno-methodologically.

> In contrast to what we might call 'mainstream' narrative analytic work, an alternative research tradition based in conversation analysis and discursive psychology examines narratives (i.e. stories and story elements) as productions tailored for the sequentially organized occasions of their telling (e.g., Edwards, 1997; Jefferson, 1978; Ryave, 1978). The interest is therefore in *how* stories are told – how they get embedded and are managed, turn by turn, in interaction – and what conversational actions are accomplished in their telling (e.g. complaining, justifying, flirting, testifying, etc.) (Stokoe & Edwards, 2006, p. 57)

Recent research in mathematics education calls for further study on how narrative intersects with mathematics learning (de Freitas, 2004; Doxiadis, 2003; Drake, Spillane & Hufferd-Ackles, 2001; Povey, Burton, Angier & Boylan, 2004). Doxiadis argues that a new vision of 'doing mathematics' might also incorporate the telling of mathematics experiences in a narrative mode, a kind of 'paramathematics' that situates mathematics in story (Doxiadis, 2004). Povey &

ENACTING IDENTITY THROUGH NARRATIVE

Burton suggest that such narratives are crucial for making sense of why so many 'fail in their attempts to learn mathematics and, in particular, why so many of these unsuccessful learners are predominantly found in particular communities'. (Povey, Burton, Angier & Boylan, 2004, p. 43) But none of these researchers have examined the role of story in the mathematics classroom as a form of identity enactment, nor the ways that teacher stories disrupt institutional discourse in classroom practice.

THE PARTICIPANTS AND THE STORIES

The four participants are Roy, Janet, Mark and Leslie. They teach in a rural school in Canada. The school population is over 95% white. It is not a high-needs school, but there is significant socio-economic diversity within the student population. Classes are each 80 minutes long, and class size is about 30 students. Each participant was observed on five occasions. Participants are presented in terms of increasing frequency of personal narrative discourse. During our observations, Roy used no personal narratives, Janet used one personal narrative, Mark used three personal narratives, and Leslie used six personal narratives.

Roy

Roy was the chair of the mathematics department. He had been teaching for over thirty years. He taught the upper level grade 12 academic classes. During the five observations, Roy did not share any personal narratives with the class. From beginning to end, he employed only administrative and mathematical discourse, with the usual amounts of embedded English grammar. His instructional style was to complete homework questions on the blackboard if students requested them, and to then complete a series of problems on the next textbook topic, again on the blackboard. He did not incorporate metaphorical language or analogy or other contextual language. His vocabulary consisted only of the parameters given by the particular problem under discussion. Although he was teaching 'applied' problems about rates of change, his focus was on the algebraic procedure, and the applications came directly from the textbook problems. The only traces of 'I' statements in his classes were those that pertained to the procedure of completing problems, or to his evaluation of a procedure, a problem, or student effort. Roy's class was the advanced University Preparation course in calculus. Roy's use of contextual and administrative registers usually pertained to student academic trajectory and the future scholastic demands of university 'life'. Observation notes indicated that students eagerly complied with the learning agenda, and freely submitted to the procedural discourse. Mastery in this class was extremely valued. Roy enacted the role of the expert whose mastery was never in doubt. The absence of personal narratives speaks to the process of enculturation by which students at this level have gained full membership in the 'expert' community, have absorbed the rules of the discourse, and do not have to risk (nor be addressed through) an embodied 'I'.

145

ELIZABETH DE FREITAS

Janet

Janet had been teaching for 13 years. She taught a grade 10 academic class. During the five observations, Janet shared only one personal narrative with the class. She spent more time on classroom management talk than the other participants. She used very unsituated examples in her instruction (emphasis on sign manipulation), but she did try on occasion to give motivating contexts for the mathematical material ('Suppose you want to build a roof'). Her lessons were delivered using overhead projector, digital projector and blackboard. The students copied notes as she revealed them on the screen. She spoke to the whole class as she disclosed the written material and diagrams. Whole class instruction was followed by individual work. Below is the only personal narrative that Janet shared while she was observed. I have included the procedural discourse that contextualizes the narrative, so that the reader can see the way that Janet shifted back and forth between the registers.

(After 4 minutes of requests for 'hats off' and 'put your calculators away', and 3 minutes of announcements about the day's agenda, she asks the students to complete two calculations on the blackboard. The first calculation is 294 x 25. The second calculation is 42360/20. She prepares her slides while they settle down and attempt the calculations.)

Janet: Alright, has everybody finished the first problem? Ok. Let's just take a look at number 1. Because it's not necessarily easier but a little less mess than that other one. Alright. Is it a fair assumption that by the time you've hit grade 10 academic math you should be able to multiply those out.

Students: Yes.

Janet: Ok. Perfect, so what do you do? Where do you start?

Students: The bottom right.

Janet: The bottom right? Times each of the top. Right, you're going to get zero there. And then you go down to your next row. You put a placeholder for that one and you start the next one and so on. Is that what everybody did? Used placeholders and worked it all out? What did we get for an answer?

(Most of the class responds)

Janet: 7350? How many got it? Excellent. Ok. That is encouraging. Alright, now there's a method to my madness in having you do this today. Ah, twofold. Obviously you should be able to multiply and divide in grade 10. But you would be surprised at how many people can't. I remember, I think I may have told this story before I went to get gas. This happened last summer. And I gave the

146

ENACTING IDENTITY THROUGH NARRATIVE

person like, I don't know, it cost 35 dollars to fill my car and I gave them 50 and they couldn't figure it out. And it was weird, because like within a 2-week span every time I went to buy something somewhere, groceries, I kind of ran into the same problem. People, if the machine wasn't working right or you gave them like, say it came to 20 dollars and 46 cents and you gave them $25.46, it threw them off. They didn't know what to do, that sort of thing. So it was kind of enlightening to me that, you know, not everybody is getting these basic math skills. So I'm glad and impressed that you guys can multiply. So, that's a good thing. The real reason I had you do this is, because how long did it take you just to do problem number 1?'

Student: A long time.

Janet: A while. If I said now that you can use your calculators, how long would it take you?

Students: seconds

Janet: Or less, right? So, if you do not bring a calculator every day for trigonometry, you'll be doing that all class. I'm serious. So, the method to my madness is, you will bring a calculator every day after seeing how much torture it is trying to multiply and divide those numbers out.

Janet's story is explicitly functional. First, the story is the explanation as to why she is asking them to perform calculations 'long hand'. It functions as an explanation for the mathematical task. Her story recounts an experience that has made her worry about basic numeracy skills in the local population. She says, 'I think I may have told this story before', pointing to its ritual status as a story of moral significance. Stories are repeated in this way when they function as parables or moral lessons. By pointing out the repetition, she reminds the students that this story is essentially a lesson about life. The story also functions implicitly as a lesson about numeracy and socio-economic positioning. As a moral lesson, the story warns the students that, without numeracy skills, they are no better than the unskilled gas attendants and grocery cashiers whom she encounters. Her grade ten class will be divided the following year into university track students (to be found in Roy's class) and college or other bound students. The story is a way of reminding them of the material consequences of their performance in school mathematics.

Janet shifts between the narrative discourse and the procedural by saying 'The real reason I had you do this...' thereby bracketing the narrative into a separate enclave of less value (as it turns out, the story is a red herring, because she actually wants them to rely on calculators during trigonometry). But her emphasis on procedure is mirrored in the story she chooses to present to the class, a story about procedural mastery of multiplication. Note that she is concerned that her

ELIZABETH DE FREITAS

encounters at the gas station and elsewhere point to others' inability to perform mental maths calculations, and yet she asks the students to perform longhand calculations. The disconnect between the story and the task is compounded when she states that her 'real' purpose is to help them see the value of calculators, since the story admonishes those who become too reliant on calculating machines. The contradictions regarding her stated purpose underscore the many different functions of the story.

Janet's personal narrative is highly disembodied. Her story conveys no intimacy and no vulnerability on her part, but rather functions as a lesson about social position and subjectification. As such, it breaks with one of the usual aspects of personal narrative – to convey the vulnerable 'I'. She is the authority in the room and uses the story to communicate both her power as moral judge and the power of school mathematics to determine socio-economic status. The paradox of her own subject status is in her disembodiment. She enacts or performs an identity of mastery which she uses to control the students. Her personal narrative functions to enforce her control, by pointing to the ramifications for students if they do not submit to the rules of the discourse. Thus, her desire to control the students is implicated and given larger cultural significance through the narrative performance.

Mark

Mark had been teaching for 10 years. He taught grade 11 Academic math. The ratio of male to female was approximately 1:1, but a group of five male students dominated the student talk during whole class discussion. Mark kept the students busy with opening mental math exercises or puzzles, closing pop quizzes, 'life questions' if time permitted, and lots of teacher-centered procedural demonstrations on the blackboard. Mark embedded many references to sports throughout his lessons, and he had an ongoing conversation with the five boys about the national hockey league results. As he proceeded through the many examples on the blackboard he regularly categorized each question in terms of difficulty by using a 'rottweiller' rating system. His personal anecdotes were mostly grounded in his impressions about particular sport events and were directed at the five male students. There were three personal narratives shared with the entire class during the five observations. One pertained to writing a reference letter to a student, and functioned as an explicit parable about the importance of performing well in mathematics. Another was about his experience travelling in the Czech Republic where his passport was taken from him at the border and he worried that he would be imprisoned. The third is found below:

(A Sudoku puzzle is on the blackboard. Mark chats for five minutes with a group of male students about hockey scores before addressing the class. A teacher arrives at the door during the first 5 minutes and hands Mark a photograph. They chuckle and exchange a few words.)

148

ENACTING IDENTITY THROUGH NARRATIVE

Mark: OK. Folks can you take that Sudoku into your notes.

Mark: You want to give me a little sympathy. You can see my grade 1 picture here. I have my Montreal uniform on there with all the other ignorant Toronto fans. Actually, something like that kind of similar happened when I moved here. I moved here when I was seven years old. In grade two I went to class my first day at West Henley School. And the school I went to in Montreal you had to wear a uniform. These little grey trousers and a little blue blazer and a tie. And my mother, god bless her heart, sent me to school in the same uniform. So I walked down to West Henley School. And I got there. And everybody's in there in a pair of jeans and a t-shirt and I'm this idiot at the back of the class with a blazer and a tie and stuff and so I ran home at lunch crying. (laughter from class). (more loudly) And that's why I'm the teacher today, to put a little hell into your lives. (2 seconds pass)

Mark: Ok. So take this down please. Hint here. Just if you start with the 5s and 6s this will help you try to solve this. Remember when we're doing these, each row and column and each box has to contain the numbers one through nine just once.

Mark shifts back and forth between the personal narrative and the procedural discourse, but makes no attempts to blend these or to seek intersections between them, as in the case of Janet. His story (as with the other two we recorded from him) is not directly related to the mathematics content. He presents himself in anecdote and rhetorical style as someone with a life history of adventure, but he doesn't share everyday stories unless they pertain to ongoing televised sports competitions. He invests in his social identity as a hockey fan for a particular team, and defines himself against the other 'enemy' team. Mark invests in a masculine sports identity in classroom discourse, and often uses the term 'the ladies' in class. Mark's contextual discourse cited gender more frequently than the other participants. For instance, in recounting a personal anecdote about his past experience working at a boarding school, he said 'And the guys, I worked in a guys house, they seemed to be easier to deal with, because guys would come straight up to you and go 'F Off' and they get it off their chest. And girls, they go da da da da and behind you they're saying you're the biggest -----'

The narrative triggered by the picture of Mark in his Montreal Canadian hockey jersey in grade one, tells of his personal anguish as a small child at a new school. It is a story about the agony of school culture and the incredible emotion experienced by those who feel like outsiders. The other story he tells about the Czech border is similar in its focus on his anguish around identity or loss of alliance. He presents himself as vulnerable in these stories, as someone who invests passionately in social alliances or affiliations (nationalities, hockey fandom, school culture). Mark is performing an identity in these personal narratives. It is not that he chooses this identity, but by repeated citation of this identity in and through discourse, he comes to identify it as fixed and inherently meaningful. According to Butler, this coalescing of identity is never felt to be sufficient, no matter how strongly articulated or defended, because it is always already threatened by that which it aims to exclude. One must endlessly enact this identity through speech acts that sustain it. Reading Mark's classroom discourse through a gender lens would doubtless shed light on one of the particular differences he hopes to exclude. But my focus here is the relationship between the procedural discourse and the personal narrative. Mark's storying of himself is a performative enactment of himself as embodied. He counters the disembodied absence of procedural discourse with the embodied discourse of personal narrative. Mark presents himself (to his students and to his own self-regarding gaze) as someone who desires recognition. Redman (2005) (drawing on the work of Graham Dawson), argues that personal narratives 'should be understood as inevitably dialogic or relational – that is, as seeking recognition (as like or different) from significant social others in these worlds'. (Redman, 2005, p. 35) Mark's stories are about his difference from others, and his need for recognition. There are other psychological dynamics expressed through his personal narratives, such as the process of splitting and erasing his difference as he acculturates to the local school culture where no one wears uniforms.

When examining the shift to the personal narrative register, one hears a certain awkwardness: *'Actually, something like that kind of similar happened when I moved here.'* The word 'actually' marks the introduction of reality into the classroom discourse, but the messy grammar of comparison ('something like that kind of similar' – with reference to his wearing a Montreal hockey jersey in the photograph) points to the rough transition between the Sudoko puzzle and the personal narrative register. He closes the narrative with the coda – 'and that's why I'm the teacher – to put a little hell into your lives.' And then he smoothly shifts into the procedural discourse and explains the method for solving the Sudoko puzzle. The splitting at this moment in his identity may in fact be a point of suturing when his social position as teacher is stitched together with the enactment of procedural proficiency. As a point of suturing, one can ask whether the enactment of a disembodied self through the procedural discourse is a form of introjection, whereby Mark internalizes that which was once threatening and other but is now his to enact in the classroom. That is to say, the power formations of school culture that subjected him to humiliation as a young boy are strongly introjected and later performed through his enactment of 'the teacher'. In this way, the code for making sense of the story ('And that's why …') involves reading it as supportive of his mastery identity. In situating the narrative within the classroom discourse, one sees how the enactment of the vulnerable 'I' functions to legitimate the 'I' as authority.

Leslie

Leslie had been teaching for 7 years. She taught a grade 11 'Life mathematics' course. Poor attendance was an issue. During the five observations, Leslie taught from the front of the classroom, writing examples on the blackboard and asking the

ENACTING IDENTITY THROUGH NARRATIVE

students for answers. Her questions shifted back and forth between personal questions about student experiences (both related and unrelated to 'Life Mathematics') and questions about factual or procedural issues in the content. She struggled to keep student attention. She frequently introduced personal anecdotes into her talk, often about her family. The following is one paradigmatic story in Leslie's classroom discourse.

(After 7 minutes of administrative discourse (exam schedule), Leslie asks 'Ok! How many go to the races in the summer? You know the races?')

Student: What races?

Leslie: Horse races. When you're looking at the horse race, what do you see on the board? When they have the horses all …

(An announcement interrupts the class)

(Students walk in late)

Leslie: Guys, class starts at 8:50. If you're gonna be late, you'd better bring a note. You missed my speech about how there's 11 days left and to make sure you're here on time and all the rest.

Student: I didn't even think I was going to, like, make it. I was ready to go back to sleep.

Leslie: We don't need all the stories. Ok, um, Brad, you were saying that the horse races, again. I'm not 100% accurate on this because I don't go to the horse races but I have been there a time or two. Ok, what would this mean?

(Leslie writes on the board 1:100. She continues to question the students about the ways in which odds in favour of a horse winning is calculated. Then she talks about odds in favour and against in the abstract case. Twice more she refers to horse racing and mentions that she doesn't know much about them: 'I don't know, anybody, who goes to the races a lot? Mike? What are the numbers usually like?' and then 'Oh. Anybody a horse person? I'm not so I can't really say I've seen those numbers on there when I go to the exhibition, to walk through there, the horse races.' A few students speculate about the numbers (no use of hands to mark the right to speak).)

Leslie: Yeah. Anyway, like I say. I 'm not up on horse racing to tell you, but I do know that those numbers are telling what are the odds, and the greater the odds, the higher the payout. I do know that much. My husband has a good friend who's big into horse racing. They went away to school one year, they went down to the states where it's cool and they went to the horse races one night, and there was a horse there who the guy remembered being back (in his

ELIZABETH DE FREITAS

> hometown), years ago, and what a good horse it was. So, they had like 20 bucks each and decided to throw it on to see what happens and the odds were very high that he would not win. And, so anyway, they won. They won like 250 bucks each or something like that. When you're students away somewhere that's a lot of money.

(An individual student near the front says something to her and they talk while the rest of the class cannot hear. Leslie then begins writing on the board. The students then begin recording what she is writing)

> Student: What is the word right after ...?

>> (Leslie proceeds to talk to the entire class about the procedure for calculating and recognizing odds and probability. Her description of the rules for representing probability and odds are somewhat confused as she speaks: 'When we're looking at probability, it was always a fraction. It was always like 1 out of 10 or 2 out of 6 ... ok each of them would be a number between zero and 1 and they would be written as a ratio...')

Leslie tells stories about her family. She presents herself as a mother and wife. Her anecdotes convey her preferences and her knowledge about everyday matters. A number of utterances communicate her unfamiliarity or lack of knowledge with the rules of horse racing. These anecdotes set up her vulnerability as someone who is willing to learn from her students. The course she teaches lends itself to the personal narrative register, because of the curriculum resources, but nonetheless she might have used stories about others instead of her own family. In this example, when she shifts to the personal narrative register, her confidence about what she knows increases. She is demonstrating that knowledge gained from personal experience is more reliable than other kinds of knowledge. Unfortunately, she fails to say 'odds against' in the utterance: 'the greater the odds, the higher the payout', and thereby suggests the opposite and incorrect correlation between odds and pay-out. But it may be that the actual mathematics embedded in the story is less important than the other messages embedded in the story. Leslie shifts to the personal narrative register in order to present herself as socially and physically positioned.

The story recounted in this excerpt is about her husband's experience 'away' (in another country) as a student without money, making a bet on a long shot because of the connection between the horse and his hometown. It's not clear why she decides to tell the story, except to entertain the students or perhaps reveal a 'real life' situation where evaluating odds matters in terms of money. The narrative, like the many anecdotes about burgers and other local items, presents her as an individual with a particular life history. It is also a story about going away to school, which is an experience associated with academic success, particularly in this rural community, and even more so in the 'Life Mathematics' class. Much of the talk in this course pertains to making, saving and judiciously spending money. There are chapters in the textbook about balancing a cheque book, assessing bank loans, and how to raise money to buy a car. And yet the story seems to convey the very opposite of a moral lesson about frugality and sound money sense. In the story, her husband and his friend enjoy the privilege of a post-secondary education and the accompanying pleasures of making high-risk and playful gestures with their money. She closes the story for the class with an evaluation of the value of the winnings. When she shifts back to the procedural register she prefaces it with 'And these are definitely not based on fact, these are just examples,' thereby highlighting the radical disjuncture between the two registers. The classroom examples are inauthentic, whereas the story of her husband's successful gambling represents 'the real.

Leslie enacts the vulnerable 'I' to create a relationship of trust with her students. Her story also positions her as the wife of someone who is from the community (an important issue of membership in rural contexts) and whose husband is sufficiently privileged to pursue post-secondary education in another country. The story about gambling on the horses represents a disruption of the dominant cultural message of frugality and balance found throughout the 'Life Mathematics' course. Because the students in this course have low socio-economic status, relative to the rest of the school and the surrounding area, the story addresses them in terms of class structure and privilege. When this story is told within this context, it tacitly conveys normative messages about access and opportunity denied to these students. The 'real' of this story, in the context of apparently 'real' life mathematics, communicates to the students the inequity of their own subject position. Obviously this is only one possible reading, and there are a multitude of others – as is the nature of interpretation - but it seems crucial that we recognize this possible reading and begin to grapple with the ways in which these students might internalize the messages within these kinds of stories.

CLOSING REMARKS

Teacher identity is mapped onto school culture through the telling and re-telling of stories (Clandinin & Connelly, 2000; Clandinin & Connelly, 1995). Teachers modify and multiply these life stories as they negotiate their position on the professional teaching landscape. Narrative is therefore a personal site for identity construction and enactment. Through the process of narrating, teachers are often able to contextualize their experiences within the power economy of education, thereby enacting (and sometimes naming) the conditions that gave rise to the accounts. The narratives in this study were not explicitly elicited from the participants, and hence they are not 'life history' narratives crafted as a self-conscious response to the question: 'What is your story?' On the other hand, these narratives are precisely the stories that teachers 'choose' to enact in classrooms where they present themselves in varying degrees of embodiment and socio-cultural positioning. These stories are used by the participants in important ways as they negotiate the classroom discourse. My focus here has been on the function of these stories in the mathematics classroom – on what these stories *do* when used in context.

Each of the four participants used personal narrative differently in their classroom discourse. At one end of the spectrum, Roy, the veteran chair of the department, stays fixedly within the procedural discourse, while teaching students

ELIZABETH DE FREITAS

university bound. In so doing, he enacts a pure identity of mastery that represents the ultimate success of school mathematics. Janet uses only one dispassionate and disembodied narrative to impart a moral lesson about socio-economic status and schools. Mark enacts an identity of remembered vulnerability so as to reclaim his gendered authority. While Leslie presents an embodied presence throughout the procedural discourse, and offers family stories that implicitly contradict the cultural messages of the curriculum. By employing a close textual analysis, I have tried to show how different forms of identity are enacted in these personal narratives, and that these stories often function to enforce the legitimacy of the dominant procedural discourse.

It is important to note that this study was an analysis of classroom discourse as the trace of power relations across subject positions. I was not examining language as a way of explaining the psychological interior space of the teachers, although I was speculating on the psychoanalytic mechanisms that produce particular identities. I tried to do so, however, by tracing the exterior shape of the classroom discourse, and listening to the ways in which identities were located within and through it. Stories are told when a teacher deems it fortuitous or appropriate to interrupt the procedural discourse, but it's crucial to recognize the perceived spontaneity of these stories in the classroom, and to note that this perceived spontaneity marks the narrative as a kind of psychoanalytic trace. It is precisely because of this perceived spontaneity that stories in the classroom are such powerful vehicles for tacit socio-cultural messages of all kinds.

I have argued that teacher identity is enacted in the classroom through various discursive registers. The mastery identity is enacted through procedural discourse and represents the dominant identity in this study. When teachers shift back and forth between procedural discourse and personal narrative they perform radically different identities. The 'I' of machine talk is suddenly juxtaposed with the vulnerable 'I' of the embodied self. At the same time, each enactment conveys normative messages about the legitimacy of particular subject positions in the classroom. In particular, the personal narrative positions the teacher according to race, gender, ethnicity and class (the 'I' as member of the community) and thereby addresses the students in these terms. This embodied aspect of narrative is what makes narrative such a powerful form of pedagogy. Teacher personal narratives 'teach' students about socio-cultural positioning within math classrooms. I have shown that one possible reading of these narratives reveals their role in communicating messages about socio-economic status in relation to school mathematics. In each case, the personal narratives functioned to enforce the legitimacy of the dominant procedural discourse. I am not suggesting that we discourage teachers form telling these stories, but rather that we attend to the nuanced meanings that are embedded in them, and examine their relation to other discursive registers. If school mathematics is often less about understanding and more about habit (Tate and Rousseau, 2002), then we need to interrogate the classroom practices by which those habits are inscribed onto identity.

ENACTING IDENTITY THROUGH NARRATIVE

REFERENCES

Adler, J. (2001). *Teaching mathematics in multilingual classrooms*. Dordrecht: Kluwer.

Bhabha, H. (1994). *The location of culture*. London: Routledge.

Butler, J. (1997). *The psychic life of power: Theories in subjection*. Stanford, CA: Stanford University Press.

Clandinin, D. J., & Connelly, F. M. (2000). *Narrative inquiry: Experience and story in qualitative research*. San Fransisco: Jossey-Bass Publishers.

Clandinin, D. J., & Connelly, F.M. (1995). *Teachers' professional knowledge landscapes*. New York: Teachers College Press.

de Freitas, E. (2004). Plotting intersections along the political axis: The interior voice of dissenting mathematics teachers. *Educational Studies in Mathematics, 55*, 259–274.

Doxiadis, A. (2003). *Embedding mathematics in the soul: Narrative as a force in mathematics education*. Opening address to the 3rd Mediterranean Conference of Mathematics Education. Retrieved from www.apostolosdoxiadis.com/files/essays/embeddingmath.pdf

Doxiadis, A. (2004). *The mystery of the black knight's noetherian ring*. Key note address at the Fields symposium on Online mathematical investigation as a narrative experience, University of Western Ontario, June 11, 2004.

Drake, C., Spillane, J. P., Hufferd-Ackles, K. (2001). Storied identities: Teacher learning and subject-matter context. *Journal of Curriculum Studies, 33*(1), 1–23.

Fairclough, N. (2003). Analysing discourse: Textual analysis for social research. New York: Routledge.

Hall, S. (1996). Introduction: Who needs identity? In S. Hall & P. de Guy (Eds.), *Questions of cultural identit* (pp. 1–17). London: Sage Publications.

Labov, W. (2006). Narrative pre-construction. *Narrative Inquiry, 16*(1), 37–45.

Labov, W., & Waletzky, J. (1967). Narrative analysis. In J. Helm (Ed.), *Essays on the verbal and visual arts* (pp. 12–44). Seattle, WA: Washington University Press.

Malloy, C. (2004). Equity in mathematics education is about access. In R. N. Rubenstein & G. W. Bright (Eds.), *Perspectives on the teaching of mathematics* (pp. 1–14). Reston, VA: NCTM Publishing.

Povey, H., Burton, L., Angier, C., & Boylan, M. (2004). Learners as authors in the mathematics classroom. In B. Allen & S. Johnston-Wilder (Eds.), *Mathematics education: Exploring the culture of learning* (pp. 43–56). New York: Routledge-Falmer.

Redman, P. (2005). The narrative formation of identity revisited: Narrative construction, agency and the unconscious. *Narrative Inquiry, 15*(1), 25–44.

Sasaki, B. (2002). Toward a pedagogy of coalition. In A. A. Macdonald & S. Sanchez-Casal (Eds.), *Twenty-first-century feminist classrooms: Pedagogies of identity and difference* (pp. 31–58). New York: Palgrave Macmillan.

Stokoe, E., & Edwards, D. (2006). Story formation in talk-in-interaction. *Narrative Inquiry, 16*(1), 56–65.

Tate, W., & Rousseau, C. (2002). Access and opportunity: The political and social context of mathematics education. In L. D. English (Ed.), *Handbook of international research in mathematics education*. Mahwah, NJ: Lawrence Erlbaum Associates, Publishers.

Walshaw, M. (2004). A powerful theory of active engagement. *For the Learning of Mathematics, 24*(3), 4–10.

Young, K. (1999). Narrative embodiments: Enclaves of the self in the realm of medicine. In A. Jaworski & N. Coupland (Eds.), *The discourse reader* (pp. 428–441). New York: Routledge.

Elizabeth de Freitas
Department of Curriculum and Instruction,
School of Education
Adelphi University
New York

PART FOUR

THE RESEARCH FILTER

KATHLEEN NOLAN

7. IMAGINE THERE'S NO HAVEN: EXPLORING THE DESIRES AND DILEMMAS OF A MATHEMATICS EDUCATION RESEARCHER

INTRODUCTION

Schools like to produce teachers in their own image, or so it appears in some recent instances of pre-service teacher education in secondary mathematics. Such instances, this chapter contends, perpetuate and further exasperate the existing chasm between theory and practice in the education of mathematics teachers and provide a haven for 'teaching as we were taught'. What hope is there then for non-traditional teaching practices knocking at the door of this haven, especially when this haven is so reminiscent of the teachers' own largely successful experiences as learners in mathematics classrooms? By resisting the status quo held in place by the mantra of 'if it ain't broke, don't fix it', might it be possible for these becoming teachers to transcend the *habitual* to think the *possible* in mathematics classrooms. This chapter is written from the perspective of a mathematics teacher educator and researcher, as she grapples with her desire to dismantle the haven of secondary mathematics teaching and learning through non-traditional pedagogies and assessments. This reflexive piece highlights the researcher's efforts to support pre-service teachers' professional growth while, at the same time, propose counter-narratives to dominant school traditions and images of mathematics knowledge. In desiring to go beyond just *imagining* and talking about more reflective, inclusive, creative, and critical mathematical practices, the researcher, along with her research agenda, are met with resistance and potential ethical dilemmas.

From the perspective of a teacher educator, encouraging pre-service teachers to question dominant school traditions for what it means to know (in) mathematics and to consider alternative approaches to pedagogy and assessment in mathematics is a challenging task. In spite of introducing such new strategies during teacher education programs, traditional textbook and teacher-directed approaches prevail in mathematics classrooms. According to several researchers (Jaworski & Gellert, 2003; Lerman, 2005), such approaches still dominate because of a number of socio-cultural issues relating to classroom culture, the perceived nature of mathematics, and personal epistemological beliefs.

It often seems as if status quo practices in the teaching of mathematics are held in place by the mantra 'if it ain't broke, don't fix it'. What is the 'it'? Skovsmose (2008) writes about it; Brown & McNamara's (2005) teacher trainees talk about it;

T. Brown (ed.), The Psychology of Mathematics Education: A Psychoanalytic Displacement, 159–181.
© 2008 Sense Publishers. All rights reserved.

many of us have experienced it. There is a hegemonic sway in high school mathematics classrooms, working to preserve these status-quo practices that, to many, do not appear 'broke'. Skovsmose (2008) calls it the 'exercise paradigm':

> School mathematics can be characterised as exemplifying the *exercise* paradigm: a large part of students' activities is concentrated on performing exercises. Mathematics lessons often follow the same pattern. First, the teacher presents a new topic, which may include a careful exposition of some details... Second, the students are asked to solve particular exercises... Third, a part of the lesson is reserved for the teacher to control the students' possible learning and understanding. Exercises are often then checked and worked out at the blackboard (p. 167).

In addition, Brown & McNamara's (2005) teacher trainees

> revealed harrowing memories of being recipients of transmission styles of mathematics teaching in schools. It seemed that this style of teaching accentuated any difficulties with mathematical learning. Yet their capacity to radically reconceptualise mathematics as a discipline and its teaching seemed limited to enacting pseudo-transmission style where the approach was laced with motivational niceties. (p. 121)

In this chapter, I describe my perceptions of 'it' as a haven—a comfortable place in which to reside for both new and experienced mathematics teachers alike. And, I provide a glimpse into my desires, and corresponding dilemmas, associated with attempts to dismantle this haven.

The chapter has been divided into several sections which, taken together, endeavour to tell the story of my desires and dilemmas within a research study with secondary mathematics pre-service teachers. In the first section, I attempt to bring the reader into the space of the undergraduate curriculum course where I introduce the theory and practice of alternative pedagogies and assessments for high school mathematics classrooms. After several semesters of teaching this course and encountering theory-practice chasms and disillusionment that I seemed unable to ignore any longer, I began a research study, which I briefly describe in section two of this chapter. The theory proposed for how the project *would* proceed, however, differed dramatically from the actual practice of that project once it was underway. So, in the third section of this chapter, I shift the reader's attention to a discussion of the realities of the research project - once it began to involve real research participants and actual high school classrooms. The chapter then moves into a discussion of the research data, not by any thorough analysis of the data but by a reflexive (and dual) process of 'reading' research data. The final

Main Entry: **ha·ven**
Pronunciation: 'hA-v&n
Function: *noun*
Etymology: Middle English, from Old English *hæfen;* akin to Middle High German *habene* harbor
1 : HARBOR, PORT
2 : a place of safety : **REFUGE**
3 : a place offering favorable opportunities or conditions
- **haven** *transitive verb*
[http://www.merriam-webster.com/dictionary/haven]

IMAGINE THERE'S NO HAVEN

section of this chapter interrogates and interpellates[1] my own research agenda and its potential for dismantling this haven of the habitual.

POST-INTRODUCTION

As a mathematics teacher educator and researcher, I work with/in my desire to dismantle the haven of secondary mathematics teaching and learning by grounding socio-cultural and post-structural theories in education in non-traditional pedagogies and assessments in a teacher education program. This text is constructed as a reflexive piece to highlight the desires and dilemmas that emerged as I strived to support pre-service teachers' professional growth but at the same time, to propose counter-narratives to dominant school traditions and images of mathematics knowledge. In desiring to go beyond just *imagining* and talking about more reflective, inclusive, creative, and critical mathematics education practices, my research agenda was met with resistance and ethical dilemmas.

The opening of each section of this chapter is framed in a playful dichotomy of desire/dilemma, where I articulate my longings, my hopes, for secondary mathematics education, while simultaneously expressing the undesirable or unpleasant opponents facing me and my desires.

desire...

Main Entry: **[1]de·sire**
Pronunciation: di-'zI(-&)r, dE-
Function: *verb*
Etymology: Middle English, from Anglo-French *desirer,* from Latin *desiderare,* from *de-* + *sider-, sidus* heavenly body
1 : to long or hope for **:** exhibit or feel desire for
2 a : to express a wish for **: REQUEST b** *archaic* **:** to express a wish to **: ASK**
3 *obsolete* **: INVITE**
4 *archaic* **:** to feel the loss of
intransitive verb **:** to have or feel desire
synonyms WISH, WANT, CRAVE, COVET mean to have a longing for.
[http://www.merriam-webster.com/dictionary/desire]

dilemma...

Main Entry: **di·lem·ma**
Pronunciation: d&-'le-m& *also* dI-
Function: *noun*
Etymology: Late Latin, from Late Greek *dilEmmat-, dilEmma,* probably back-formation from Greek *dilEmmatos* involving two assumptions, from *di-* + *lEmmat-, lEmma* assumption -- more at LEMMA
1 : an argument presenting two or more equally conclusive alternatives against an opponent
2 a : a usually undesirable or unpleasant choice **b :** a situation involving such a choice; *broadly* **: PREDICAMENT**
3 a : a problem involving a difficult choice **b :** a difficult or persistent problem
[http://www.merriam-webster.com/dictionary/dilemma]

KATHLEEN NOLAN

In articulating my desires (and corresponding dilemmas), I acknowledge that '(d)esire goes beyond rationality and to a large extent is part of the mysterious, the poetic, the ineffable - in a realm not readily pinned down with words, not readily amenable to logic and rationality'. (Davies, 2000, p. 37)

> ... desire is spoken into existence, it is shaped through discursive and interactive practices, through the symbolic and the semiotic. Desires are constituted through the narratives and storylines, the metaphors, the very language and patterns of existence through which we are 'interpellated' into the social world. (Davies, 2000, p. 37)

A slightly different perspective on desire, based on Lacanian notions, is offered by Brown & McNamara (2005) in suggesting that '... there is always a gap between aspirations and outcomes. It is this gap that locates desire, the essential point of impossibility, which governs life. It motivates people's conceptions of who they are'. (p. 109) While my attempt in this chapter is to articulate my journey of identifying these gaps – the desires and the dilemmas that motivate me in my research life – I am aware that such an attempt is quite suspect from a psychoanalytic perspective. Brown & England (2005) see that 'the task of research is not to seek truth or find a final resolution, but rather to ask how the discursive formulations have taken the shape that they have'. (p. 449) I realize that, in shaping my research into desires and dilemmas (possibly even creating a false dichotomy of my own researcher lens), I run the risk of feeling 'compelled by my own narrative to find a suitably convincing thesis at the end even if there (isn't) one'. (Brown & England, 2005, p. 452. In other words, I may feel driven to close the gap between my aspirations and an elusive and ambiguous outcome of 'better teaching' – clearly an 'essential point of impossibility'. In believing that I can first locate my desires in this gap and then seek to close the gap, I am failing to acknowledge that my research agenda, or script, has spaces outside itself – spaces that demand recognition of 'aspects of the research situation not mopped up by the story being told'. (Brown & England, 2005, p. 452) Perhaps my initiative to imagine the story not being told rests in my formulation of a dual process of reading the research data – a process that attempts to disrupt my 'story-as-usual' research narrative and to create a discursive 'doubling space' (Nolan, 2007) where desires and dilemmas are acknowledged as ever shifting and unfolding.

THE COURSE

In the undergraduate curriculum course for secondary pre-service teachers, I had explicit desires and dilemmas:

> *MY DESIRE...* to introduce students to alternative, non-traditional instruction and assessment strategies in secondary mathematics and to engage them in a critical exploration of transformed discourses in mathematics teaching and learning

> *MY DILEMMA...* the dichotomies of theory/ practice, university/school, ideal/real, absence/ presence seemed to be working to further reify the current traditional discourses

The course content focused on becoming familiar with advanced topics in high school mathematics curricula, but with a goal of exploring those advanced curriculum topics through performance-based and authentic instruction and assessment tasks. Underpinning the actual content and pedagogy of the course was the integration of 'alternative' (or non-traditional) strategies for mathematics instruction and assessment, including problem-based learning (PBL), portfolio assessment, mathematics experiments, journal writing, anecdotal records, student interviews, and self-assessment. The course was designed to provide students with opportunities (and indeed encouragement) to discuss the effectiveness of different strategies for teaching different topics with/in different learning environments and to critically reflect on the importance of aligning curriculum, instruction, and assessment in mathematics, in both theory and practice.

author reflection on language...
my research & teaching interests intersect in many ways but, what I find most challenging, is finding a language for these intersections. With my students I cannot use the language of deconstruction, poststructural, critical theory, since blank looks greet me with such utterances. Yet, I am dissatisfied with the positivistic language I use in my course outline—alternative, non-traditional, instruction, effectiveness...

*as an example, take the expression 'alternative assessment'. What immediately comes to mind is the question: alternative to what? Of course, it is alternative to the assessment practices that are currently associated with the mainstream, dominant paradigm in/of teaching mathematics— that is, a predominant focus on testing. 'Alternative' may seem to be suitable language for my students but in the wor(l)ds of educational theorists, to speak of an alternative is 'to other'. While 'othering' is considered "an ideological process that isolates groups that are seen as different from the norm of the colonizers" (Dimitriadis, & Kamberelis, 2006, p. 186), its connection to this situation is clear: Such commonly used language may be 'other thinging' the **possible** in mathematics education and thus drawing easy criticism to the thing that is not **habitual?***

In the course, students were assigned the task of constructing a unit plan - one that highlighted non-traditional teaching and learning experiences. Since they had opportunities to start designing their unit plans well in advance of their 3-week pre-internship field experience, I was hoping (*while also slightly dreading*) that they would have the chance to 'try out' at least one of their lessons while in the field. At first, students were somewhat reluctant to 'buy into' the strategies, because they had experienced success with traditionally taught high school mathematics. The strategies clearly represented a paradigm shift in mathematics teaching and learning for these pre-service teachers. Their perceptions of what it means to know, to teach, and to learn mathematics did not readily enable (let alone encourage) them to integrate these new and different ideas into practice. The mantra of 'if it ain't broke, don't fix it', while not explicitly verbalized, was definitely visible in

KATHLEEN NOLAN

their eyes and attitudes at the onset of the course. Through class activities and discussions, however, I felt confident they were convinced...
– that, as mathematics students, they likely represented the top 10% (in terms of grades) of students in their high school mathematics classrooms and that,
– while lecture and drill-and-practice techniques may have worked for them, such a teaching/learning paradigm generally leaves the remaining 90% behind in the dust and debris, and that
– there are other ways of knowing (in) mathematics and, therefore, other ways of assessing knowing besides the traditional procedure-driven and answer-focused tasks and tests.

Before they departed for their classroom field experience, there was an air of optimism. I was hopeful that these becoming teachers might work to transcend the *habitual* in order to think the *possible* in mathematics classrooms. When they returned from their classroom field experience, however, there was a coolness in the air. This coolness was initially fraught with much unspoken tension. But then the students spoke out. In fact, as the instructor, I then encountered substantial student resistance based in their perceptions of the reality of mathematics classrooms, curricula, and students. They spoke out against the unit plan course assignment, against the course objectives, and against me for, essentially, wasting their time. In their verbal rebellion against me and the course, they said, 'these things are not happening in high school math classrooms'. They demanded more 'practical' things (*more than my big ideas and lofty ideals, I guess*). They wanted to spend more time planning activities directly from the curriculum and the textbook – ones that would use the familiar teacher-directed strategies in their lesson plans and that would more readily feed into the traditional paper and pencil tests that (they felt) were obligatory to give at the end of each topic or textbook section. Arms folded and minds focused on their upcoming four-month internship, they could not imagine how the unit plan assignment, full of such non-traditional idea(l)s, would be of any use to them as high school mathematics teachers – teachers like the ones from whom they learned school mathematics and teachers like the ones with whom they just spent three weeks.

After several semesters of experiencing student resistance, class after class, along with my own personal disillusionment and doubt, I proposed a research study where I could explore some of the issues involved. The study was designed to respond to these student 'rebellions', to explore what students actually need to make transitions between university theory and school practice. In spite of student resistance, I refused to believe that the university course could function only in a theoretical landscape, with little practical implications. I echo Vithal (2000) in saying, 'My research interest lies in making a concerted effort to introduce prospective teachers to a particular theoretical landscape and its associated practices and then to examine its re-contextualisation when facing the reality of classrooms'. (Vithal, 2000, p. 3) Even more than this, however, the research study was designed *for me* - I desired to understand what I could do, as a teacher educator, to dismantle the comfortable haven working to maintain status quo teaching and learning practices in high school mathematics classrooms.

THE RESEARCH: IN THEORY

MY DESIRE... to ask the question: What happens in a secondary mathematics classroom when pre-service teachers who have been introduced to alternative and innovative instruction and assessment strategies in a university-based curriculum course attempt to realize the strategies in practice?

MY DILEMMA... the students' perceptions of what it means to know, to teach, and to learn mathematics did not readily enable (let alone encourage) them to integrate these new and different ideas into practice.

Description of the Study

The research study was designed as a case study to investigate the experiences of several pre-service teachers during their four-month internship in secondary school mathematics classrooms. As mentioned previously, the study emerged out of a recognized disconnect between the theory of the university-based curriculum course on alternative instruction and assessment and the practical implementation of these ideas in mathematics classrooms. From my perspective as both a teacher educator and researcher, I designed the study as a means to assist pre-service teachers as they negotiated their way through the theory/practice transitions – ways to enable teachers to resist the strong current of tradition once inside the classroom walls. Desirable transitions between theory and practice demand fluid movements between university and school, including a more reflective and mutually supportive relationship between practicing teachers, teacher educators, and pre-service teachers.

The question posed in the study was: What happens in a secondary mathematics classroom when pre-service teachers who have been introduced to alternative and innovative instruction and assessment strategies in a university-based curriculum course attempt to realize the strategies in practice? The project aimed to create the conditions in which pre-service teachers would have opportunities to try out the new strategies learned in the curriculum class while under the guidance and support of an experienced cooperating teacher as well as myself, in the role of advisor/ mentor. My intent was to create a feedback-oriented internship that would enable pre-service teachers to express their concerns, beliefs, challenges and successes as they negotiated transitions from the theories of the course to the practices of the mathematics classroom.

My main criterion for selection of pre-service teacher participants was that they expressed a willingness to incorporate alternative instruction and assessment practices into their internship classroom. As participants in this case study research project, their role was to be three-fold. Firstly, they were asked to work with me to design a plan for their internship semester, which would describe the specific alternative instruction and assessment strategies they wanted to try in their mathematics classroom throughout the semester. Secondly, participants were asked to participate in three (3) individual conversations with me as well as one (1) focus group discussion with myself and the other participants in the study during the

KATHLEEN NOLAN

semester. Finally, participants were asked to maintain an ongoing reflective artefact in the form of a written journal or a weblog, which the researcher would have access to at the end of the semester.

Theoretical Framework of the Study

To explore learning through socio-cultural lenses means to open the nature(s) of learning to scrutiny by (1) viewing learning as situated with/in the social interactions of members of a social group (Bauersfeld, 1988), (2) understanding cognition to be both in the minds of individuals and distributed across communities of practice (Bohl & Van Zoest, 2003; Eames & Bell, 2005), (3) exploring how particular practices of schooling are implicated in the constitution of teacher and student identities (Walshaw, 2005) and, (4) exploring how meaning is negotiated through the cultural tools (especially language) that operate within school discursive practices (Lerman, 1994; Radford, 1997). In addition, research with/in a socio-cultural framework can highlight the importance of a critical mathematics education (Skovsmose & Borba, 2004) by drawing attention to assumptions that remain unquestioned while highlighting possible alternative images of mathematics practices and discourses (Nolan & Simmt, 2006).

Unquestioned assumptions came to the foreground more in this study than was originally anticipated, functioning as obstacles to change. Begg, Davis & Bramald (2003) describe how it is necessary for teachers to 'overcome the momentum of habit', suggesting that certain teacher habits are 'tied to our long history with traditional schooling practices and are supported by such things as curricula, evaluation regimes, and student expectations (and that) changes in practice involve more than conscious decisions to do things differently'. (p. 622)

As alluded to in the introduction of this chapter, the research project did not proceed as planned in that I encountered several twists, turns and road blocks during my study of theory-practice transitions. My research desires had to be modified in the face of several practical research dilemmas.

THE RESEARCH: IN PRACTICE

MY DESIRE... to support pre-service teachers' professional growth while, at the same time, proposing counter-narratives to dominant school traditions and images of mathematics knowledge.

MY DILEMMA... the pre-service teachers did not seem open to counter-narratives and expressed the need to master the current (dominant) narratives first. Expansion into alternative (critical and non-dominant) realms seemed contingent on first immersing oneself in the narratives of the dominant paradigm.

*MY DESIRE...*to dismantle the haven

MY DILEMMA... 'if it ain't broke, don't fix it'

In this section of the chapter, I discuss why and how I changed the research project; several papers have thus far emerged from this ongoing research project, each with a different focus. For example, in Nolan (*forthcoming*), I draw out themes from the data that highlight regulative discourses in operation, while in Nolan (2006), I highlight experiences that point to how the research was resisted and 'explained away'. (Skovsmose, 2005) The path I take in this chapter is a more reflexive one.

Imagining and creating modified discourses of/in mathematics education is not an easy task for novice teachers who find themselves faced with the conservative power of school tradition and culture. Since alternative approaches to instruction and assessment often fly in the face of current status quo practices, they highlight the obstacles to change in the teaching of mathematics. As previously mentioned, the alternative instruction and assessment strategies

author reflection on 'willingness' and agency…

At the time of choosing to 'abandon' my original research agenda, I was disappointed that the preservice teachers' initial willingness to make an effort to incorporate alternative instruction and assessment remained at that level—a <u>willingness</u> to cooperate, so to speak, but not a personal and/or professional <u>investment</u> in doing so. But why would I expect such an investment? After all, it is the value of <u>my</u> research agenda about which I was attempting to convince them. Why should they buy into it? Perhaps, however, I can never really know much about the level of their investment and agency in the research project since there is another shifting discourse in all of this—one that acknowledges how their investment and agency is already embedded within a web of power relations between myself (as teacher educator, faculty advisor, and researcher), the university, and the cooperating teacher.

introduced in the university course represented a paradigm shift in mathematics teaching and learning for pre-service teachers. Since their experiences and perceptions of what it means to know, to teach, and to learn mathematics did not prepare them to integrate such new and different ideas into practice, I was not entirely surprised (or even initially discouraged) by the reluctance of my participants to dive headfirst into the study and try several forms of alternative instruction and assessment strategies in their internship classroom.

I was surprised, however, that my research 'agenda' was met with so much resistance. For example, during my first planning meeting with the interns and their cooperating teachers, I discussed the importance of creating student-centred and collaborative mathematical problem solving classrooms. One cooperating teacher promptly responded to this by saying, 'I tried teaching in more constructivist ways where the students try to solve the problem on their own, but the students said they preferred it if I just did an example first and then they could follow it to do more.' I wanted to talk to her about how, I believe, students have learned to follow the rules of the game over many years and so it is expected that they would resist suddenly changing the rules and/or the game without understanding why, but I remained silent. In remaining silent, I took a step backward from my research agenda. I felt I was intruding on the comfortable

KATHLEEN NOLAN

haven that had been established through the pre-service teachers' own largely successful experiences as learners in mathematics classrooms, along with the cooperating teachers' subtle expression of the mantra 'if it ain't broke, don't fix it'. In fact, I felt this mantra became the subtext for much of the resistance I felt in trying to conduct my research.

It suddenly became clear to me that I had more ownership and desire invested in this mentorship approach (and, in fact, probably also in the alternative instructional and assessment approaches) than any of the interns or cooperating teachers had. Thus, I truncated my research project to one interview during internship and then one post-internship interview or focus group conversation, but I dropped the mentorship approach to planning and implementing alternative pedagogy and assessment. With such a truncated research agenda, issues of data collection and analysis come to the fore. In the next section, I introduce a duality of lenses, laden with 'guilty readings' (Britzman, 2003), in the interpretation of data excerpts. I 'work the ruins' (St. Pierre, 1999), so to speak, of my research data.

THE RESEARCH: THROUGH DIFFERENT LENSES

MY DESIRE… to read the data through a critical lens, and at the same time, through a lens of possibility in an attempt to open myself to seeing more than I might normally see—to notice possibilities.

MY DILEMMA… I may be blinded (and too preoccupied) by being overly critical of the habitual

Based on my truncated research agenda, I asked the question of how I should 'read' my data. In many respects, this question became an ethical one for me. I felt 'never satisfied' with the interns' theory/practice transitions when observing them in their internship classrooms – probably because I was always viewing the data through a critical lens. I began to wonder what kind of transformations I might be looking for, hoping for. Did I desire too much change, too quickly? I think I *was* expecting

author reflection on being critical…

I definitely experience resonance with a critical interpretive framework… but often, I think, when I use the word critical I am using it 'loosely' in the methodological and theoretical sense. I think I am 'being critical' in the sense of being pessimistic; of thinking teachers are resisting change because it is easier for them to do so; of believing that the 'real' work of teaching (a concern for equity, inclusion, student voice and empowerment) is being ignored from within the comfortable haven.

BIG things to be happening and, in positioning myself in this manner, I was missing the smaller things (the 'little stories', Nolan (2007)) that were unfolding. Perhaps these little stories were gradually dismantling the haven. How should I know? Was my critical agenda getting in the way of viewing *what is possible*, which may already have begun to emerge from within *what is habitual* in mathematics classrooms?

IMAGINE THERE'S NO HAVEN

In this section, I present a brief interpretive analysis of a few data excerpts, in an attempt to 'read' the data through two different lenses: one that is critical of *the habitual* and one that makes an effort to notice *the possible*. Each pre-service teacher conversation excerpt is read through these two lenses, juxtaposed immediately following the excerpt. As post-structural research methodologies suggest, it does not take different data or different readers to see/hear different interpretations with/in the same text.

> Just as there are multiple readings of any text, so there are multiple readings of ourselves. We are constituted through multiple discourses at any one point in time. While we may regard a move we make as correct within one game or discourse, it may be equally dangerous within another. (Davies, 2000, p. 62)

The research conversations were shaped around five main interview and focus group questions. In the next few pages, I present the questions, along with the conversation excerpts and the dual lens analysis for each question.

1. What is the most risky (or, out-of-your-comfort-zone) pedagogy or assessment strategy you have tried (or are trying) during your internship?

   > I do journal entries... that would be a good thing to put on a test. I don't know if I'll be able to do that (now) but that's something that I will do in my own class, but this isn't my own class. That's the thing. My coop's really good but it's just... I know that she probably feels that, you know, when you step out the box you've been in for twenty years it's hard. So when she's watching and not knowing what's going to happen, not knowing if the kids are going to learn better – nobody likes not knowing. Especially when you have to teach these kids for the next four years, right?

   > It's just like when I was growing up— with my mom there was always a particular way to fold the towels. According to my mom, this was not only a best way to fold towels, but a correct way. It's like that with (my coop) in teaching math— she's been teaching for a long time and she knows the best way to do it. I just don't think I can go against that right now. (Nadine, intern conversation, October 2005)

*lens of **the habitual**...*

Nadine feels that the effort involved in trying to convince her cooperating teacher that group problem solving is a valuable instructional strategy, and a way to supplement the traditional individual class work on mathematics problems, is just not worth it (now). I believe this situation is further reified by Nadine's already sceptical view on the value of such changes in instructional approaches. Pre-service teachers are interpellated into the discourses of schooling and mathematics, and part of this includes compliance with the belief (fact or myth?) that more experienced teachers 'know best'. In Skovsmose's (2005) language, this intern was

169

KATHLEEN NOLAN

able to 'explain away' any desire of her own to implement alternative practices in her mathematics internship classroom by directing attention to the desires and experiences of her cooperating teacher, in addition to the unsaid university expectation that the intern 'not make waves' in her internship classroom.

lens of *the possible...*

In discussing the introduction of reform-based and constructivist approaches to the teaching of mathematics, Manouchehri (1998) states that 'the longer teachers had taught using traditional approaches, the more they questioned the value of the (reform-based) programs and their relevance for their work'. (p. 279) Teachers— probably not unlike Nadine's cooperating teacher— felt that these new approaches 'lacked substance' and actually viewed them 'as an affront to the strategies, methods, and materials they had developed and used for some time and what they considered legitimate mathematics'. (p. 279) Is it *possible* that Nadine is concerned about stepping on her coop's toes, as she tries out her own dance steps, and so has made a conscious decision that it is not worth it at this beginning point of her career? Is it *possible* that the sub-text of this intern's comment may actually be that she notices how rigid the cooperating teacher is and that, by merely noticing this, the intern has already taken steps toward criticality and reflection on the emergence of new mathematics education discourses and her own teacher identity?

> ... a multitude of discourses is constantly at work constructing and producing our identity. Our identity therefore originates not from inside the person, but from the social realm, where people swim in a sea of language and other signs, a sea that is invisible to us because it is the very medium of pure existence as social beings. (Burr, 1995, p. 53)

2. What are your thoughts right now on why you would teach differently from how you were taught, since you experienced success in your own school mathematics learning? In your internship, what was your motivation for doing things differently and how easy was it for you to shift from having learned in that (traditional) way to planning and executing lessons, which teach the concepts differently?

Well, I wanted to be a teacher since I was in grade one. So I've always kind of— even during my high school experience— looked at things a little bit from a teacher's eyes, because that's just what interests me. I wanted to help people learn. Especially in high school, all of my senior math and science teachers—my math, biology, physics, and chemistry teachers—were mostly all phys ed teachers. Some of them tried, and some of them— you knew they wanted to be teaching phys ed, and they're just teaching that class because it was assigned to them.

Like, I got it, because I could learn from the textbook. I didn't need anyone telling me anything. But there were students in my class that didn't get it. So I would often help them, and try and come up with

170

IMAGINE THERE'S NO HAVEN

creative ways of explaining it to them, or making it make sense to them. And I just kind of always thought there must be a better way to do it, that's more engaging to students.

Some students just don't like math. But I've always been fascinated by math and how it explains so much in the world, and all the connections between everything you learn, which I kind of discovered myself. I was never really guided towards making those connections.

I guess I think it's a shame that so many students end up hating math. Like so many people end up hating math that they just won't even deal with it in their adult life. And I don't think it needs to be that way, because it can be really fun and engaging and they can investigate stuff themselves. It doesn't just have to be 'memorize this rule and do it'. So, as far as the planning part of your question, I found – I find planning very difficult because I don't have any experience with it. And to some extent, I really don't know where to start in certain cases. Like some things I've seen in university or we've discussed in university, and that's a huge help. But some things that I want to try, I just really have no idea where to go. So it takes a long time just to set them up. It doesn't discourage me, per se, but I did a lot less of that kind of instruction than I would have liked to (in my internship), because I didn't have the time. I had to balance incorporating that into some classes, and you know, still getting enough sleep at night, which I didn't really do anyway. But I mean, having a bit of a life outside of teaching... because as much as I love it, I already know that if I continue on that path, I'd get burnt out right away.

So that's kind of one of my biggest frustrations. I'm totally sold on the idea that math should be taught differently. I just don't always know how to do it, especially at the senior level. I think a lot of the stuff that we've talked about in math education classes has been more grade nine, ten focused, because those are the ones that are really kind of obvious. Like you can use fraction strips, and you can use so many representations for fractions. But what about math A30, B30, C30 (advanced high school) topics where, you know, we don't even know what's available sometimes. And even when we do, we wouldn't know how to apply it to the content. (Andrea, intern interview, January 2007)

*lens of **the habitual**...*

Andrea appears to be grasping for a reason that excuses her from trying different approaches in her internship classroom – namely, that in university she was not *shown how* to teach differently. There is an apparent contradiction here. Earlier in the conversation excerpt, Andrea indicates that she was *shown how* all through her school mathematics experiences and, as a result, she lacks connections and

KATHLEEN NOLAN

meaning. Now she desires to be *shown how* again, in order to be able to teach differently. On the one hand, Andrea indicates a desire to teach according to constructivist, collaborative, problem-solving approaches (because, she says, it is more meaningful and leads to a deeper understanding of the concepts). On the other hand, however, it seems Andrea is not making a connection to her own learning about how to teach differently—she does not appear to value a constructivist, problem-solving approach to learning how to integrate new pedagogical and assessment approaches and wants to be *shown how*. Her dislike of uncertainty is expressed when she says: '… we don't even know what's available sometimes and even when we do, we wouldn't know how to apply it to the content.'

In asking the question of how teacher educators might best approach the preparation of teachers with the goal of embracing uncertainty and complexity, Gordon (2006) suggests:

> The fact that a measure of uncertainty is inherent in every student-teacher interaction reinforces the point that we should embrace rather than shy away from moments of confusion. By embracing confusion, both teachers and students will gradually learn to take advantage of moments of perplexity in order to dig deeper, consider alternative ideas, and attempt new methods that have not been explored yet. (p. 21)

*lens of **the possible**…*

It seems clear that Andrea has a desire to disrupt traditional practices. She expresses frustration with the obstacles—such as time, experience, and knowledge—that she perceives are in the way of achieving this. For example, at this moment, she acknowledges that her (mainly) procedural knowledge of a particular concept does not readily connect with the multitude of pedagogical approaches that are available to her. As in intern, perhaps this is as good as it gets (for now), given the many constraints and expectations acting on her. In this brief conversation excerpt, she shows signs that 'it **is** broke' and that she is consciously avoiding merely gluing the pieces back together to obtain an incoherent blend of transmission teaching and disconnected pedagogical activities. Brown and McNamara (2005) write about elementary teacher trainees working so hard to imagine teaching mathematics differently that the pedagogy (the *way* a concept is taught) actually replaces the content (the mathematics concept itself and its connections). He states that he has 'seen students 'talking the talk' without connection to content'. (p. 127) At least Andrea is on a journey that imagines what is *possible* when/if these connections are made.

> We do not know what we can speak/write into existence until we've done it, since even those imaginary worlds through which we conjure up a possibility different from this world are discursively produced. We need to write and

speak utopias, we need to rewrite the past and the present, we need to write and speak all of our selves, not just our minds or our bodies, to *imagine* who we might be... (Davies, 2000, p. 54)

3. (a) What is it about being a math teacher that is important to you; that is, what kind of math teacher do you want to become?

> I want to create a safe environment where they feel responsible for each other and for each others' learning. Where that selfish math—you know, you're the best math dweeb in the world— isn't the goal. It's that we all are good problem solvers, thinkers. General proficiency. I don't know how to create that. I don't even know how to do that. (Nadine, focus group conversation, December 2005)

> I just wish that every single kid in my class would care enough to ask questions. Like, if someone has a question in class, I get so pumped— they're paying attention, they understand, they have a question, you know! And knowing that they're not afraid to ask questions. I value that. I appreciate that they will ask me questions, like 'I didn't really get that'. (Jane, focus group conversation, December 2005)

*lens of **the habitual**...*

Brown & McNamara (2005) state that: 'Such happy resolutions to the supposed skills required to teach mathematics (being 'sensitive', 'patient', supportive) it seems, can provide effective masks to the continuing anxieties relating to the students' own mathematical abilities'. (p. 112) In their study, Brown & McNamara (2005) work with elementary teacher trainees—students who generally expressed considerable anxiety about their own school experiences of learning mathematics. The pre-service teachers with whom I worked in this study were planning to teach mathematics at the secondary level; hence, they generally expressed positive school experiences and seldom acknowledged any level of anxiety about learning or teaching mathematics. So, it seems unusual to me— at the secondary level in particular— that the kind of mathematics teacher they want to become revolves around a nurturing approach. As secondary mathematics teachers, where is the passion for mathematics? Where is the welcome challenge of problem solving? Why does the goal of ensuring that their students 'feel responsible' become a priority? Socio-cultural theories acknowledge that learning takes place with/in the social interactions of the members of a group, and so social discourses related to mathematics learning are key, but the images conjured up in these pre-service teacher quotes seem more about discourses of being liked and accepted as a teacher; about being asked questions by the students that can be answered by the teacher; and about creating a safe, peaceful classroom environment where no-one strives to be a 'math dweeb' yet all reach 'general proficiency.'

KATHLEEN NOLAN

*lens of **the possible**...*

To be honest, I find that locating the *possible* in these excerpts is limited for me. I *understand* how good it feels to provide answers to students' questions—to remove, so to speak, students' uncertainty and frustration with not knowing. I *understand* this but I grapple with it constantly. At the moment, however, my lens is scratched (*likely with the recent poor course evaluations I received when I attempted to introduce Gordon's (2006) notion of embracing uncertainty and complexity into my classes*) to see the *possibilities* for embracing confusion and shirking my desire to be liked as a teacher. In the words of Gordon's (2006) own experience:

> Concerned with addressing my students' needs and wanting them to like me, I usually yield to their requests for more prescriptive instructions and guidelines than I am comfortable with (and)... I often attempt to immediately clarify students' confusions and alleviate the doubts that emerge regarding the basic concepts we are learning. As such, I struggle with the challenge to embrace uncertainty, often preferring simplicity over-complexity and clarity over-confusion. (p. 19)

> 3. (b) How would you say your internship has fed into your identity as a mathematics teacher... the kind of teacher you want to become?

> Well, the only other thing I have to say is, like some of the question you've been asking, I find it a bit of a challenge to answer because where I am right now, I'm still kind of developing my theory of what education is. And not even just as a teacher, but like policy wise– like what I think it should be— and those kind of things. I don't know that yet. I'm just kind of sorting that all out. It's all kind of theoretical in a way.

> And then you're looking at bigger questions, like what is the goal for a system-wide education system? Or a public education system. Is it entirely for the students' learning? Or are there other kinds of, you know, what do they call it? The hidden curriculum? I mean, how much are things going to shift, because there are certain government and society interests in this as well? It's not all – unfortunately, it's not all about the well-being of the students. (Andrea, intern interview, January 2007)

*lens of **the habitual**...*

This conversation excerpt (taken along with one in the next question where Andrea indicates her desire and need to 'walk the walk' during internship) have me concerned that a critical questioning of policy, hidden curriculum, and other 'theoretical' issues can only occur later, not right now. In other words, as I wrote in an earlier section of this chapter, the students did not seem open to counter-narratives just yet, not until they had first mastered the current (dominant) narratives. Expansion into other (critical and non-dominant) realms seemed contingent on passing through and soaking up the narratives of the dominant paradigm first. Again, however, I ask the question: in looking for the BIG transformations to be happening (straight out of their internship), am I missing the small, but still audible, knocks at the door of the haven?

*lens of **the possible**…*

It seems possible to me that Andrea understands what Burr (1995) articulates so well:

> The discourses that form our identity are intimately tied to the structures and practices that are lived out in society from day to day, and it is in the interest of relatively powerful groups that some discourses and not others receive the stamp of 'truth'. (p. 55)

By voicing the expression 'what I think it should be', Andrea exhibits considerable promise in viewing education through a lens of her own for what *is possible*. She is searching (or, at least, poised to search) for the discourses available to her, each potentially offering different and promising possibilities. At the moment, however, the answers to the big questions on policy, hidden curriculum, and her own theory of education, along with the critical question of 'in whose interest?', still form somewhat of a 'black box' for her.

4. What are your thoughts on changing the structure of internship so that more flexibility is built in and there is more time for a mentorship approach to your classroom practice experience? What would be a useful internship model? If you want to teach math differently, is it possible that you don't actually need to walk in [a cooperating teacher's] shoes for three weeks?

It was a very important part, to do the walk, because – I mean, that's when you know what it's going to be like. I mean, it's not going to be exactly like that, because there's still internship things that you have to do that you wouldn't do as a actual teacher, like the – you know, meet targets and that kind of thing. You wouldn't do them on such a formal level, anyways. But it was stressful, but it – I think you need to do it, because – I mean, going back to pre-internship, I didn't think I could teach four classes a day. I thought that I'd go crazy before I ever had enough time in the day to plan and teach four classes a day. And then I proved to myself, yeah, I can do it. I can do it for a whole month straight.

I think – where I am, I mean, I needed that four months in school. Like that was the most meaningful thing I learned at university. And the focus – I mean, as much as I want to change the way math is taught, and would love support doing that, I also need to know what it's like to be a teacher

KATHLEEN NOLAN

and learn what it's like to be a teacher, in dealing with the every day stuff. So I think the experience as it is, is really good. As far as mentorship goes, like some of it can be done during school time, because I'm at the school anyway, and it would just be one less class I observed or –

Well, I guess the other thing I was going to say— and I mean this is kind of the ideal situation— is if you can get placed with a teacher that can... that the cooperating teacher themselves can support you in what you're doing. So you don't need somebody from outside coming in to mentor you. It's just your co-op that's already doing those things, or has done them. My co-op hadn't, but he was very open to letting me try anything, and supporting me as much as he could in that. So that was really useful. (Andrea, intern interview, January 2007)

*lens of **the habitual**...*

'... already doing those things, or has done them' is an appropriate theme for a critical analysis of this conversation excerpt. In my mind, one of the weaknesses of such an extended, four month internship is that—either implicitly or explicitly— the intern is expected to walk in the shoes of her/his cooperating teacher, who was (probably) previously expected to walk in the shoes of her/his cooperating teacher, and so on. Is this not how traditions become entrenched and hegemonic? (That towels should be folded at all, let alone one particular way, *could* be called into question... couldn't it?)

... the words one utters, and the interactive practices in which one engages, do not gain their meanings through any individual's intentions. Rather it is through the discursive and interactive practices that we are interpellated into the collective and through which we become speaking subjects. We take the words we speak to be our own at the same time that they speak us into existence. (Davies, 2000, pp. 39-40)

In teacher education programs, is the subtext made available to our student teachers such that, as a professional courtesy to the teacher who volunteers to 'cooperate', they should not openly question or oppose that teacher's practice? Through such an internship structure, are we reifying the view that many pre-service teachers already express in saying: '(internship) was the most meaningful thing I learned at university'? Britzman (2003) also grapples with this conundrum in her critique of the messages being sent by teacher education programs:

Like most people in teacher education, (the student teachers) were deeply invested in the idea that experience is telling, that one learns by experience, by being there, and not by theories. If this were not the case, why have such a long internship? (pp. 252-253) *lens of **the possible**…*

'as much as I want to change the way math is taught…' shows possibility, does it not? Perhaps it is overly naïve to believe that, after so many years of traditional math experiences, interns merely want to mirror these experiences when they become teachers. While **I** may desire change to be visible and clearly audible from the get go (that is, as soon as pre-service teachers are launched into their internship), it **is** *possible* that the critical questioning of traditional mathematics classroom experiences only begins as a whisper for these pre-service teachers, not yet loud enough to register on my decibel scale.

> If one's body has learned to interact with the world in certain ways, then these ways may need more than access to new discursive practice to change them. Or the means of translating an idea into everyday practice may not easily be achieved, one's life-practice-as-usual or life as the practical expression of old familiar discourses always coming more readily to hand. (Davies, 2000, p. 65)

I believe it is possible, with a new configuration of the internship experience (*dare I say one quite **un**like many current ones?*), for new teachers to walk in newly imagined and constructed teacher shoes— not in *opposition* to experienced teachers, but right alongside them. In mathematics education research, there is a loud cry to study the induction and mentoring of novice teachers through educative mentoring by, and joint reflection between, exemplary support teachers, tutors, and teacher educators (Feiman-Nemser, 2001; Jaworski & Gellert, 2003).

5. If you could change one thing about your internship experience, what would it be?

> I just wish I would have maybe planned the whole semester better just because I was thinking I'd have all this time to do all this stuff. But then when it came down to it I was planning and then my three week block came and now it's Christmas. Yeah, I didn't realize how fast it would go, I guess. Like I would have liked to see a lot more teaching (in other classrooms) than I did. (Nadine, focus group conversation, December 2005)

> Considering I hadn't taught Math 10 before, I'm doing it right from scratch. I did the whole course right from scratch. And like for me, that was so valuable to just start. I made all the math notes, all the quizzes, all the tests. Everything. All my assignments. All my homework checks. Everything. The whole thing I did from scratch. So for me, that was so valuable just to be able to sit down with one course and I wish that I had the time to do that for Math 9, Math A30, B30, C30, Calculus even, and that when I was done university I'd have two binders for each course and at least I'd have a whole— not unit plan— but a course plan for everything. I know that probably takes a long time because it took four

KATHLEEN NOLAN

> months to do the math 10 one but ... (Sharon, focus group conversation, December 2005)

lens of the habitual...

In addition to Nadine's and Sharon's comments, another intern also made reference to an overall goal of creating/obtaining a 'magic binder'—one that contains complete course notes and questions and quizzes and tests; one that, once designed, could be used every time that course is taught, in every classroom with every student from here to retirement (or so it seems). 'From scratch' seems to be spoken with disdain, as if prefabrication is a more desirable state of affairs. But it makes me wonder: where is the teacher agency that so many new teachers about to embark on a new life journey would choose to traverse such old, established pathways?

> If people are products of discourse, and the things that they say have status only as manifestations of these discourses, in what sense can we be said to have agency?... Our hopes, desires and intentions become the products of cultural, discursive structures, not the products of human agents. (Burr, 1995, p. 59)

> For an individual entering into training his or her sense of agency is modified, understood differently, against an emergent understanding of a new environment and how he or she will be received. This entails a tricky meeting of a newly conceived agency rooted in personal aspirations and an expectation that he or she will be told how to teach. Agency on the part of the trainee mingles with dependency and gets shaped by the form of external demands encountered. (Brown & McNamara, 2005, p. 165)

lens of the possible...

My above analysis, though the lens of the habitual, risks being labelled by the reader (and quite aptly, I might add) as emerging from a structuralist perspective. That I would infer agency is an object that exists and can be obtained, and that, once obtained, one should then be in a position to articulate exactly what it looks and acts like—this is indeed the impression one might take from my analysis above. I seem to be saying that pre-service teachers with 'real' agency would choose to forge their way into new territory, and would not be lead astray by the old, stifling practices. From a poststructural perspective, however, I do understand that shifting discourses, with moments of obvious self-contradiction and doubt, are aspects of our multiple subjectivities, feeding into our multiple and conflicting identities. In the midst of all this, Davies (2000) reminds me that '(a)gency is not spoken into existence at any one moment. It is fragmented, transitory, a discursive position that can be occupied within one discourse simultaneously with its nonoccupation in another'. (p. 68) Agency constitutes, and is constituted by, what is *possible*— if not now then possibly in the next moment.

THE CONCLUSION: IN MY OWN IMAGE?

MY DESIRE... to teach a course (or two) (and conduct a research study) that could bring about significant changes to the cultural and discursive practices of schooling that currently stifle innovative instruction and assessment in mathematics while working to maintain the power of dominant school traditions and images of mathematics knowledge.

MY DILEMMA... figuring out who the research is for: High school math teachers? High school math students? My students? Me and my own personal agenda?

If I am suspicious that schools work to produce teachers in their own image then I might want to reflect on how my research agenda seeks to produce teachers in *my own image*. I am motivated by (my) research that, I believe, seeks to improve the teaching and learning of mathematics— but not to 'improve' in any measurable sense of the word as I have little interest in quantifying such things. In seeking these improvements, I know there are no easy transitions between theory and practice; there are no easy relationships between the school discourses that constitute, and at the same time are constituted by, mathematics teachers; 'there is no absolute improvement, just a recharging of life'. (Brown & Jones, 2001, p. 179)

author reflection on the lens dichotomy...
In Nolan (2007), I offer a description of metonymic spaces of doubling as a to-and-fro movement between dichotomous elements, such that one element is not privileged over the other but that both elements are constituted by, and constituting, each other simultaneously. In a sense, this is what I have been trying to do in this text—to explore familiar storylines through the lens of being critical of the habitual and, at the same time, through the lens of noticing what is possible, with the hope that the to-and-fro movement opens in-between spaces I have not yet considered and shifting discourses I have not yet imag(in)ed.

Ultimately, my desire, as a mathematics teacher educator, is to dismantle the haven of current secondary mathematics teaching and learning practices. The haven, I believe, is where we locate the myths inherent in perceptions of what it means to teach, to learn, and to know mathematics. In my research, I have grounded this desire in an exploration of alternative pedagogies and assessments because it is the only way I know, at the moment, to *imagine* more reflective, inclusive, creative, and critical mathematics education practices.

In this chapter, I attempted to move beyond my critical tunnel vision with the introduction of two different lenses through which to view my research conversations. It is my hope that, as a result of the to-and-fro movement between images formed through these lenses, spaces in which to imagine new possibilities might emerge. Davies (2000) suggests that

KATHLEEN NOLAN

... the means for moving beyond the old ways of thinking and speaking... (lie)... first with an analysis of how existing discursive practices trap us into the worlds we are trying to move beyond, and second with the collective development of discursive practices that bring into being those new, almost unimaginable possibilities...(p. 38)

Given the intense motivation and perseverance required to resist the strong current of tradition once inside the secondary mathematics classroom walls, it is in a sense of self and agency that we may move beyond/within what is *habitual* to imagine what is *possible*—to imagine there's no haven (it's easy if you try?).

Agency is never freedom from discursive constitution of self but the capacity to recognize that constitution and to resist, subvert, and change the discourses themselves through which one is being constituted. It is the freedom to recognize multiple readings such that no discursive practice, or positioning within it by powerful others, can capture and control one's identity. (Davies, 2000, p. 67)

REFERENCES

Bauersfeld, H. (1988). Interaction, construction, and knowledge - Alternative perspectives for mathematics education. In D. A. Grouws & T. J. Cooney (Eds.), Perspectives on research on effective mathematics teaching: Research agenda for mathematics education (Vol. 1, pp. 27–46). Reston, VA: NCTM and Lawrence Erlbaum Associates.

Begg, A., Davis, B., & Bramald, R. (2003). Obstacles to the dissemination of mathematics education research. In A. Bishop, et al. (Eds.), Second international handbook of mathematics education research: Part two (pp. 593–634). Dordrecht, The Netherlands: Kluwer Academic Publishers.

Bohl, J. V., & Van Zoest, L. R. (2003). The value of Wenger's concepts of modes of participation and regimes of accountability in understanding teacher learning. In PME 27 (pp. 339–346). Honolulu, HI: University of Hawaii.

Britzman, D. (2003). Practice makes practice: A critical study of learning to teach (Rev. ed.). New York: State University of New York Press.

Brown, T., & England, J. (2005). Identity, narrative and practitioner research: A Lacanian perspective. Discourse: Studies in the Cultural Politics of Education, 26(4), 443–458.

Brown, T., & Jones, L. (2001). Action research and postmodernism: Congruence and critique. Buckingham, UK: Open University Press.

Brown, T., & McNamara, O. (2005). New teacher identity and regulative government: The discursive formation of primary mathematics teacher education. New York: Springer.

Burr, V. (1995). An introduction to social constructionism. London: Routledge.

Davies, B. (2000). A body of writing, 1990–1999. New York: Alta Mira Press.

Eames, C., & Bell, B. (2005). Using sociocultural views of learning to investigate the enculturation of students into the scientific community through work placements. Canadian Journal of Science, Mathematics and Technology Education, 5(1), 153–169.

Feiman-Neismer, S. (2001). Helping novices learn to teach: Lessons from an exemplary support teacher. Journal of Teacher Education, 52(1), 17–30.

Gordon, M. (2006). Welcoming confusion, embracing uncertainty: Educating teacher candidates in an age of certitude. Paideusis, 15(2), 15–25.

Jaworski, B., & Gellert, U. (2003). Educating new mathematics teachers: Integrating theory and practice, and the roles of practicing teachers. In A. Bishop, M. A. Clements, C. Keitel, J. Kilpatrick,

& F. K. S. Leung (Eds.), Second international handbook of mathematics education (Part two) (pp. 829–875). Dordrecht, The Netherlands: Kluwer Academic Publishers.

Lerman, S. (2005). Learning as developing identity in the mathematics classroom. Plenary lecture at the 27th annual meeting of the Canadian Mathematics Education Study Group (CMESG), Ottawa, ON, 27–31 May, 2005.

Lerman, S. (1994). Changing focus in the mathematics classroom. In S. Lerman (Ed.), Cultural perspectives on the mathematics classroom (pp. 191–213). Dordrecht, The Netherlands: Kluwer Academic Publishers.

Manouchehri, A. (1998). Mathematics curriculum reform and teachers: What are the dilemmas? Journal of Teacher Education, 49(4), 276–286.

Nolan, K. (forthcoming). 'For the sake of time' and other stories to teach by: Dis/positioning regulative discourses in secondary mathematics teacher education.

Nolan, K. (2007). How should I know? Preservice teachers' images of knowing (by heart) in mathematics and science. Rotterdam: Sense Publishers.

Nolan, K. (2006). Teaching becomes you: The challenges of placing identity formation at the centre of mathematics pre-service teacher education. PME 30, Prague, CZ.

Nolan, K., & Simmt, E. (2006). Socio-cultural dimensions of mathematics learning: A working group. Proceedings of the 27th annual meeting of the Canadian Mathematics Education Study Group (CMESG), Ottawa, ON, 27–31 May, 2005.

Radford, L. (1997). On psychology, historical epistemology, and the teaching of mathematics: Towards a sociocultural history of mathematics. For the Learning of Mathematics, 17(1), 26–33.

Skovsmose, O. (2008). Mathematics education in a knowledge market: Developing functional and critical competencies. In E. de Freitas & K. Nolan (Eds.), Opening the research text: Critical insights and in(ter)ventions into mathematics education (pp. 159–174). New York: Springer.

Skovsmose, O. (2005). Foregrounds and politics of learning obstacles. For the Learning of Mathematics, 25(1), 4–10.

Skovsmose, O., & Borba, M. (2004). Research methodology and critical mathematics education. In P. Valero & R. Zevenbergen (Eds.), Researching the socio-political dimensions of mathematics education: Issues of power in theory and methodology (pp. 207–226). Boston: Kluwer Academic Publishers.

St. Pierre, E. (1999). Working the ruins: Feminist poststructural theory and methods in education. New York: Routledge.

Vithal, R. (2000). Re-searching mathematics education from a critical perspective. Paper presented at the Biennial International Conference on Mathematics Education and Society, Montechoro, Portugal, 26–31 March, 2000.

Walshaw, M. (2005). Pre-service mathematics teaching in the context of schools: An exploration into the constitution of identity. Journal of Mathematics Teacher Education, 7, 63–86.

Kathleen Nolan
Faculty of Education
University of Regina
Canada

TONY COTTON

8. 'WHAT IS IT REALLY LIKE?' DEVELOPING THE USE OF PARTICIPANT VOICE IN MATHEMATICS EDUCATION RESEARCH

Mathematics Education tends to contribute to the regeneration of an inequitable society through undemocratic and exclusive pedagogical practices, which portray mathematics and mathematics education as absolute, authoritarian disciplines.[1]

So tell me – what's the point of all this stuff you're asking us? Why would anyone want to know what we think about learning maths?[2]

INTRODUCTION

Research in mathematics education is primarily conducted for the benefit of teachers and the children they work with. Yet so often the voices of these key beneficiaries are marginalised within research to play the roles of clipped commentators, allowed in only so long as they offer sound bites that sit neatly in the researcher's preferred story. The two quotes which open the chapter offer a view of the gap between 'researcher' and 'researched' as perceived by some of the young people who are in the position of learning mathematics in school.

If we are to find ways of making research more democratic we need to find ways of stepping out of this mould. Framed as research is, in its own culture of regulative practices, the social specificity of research makes any claims it might proffer to a wider truth seem somewhat problematic. Indeed such claims to truth may in themselves become oppressive, leaving the researchers to sulk about their own complicity. The purpose of research might be viewed alternatively, however, as being about opening spaces that allow us all to think about how our worlds may be changed. This chapter will examine ways in which researchers can work with pupils and teachers to develop an authentic 'voice' that speaks to researchers, academics, administrators, and those who have responsibility in policy formation. By privileging experience over theory as a basis for understanding, space is made for marginalised or 'silenced' groups to be heard. Using texts from recent work with pupils who have become disaffected with mathematics, a methodology is explored which both reflects 'what it is like' in these schools from pupil and teachers' perspectives and offers insights into broader educational issues. The question, which is explored later in this chapter, is 'What is it like to be a learner of

T. Brown (ed.), The Psychology of Mathematics Education: A Psychoanalytic Displacement, 183–197.
© 2008 Sense Publishers. All rights reserved.

mathematics?' This question is responded to by two groups of learners from the same school. The first group are 11 and 12 years old and just beginning their experience of learning mathematics in a secondary school in the Midlands of England. Some of this group see themselves as successful learners of mathematics and some see mathematics as an area in which they struggle to learn. The other group is made up of 15 and 16 year olds who have been placed in the lowest streams in the school. This means that they are not able to access qualifications that would open up job opportunities in the future. To a large extent they are 'disaffected' learners of mathematics.

The fact that this second group of learners have become placed in a position which closes down rather than opens up opportunities is a matter of social justice. This is the form of mathematics education referred to in the opening quote. This is the way in which mathematics education contributes to the 'regeneration of an inequitable society'. The chapter begins to explore 'what it is like' to be in this position.

ENTREZ MONSIEUR FOUCAULT

Increasing attention is being paid to ideas influenced by post-modern thinkers to develop ways of working for social justice through researching mathematics education. Recent papers have suggested that the most important thing we can do as researchers and teachers is to become aware of 'what, what we do, does'. (Cotton & Hardy, 2004, p. 277) Drawing attention to the panopticon may change the way we operate. There is an additional problem for the writer of research, the question here is 'what can we say about what we do and what does what we say, do?' The Foulcauldian notion of archaeology helps here. Foucault, describes 'archaeology' as

> an attempt to describe discourses. Not books (in relation to their authors), not theories (with their structures and coherences), but those familiar yet enigmatic groups of statements that are known as medicine, political economy, and biology. I would like to show that these unities form a number of autonomous, but not independent, domains, governed by rules, but in perpetual transform-ation, anonymous and without a subject, but imbuing a great many individual works. (Foucault, 1972, back cover)

He goes on to describe a notion of 'things said'. This revisits immediately the question of 'what can we say?' Archaeology explores how 'things said' come into being, how they are interpreted, transformed and articulated. The aim of such an archaeology is to expose the ideology present within current practice and through this description offer a view of possible futures. Such an 'archaeology' demands work from 'archaeologists'. The empirical work later in this chapter engages the young people in a personal archaeology.

So this chapter will describe a methodology that takes as its starting point the 'voice' of those engaged in the research. It suggests that the exploration of educational settings should be a collaborative activity engaging those who live and work in the settings as well as the researcher. This gives a deeper understanding of the current context within the setting and offers areas for intervention and action by all engaged in the research. It also aims to be a chapter that requires active collaboration by the young people I worked with. In particular, the chapter illustrates how such a methodology can be used to raise questions around the development of identity within the mathematics classroom and the possible tensions between perceptions of identity and effective learning and teaching. I will suggest that for some learners who become disaffected learners of mathematics their self-perception is held in tension with their perception of the characteristics of an effective learner of mathematics. I will also argue that the process of exploring identity formation can be empowering to those involved.

VOICE, NARRATIVE AND SOCIAL JUSTICE

But what is justice? Justice is allowing people to live in the way for which they evolved. Human beings have an emotional and physical need to do so, it is their biological expectation. They can only live in this way, or all the time struggle consciously or unconsciously to do so… We can express this basic need in many ways: aesthetic, intellectual, the need to love, create, protect and enjoy. These are not the higher things that can be added when more basic needs are met. They are basic. They must be the way we express all our existence, and if they do not control our daily life then we cannot function as human beings at all. (Bond, 1983, p. LXIV)

Bond's view of Social Justice echoes a Rawlsian (Rawls, 1971) conception. A socially just society would be one in which we would be happy for our worst enemy to choose our place. Perhaps a more pertinent metaphor for mathematics education is the image that a socially just mathematics education system would be one in which we would be happy for our own children, or children that we hold dear, to replace any other child within that system. If there are any children in situations in which we would not willingly place our own, injustice exists.

We would probably not choose to place our own children in the lowest streams in secondary schools in the UK. Not because of any pathologisation of the young people taught in these streams, but simply because these young people have access to a smaller range of life choices than those placed in the top streams. It is because of this that the chapter focuses on the voices of this particular group of young people. Perhaps these voices will help us explore what we should change in order to create a 'more just' situation.

Eisner (1991, p. 72) suggests that the question 'what is it like to be here?' is nontrivial and that such a question can only be answered by researchers taking a careful and rigorous approach to qualitative research. Such an approach to qualitative studies takes the issue of 'voice' as primary. Schratz & Walker (1995, p. 14) ask the question:

TONY COTTON

If we are to find ways to make research democratic then we have to find ways to break the mould that confines research to a highly selected group of specialists.

For Schratz and Walker the social specificity of research make any claims to truth problematic. Indeed such claims to truth may be oppressive in themselves and reflexivity may become the main focus of concern for the researcher engaged in democratic research. The purpose of such work is not to tell truths about the world but to open up spaces that allow us all to think about how our worlds may be changed. As Doris Lessing reminds us, truth is elusive.

> How little I have managed to say of the truth, how little I have caught of all that complexity; how can this small neat thing be true when what I experienced was so rough and apparently formless and unshaped (Lessing, 2002, p.13)

I take this passage to act as a warning rather than a roadblock. It reminds me that I should be aware of the dangers of presenting simplistic answers when attempting to (re)present the voices of the people with whom I carry out research. I should always remind myself of the 'roughness' and complexity of the research experience. I do not attempt to capture the complexity of the research process, rather I try to remain aware of the messiness as I write. I do not stop exploring the notion of what might be 'true' in the research as ... the search for 'truths' supports us in finding arenas in which to work for social justice. As Lessing suggests later in the same text

> (If) we don't believe the things we put on our agendas will come true for us, then there is no hope for us. We're going to be saved by what we seriously put on our agendas. We've got to believe in our blueprints. We've got to believe in our beautiful, impossible blueprints. (ibid, p. 553)

Narrative empowers as we find that there is shared vision which can effect change within personal spheres of influence and which can contribute towards a more just society through education. Empowerment is a contested term. What I am suggesting here is that collaborative work to form narratives which attempt to describe day to day lived experience allows individuals to describe themselves within a complex set of relationships with other individuals within the same social context and within complex institutional relationships. Through this process individuals move towards making sense of their identity within this set of relationships, rather than seeing themselves as 'helpless' and out of control.

It offers the empowerment described by Rappaport as empowerment ...

> based on divergent reasoning that encourages diversity through the support of many different local groups rather than the large centralised social agencies and institutions which control resources, use convergent reasoning, and attempt to standardise the way people live their lives. (Rappaport, 1981, p. 19)

'WHAT IS IT REALLY LIKE?'

and empowerment that

> provides niches for people that enhances their ability to control their lives and allows them both affirmation and the opportunity to learn and to experience growth and development. (ibid, 1981, p. 19)

Some of the young people we hear from in this chapter do not feel in control of their own learning within the mathematics classroom and would certainly not see their experience as mathematics learners as an opportunity to experience growth. Those who feel excluded from mathematics learning see themselves as outside an exclusive club. Their constructions of self do not include the category 'good at mathematics'. Walshaw and Cabral explore this from a Lacanian perspective (Walshaw & Cabral, 2005, p. 301). For Lacan, the construction of identity begins with a young child unaware of the social situation into which it has been born. He describes the unconscious process through which the developing child takes on the language of its surroundings through recognising there are others on which it depends, but who are outside its control. This 'taking on' of language is a means of expressing desire and meeting needs. Lacan describes the **imaginary order** of awareness, which precedes language. During this stage the child begins the process of identity separation through investing significance in particular events/objects particularly linked to the mother. This stage is interrupted when the child makes an identification with its mirror image. Through the **mirror stage** the child comes to identify with an image outside itself, this image can be its own mirror image or the image of another. The apparent completeness of this image gives the child mastery over the body.

Walshaw and Cabral also suggest that by investigating the process of learners' self-construction of identity in connection with others, processes of learning within the classroom can be exposed (ibid, 2005, p. 301). For them, the space to explore is the struggle for meaning between the teacher and the learner over what it means to be a learner – they suggest that when this gap is small the 'classroom becomes a safe place in which to speak and act'. (ibid, p. 301) The learners we will hear from offer clues as to how this space becomes unbridgeable for some young people in our schools. The view of social justice I outlined above sees justice as a basic human right – and as something that our learners will struggle for. Until they can develop the language to describe how they 'feel' about the situations they find themselves in they will continue to struggle for justice. Coming to this language is both a part of identity formation within the classroom and a process of empowerment. In the next section I also link these ideas to ideas of *techne* – or practical wisdom. This supports my argument that a methodology, which sees narrative and narrating as key can work for social justice.

FINDING VOICE

My books are a series of introductions to matters and agendas unfinished. Like memory, it has gaps, amnesias, fragments of past, fractured presoent. To

TONY COTTON

those who have not lived it, it might appear opaque; those of us living it will recognise the map. (Jarman, 1992, p. 5)

'Voice' has been defined as privileging experience over theory as a basis for understanding (Hadfield & Haw, 2000). The main concerns of those researching with 'voice' at the heart of their research being work with marginalised or 'silenced' groups; inclusive and democratic research; the challenge and critique of processes which silence; and participation and empowerment within and through the research process.

The use of 'voice' within research texts is not unproblematic. The development of powerful narratives takes work. The narrative above offers both a critical and a representative voice (Hadfield & Haw, 2000). A critical voice which seeks to challenge existing structures and assumptions about working practices. Authentication comes both from an awareness of the teller of the story as to the purpose of asserting her voice and the particularity of her experience. The theme of representation aims to raise arguments and issues that are often marginalised in policy making.

In tackling this difficulty I would like to draw on the idea of *techne*. From Aristotle, *techne* is usually translated as 'art' or 'craft' and seen in opposition to *episteme* or knowledge. This opposition sets up a false divide between the domains of theory and practice however, and it may be more useful to see *techne* as theory in practice. Nussbaum (1986) suggests we should see *techne* in opposition to *tuche* or luck. So here *techne* allows us to apply our knowledge to our world giving us some form of control rather than simply succumbing to luck. Nussbaum describes *techne* as being 'concerned with the management of need and with prediction and control concerning future contingencies'. (Nussbaum, 1986, p. 85) If we live by *techne* we possess 'some sort of systematic grasp' that will allow us to enter a 'new situation well prepared, removed from blind dependence on what happens.' (ibid, p. 85) We may argue that such a person in possession of *techne* can be described as empowered. In the Lacanian sense the 'learner personalizes rules of conduct in order to optimise existence in the classroom'. (Walshaw & Cabral, 2005, p. 310)

Martha Nussbaum (1986) suggests that from Aristotle there are four sources of *techne*: universality, teachability, precision, concern with explanation (Nussbaum, 1986).

Universality and explanation yield control over the future in virtue of their orderly grasp of the past; teaching enables past work to yield future progress; precision yields consistent accuracy, the minimisation of failure. (ibid, p. 97)

These sources of *techne* offer powerful tools with which to analyse the narratives we produce. I would also argue that the exploration of narrative using these tools is both pedagogical and a model of research as praxis. The questions we should ask of our data are: to what extent does the narrative describe a past event so that it is recognizable by those involved in the event and by an audience who have experiences of similar events; to what extent is the narrative pedagogical, does it enable work to take place which may create alternative futures? Aristotle's view of

'WHAT IS IT REALLY LIKE?'

precision would suggest that the validity of the method is in the narratives it produces.

The process I describe below worked with young people to develop a description of how learning 'felt' for them. I would argue that at the beginning of the process those learners who had become excluded from the process of learning felt out of control of the process of education. They are living by *tuche*, the knowledge of the work that they brought with them into the classroom did not offer them '*prediction and control concerning future contingencies*'. As learners come to a language of critique they can gain *techne*, through the narratives which detail what has happened to them in the past they can gain some control over their possible futures

I would also argue that drawing on the idea of *techne* allows us to return to Bond's and Rawls' view of social justice. If we feel in control of our future, if we can understand how our previous work moves us forward and if we feel in as much control as we can expect of our future(s) we are moving towards social justice. Drawing on *techne* rather than *episteme* also means that truth claims take a different form. In this case the knowledge produced can be seen as a form of critical and emancipatory knowledge described by Morrow (1994, p. 146) as 'Our individual and collective consciousness of reality in order to maximise the human potential for freedom and equality'. The following section of the chapter describes a process through which such knowledge may be unearthed.

WHAT IS IT LIKE TO BE HERE?

Yeah – we'd love to hear your story
Just as long as it tells us where we are
And that where we are is where we're meant to be

Oh, come on, make it up yourself
You don't need anybody else
And I promise I won't sell these days to anyone else but you
No one but you

(Pulp – Glory Days)

The research that follows was undertaken with two groups of students in a Midlands inner city school. It is seen as a school in 'challenging' circumstances within the city and takes many young people from disadvantaged parts of the city.

Much of the research I engage in uses schools that may be seen as difficult places in the education system. I like to work with groups who find it difficult to access education and in schools that may find it difficult to implement national education policy. Researching in these settings is problematic. The groups of students do not remain constant over a period of weeks, as attendance at school is erratic for these students. Some of these groups have become disengaged from schooling and are thus less likely to engage with the research process as the quote that opens this paper suggests. Similarly the teachers in these schools are working in very stressful situations and the likelihood that they take time off during the research period is high. Indeed, both of these things were the case in this piece of research. However, unless we engage with students and teachers in these settings the only voices we hear are in settled environments, meaning that we only hear half of the story.

I worked with a group of 12 Year 7 students, aged 11-12. These students were usually taught in a 'pod' which took a cross curricular approach to the curriculum. They had been selected by their teacher to provide a cross section of skills, abilities and attachments to learning mathematics. These students had had little experience of learning mathematics in the secondary schools. Any mathematics that they had learnt had been to support learning in another curriculum area. In contrast I also worked with a group of 15 – 25 (depending on attendance on any particular day) of Year 11 students. These students were about to sit the national examinations at 16 and were placed in the lowest achieving groups of students. The school streamed students according to prior attainment, amalgamating the two lowest achieving groups with two teachers team teaching. The current teachers suggested this was an attempt to improve behaviour in mathematics lessons.

Whenever I work with groups of learners in school I try to ensure that the sessions are worthwhile learning experiences in themselves as well as worthwhile in terms of research outcomes for me. This, for me, is an issue of social justice. So each research visit to the school consisted of activities that allowed me to develop responses from the young people about what it was like for them to learn mathematics, alongside activities that I hoped also supported them in developing as mathematicians.

The beginning of the process is about exploring who we are. If we are to describe what is it like to be here, we need to articulate how we see ourselves early in the process. The technique I use to develop this articulation is often used as a drama warm up activity. I ask every member of the group I am working with to ask me the question, 'Who are you?' I have to answer each questioner with a different facet of who I am, teacher, parent, musician, frustrated football fan, and so on. This begins to model the complex natures of our identities – it also brings to the surface those facets of identity we bring to particular situations. You may like to try this:

Who are you?
Who are you?
Who are you?

I then asked the two groups of learners to create a web diagram answering the question 'Who am I? with as many different views of themselves as they could think of. There were fascinating differences between the 11-year old and the 16-year old students. The year 7 immediately worked in small groups to talk about things about themselves that they saw as important. They drew on many categories. They described their families, the wide range of linguistic backgrounds they could draw on, their hobbies and interests. All their definitions of themselves were phrased as positive statements, including three of the group who described

'WHAT IS IT REALLY LIKE?'

themselves as 'someone who loves maths', or 'someone who is good at maths'. This group averaged 18 statements about themselves. The class teacher suggested that the ethos of year 7 encouraged celebration of linguistic diversity and an acceptance of all facets of identity – this certainly seemed to support the young people in being able to bring a positive view of themselves into school.

In contrast the group of 16 year olds who had been placed in low attaining groups found it very difficult to describe themselves at all. They needed constant support and encouragement to bring themselves into the classroom. The average number of responses from this group was 10. These described familial relationships and interests as with the younger group. None of the students described themselves in terms of their linguistic background although many were positive about their ethnic background. One student phrased this in a slightly more complex way saying, 'People say I look like an Iraqi.' In this group there were several negative comments – 3 young people said 'I am someone who hates teachers.' 4 students stated that they 'hated school uniform' and 4 other students said 'I hate maths'. Unlike the younger group this group's complex view of their identities often created a tension between their view of themselves and a view of self, which is compatible with seeing learning in school as a positive endeavour. Earlier in the chapter the struggle of negotiation between teacher and learner over what it is to learn was discussed. The young people in this study who had been placed in groups on which low expectations were placed described this tension, both during this activity and in the following session, which explored what it was to be 'good at maths'.

I asked the two groups to draw me a mind map, which described, for them, what it was to be 'good at maths'. Again most of the younger group treated this is as a collaborative activity, engaging in discussion before making their mind maps. One of the group asked me if she could work on her own. She argued convincingly that she worked better when she 'could think things through for herself.' This showed great confidence and an understanding of how she felt she best engaged with learning. The posters all used an imaginary figure or a figure from history to characterise someone who was successful in mathematics. The figures from history were scientists such as Thomas Edison, the 'imaginary' figures contained the stereotypes which have appeared in previous studies of this type. Figures with glasses, having very bad hair days! When the students described what skills these people had they listed: they do not need to use calculators; they can answer questions very quickly; they can use all the mathematical operations well; they use complex mathematical vocabulary and explain things well. This suggests that the group has a fairly narrow view of the nature of mathematics that is limited to arithmetic. They also seem to see 'being good at mathematics' as something out of the 'norm' – the 'mad scientist' or 'geek' stereotype persists. However they could all describe peers who they saw as good mathematicians, and several pointed out individuals within the group. One whispered to me that they knew one of their friends was good at maths because the teacher always asked them the questions –

191

TONY COTTON

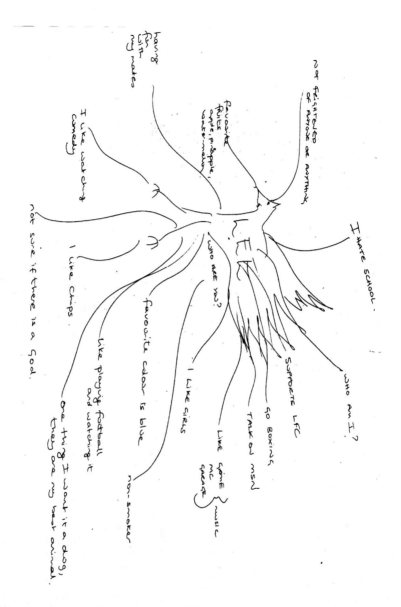

this was seen as positive as she said, 'It's great, we always let them answer the questions so we can get on quickly.'

In contrast the Year 11 students did not draw on any peers. All of the students used their current teacher as a model for someone who is good at mathematics. They described success in mathematics as mastery over content. A summary of

'WHAT IS IT REALLY LIKE?'

their discussion could be that individuals who are 'good' at maths understand the content – these individuals are also 'boring'. This view of successful learners in maths completely cut across their view of themselves as learners. In this way they cannot see any way that their identities as individuals are compatible with an identity, which would include being successful learners of mathematics. More worryingly, this was beginning to emerge with the younger group of learners too.

To further explore the young people's images of learning mathematics and their images of themselves as learners of mathematics I asked them to draw me images of 'what learning maths was like'. As in the previous activities the younger students drew a wide ranges of images, and articulated clearly how these images related to their prior experiences of learning mathematics – they could also describe their relationship to the images. However the older students could not articulate what it was like for them to learn mathematics, none of them could relate a time when they had felt successful in learning mathematics. One student told me that the activities we had worked on together during my first visit allowed them access to learning mathematics for the first time. In order to try to get the older students to engage with the question 'what is it like for you to learn maths?' I used the images that the younger students had drawn and asked them to sort them into two piles. Those that resonated with their own ideas of what it was to learn mathematics and those that didn't. This activity allowed them to begin to describe their feelings towards learning mathematics.

I used a similar process with the younger group – they sorted the set of 24 images into two groups, and then selected a key image from the group that they thought fitted their view of the process of learning mathematics. They then explained in some detail why they had selected this image. For the 11-year old pupils the key image was of a tape recorder sitting on a teacher's desk. There is no sign of a teacher. Lines emanating from the tape recorder make it clear that the tape recorder is controlling the lesson. There is also a sheet of paper resting on another desk. This is a pupil's answer sheet for a mental maths test. The pupil has written next to the image '*I like doing Mental Maths with the tape recorder in the Primary School*'. This image refers to the process, which is used by the national tests at age 11 in the UK. Pupils are asked to respond to a series of questions using mental methods. The process is standardised nationally by using a common set of questions delivered to schools on an audiotape.

The next image was selected by all the 11 year old students as being an image that they saw as representative of 'what it was like to learn maths'. When I asked them to talk more about this choice they said:

It's good because it says it clearly. The teachers take too long but the tape goes really quickly. Sometimes the teachers repeat themselves and it takes ages

I like doing them booklets[3]. Yesterday I completed one and then nearly completed another one. I completed everything

This suggests a view of learning mathematics as disembodied, literally in this case. The tape recorder was not required to take account of individual needs – it did not bring emotion into the equation. This view linked directly to the sense the young learners had that success in mathematics is measured through successful completion of tasks.

This was not a view of learning mathematics that was recognised at all by the older students. This group selected three cards; one showed a pupil sitting at a desk, almost swamped by a huge piece of paper saying 'Oh no not maths again'; another image showed a face with swimming eyes with the statement '*learning maths is some times confusing*'; their final choice was a card showing a sleeping pupil sitting at a desk with a teacher. The teacher's speech bubble contains 'Blah, blah, blah, blah, blah, ...'. The student has written on the card 'I don't like it when teachers take FOREVER to explain something and Boring (sic) teachers shouldn't teach maths'.

When we discussed these choices further the students told me that they felt teachers took too long to explain things – for these students the explanations were not supporting their learning – they said:

It just makes me confused

People get scared when they do their work because sometimes they can't solve it

When I'm doing my maths revision at home it makes me mad and it makes me confused

This suggested an image of learning mathematics as a process of confusion and frustration, which could not be alleviated by the teacher trying to explain concepts and ideas. In fact the lengthy explanations were perceived as increasing the frustration. Mathematics for these learners appeared to be confusing, frightening and enraging.

DEVELOPING A VOCABULARY OF CRITIQUE

The transition to verbalised self-observation denotes a beginning process of generalisation of inner forms of activity. The shift to a new type of inner perception means also a shift to a higher type of inner activity, since a new way of seeing things opens up new possibilities for handling them. (Vygotsky, 1986, p. 170)

I have suggested above that the data shows a group of young people who, at age 11, are able to see 'mathematics learner' as a facet of their identity, although with this group there was an emerging sense of identifying success in mathematics as external to their self-image. The group of 16-year old students, identified as 'disaffected' by the school, made no connection at all between their images of themselves and images of successful learners of mathematics. This disconnection makes any form of teacher – student relationship in the mathematics classroom very difficult. There was also a marked difference between the ways that the younger students could articulate their images of themselves – particularly in relation to school, learning and mathematics learning, and the older students who could articulate self identity but often saw it in tension with what it is to be a learner of mathematics. These students found it very difficult to articulate their relationship to mathematics and mathematics learning – except as an opposition.

The process of research allowed the students who felt disconnected to the process of mathematics to begin to articulate this sense of disconnection. I suggested earlier in the chapter that developing a sense of 'techne' allowed individuals to take some control over their lives. It removes the sense of 'blind

TONY COTTON

dependence' on the experiences that life throws at us. My hope would be that the process of research has begun the process of developing a vocabulary of critique for these young people. If we can describe what it is like for us to be in a particular situation, we can begin to think through the possibilities for change.

In the introduction to the book Tony Brown argued that a postivistically conceived world is Imaginary – in the Lacanian sense. The young people I worked with were coming to see the world through positivistic lenses. They could describe the characteristics of effective learners of mathematics – they seemed certain that people with these characteristics would succeed. Unfortunately they described themselves in opposition to these characteristics and their positivist view of identity meant that they became excluded from this world. Exploring identity with these young people offered them a glimpse of a more complex world in which identities slip and slide and are not fixed oppositions. This gives previously excluded learners room for manoeuvre, it opens up the possibility for them to find matches between facets of self-identity and their perceptions of what it is to be 'good at maths'.

NOTES

[1] This is taken from the aims of the group Mathematics Education and Society.

[2] This was a comment from one of the young people I worked with for the empirical work on which this chapter draws.

[3] Many primary classrooms in the UK use individualised programmes, which ask individual learners to work through booklets of examples in a structured way. Once the learner completes a booklet successfully they will move on to the next booklet in the sequence.

REFERENCES

Bond, E. (1983). Lear – Author's Preface. London: Eyre Methuen.
Cotton, T., & Hardy, T. (2004). Problematising culture and discourse for mathematics education research: defining the issues – tools for research'. In P. Valero & R. Zevenbergen (Eds.), Researching the socio-political dimensions of Mathematics (pp. 85–105). Dordrecht: Kluwer.
Department for Education and Skills. (2002). Retrieved from http://www.dfes.gov.uk.html
Eisner, E. W. (1991). The enlightened eye - qualitative inquiry and the enhancement of educational practice. New York: Macmillan Publishing Company.
Foucault, M. (1972). The archaeology of knowledge. London: Routledge Falmer.
Hadfield, M., & Haw, K. (2000). The 'voice' of young people: Hearing, listening, responding. Nottingham, UK: University of Nottingham.
Jarman, D. (1992). At your own risk: a saint's testament. London: Vintage Books.
Lessing, D. (2002). The golden notebook. London: Harper Collins Publishers.
Morrow, R. A., & Brown, D. (1994). Critical theory and methodology. London: Sage Publications.
Nussbaum, M. (1986). The fragility of goodness: Luck and ethics in Greek tragedy and philosophy. Cambridge: Cambridge University Press.
Pulp. (1998). Excerpt from the lyrics of 'Glory days' taken from the album. This is Hardcore. Island records.
Rappaport, J. (1981). In praise of paradox: A social policy of empowerment over prevention. American Journal of Community Psychology, 9, 17–25.

Rawls, J. (1971). A theory of justice. Oxford: Oxford University Press.
Schratz, M., & Walker, R. (1995). Research as social change. London: Routledge.
Vygotsky, L. (1986). Thought and language. Cambridge, MA: Massachusetts Institute of Technology Press.
Walshaw, M., & Cabral, T. (2005). Reviewing and thinking: The affect/cognition relation. PME 29. University of Melbourne. Australia.

Tony Cotton
Carnegie Faculty of Sport and Education
Leeds Metropolitan University

PART FIVE

EVER PRESENT AFFECTIVITY

DAVE WILSON

9. THE TRANSFERENCE RELATION IN TEACHING

During much of last year I attempted to reflect upon my teaching in a particular way. At the end of each day, or week, I sat quietly and allowed an incident from my teaching to enter my mind. Whatever that was, I tried to recapture the detail of that incident and to set it down in writing as objectively as I could. I then worked upon that fragment. My conjecture was that whatever entered my mind swiftly and easily would have some significance. The fact that they were significant I took for granted. Why otherwise, would I have remembered them? To use John Mason's expression, they were salient incidents (Mason, 1992). My task was to clarify and to articulate their significance and to draw from this some implications for my practice as a teacher. I tried to examine myself within these situations, to look at my feelings and actions. I tried to read and to reread my stories offering a variety of interpretations of the significance of them for me.

As I proceeded in this way I produced generalities based upon the particularities of my (reflected upon) experience. When my reflection evoked a fragment from my reading I attempted to discuss those readings and to reflect upon their relevance for myself. During this period, as now, I found strongly resonant the work of Lacan and his interpreters – importantly Žižek – the writings of Gattegno and recent attempts by Mason to articulate a research methodology appropriate for reflective practitioners. I used these to provide me both with the tools to interpret my experience and to help me to articulate generalities.

I found that modern psychoanalysis was a particularly rich source of readings. It has been suggested that Lacan shifted from discussing psychoanalytic practice to using psychoanalysis to analyse discourse itself during the twenty-five year course of his seminars. At some stage as the year proceeded I began to consciously use this possibility in my own reflection.

In particular I used the notion of 'transference' very heavily. From a psychoanalytic perspective, whatever relationship I am currently within, I respond as if I were in another relationship.

> The transference relationship describes distorted perceptions of counsellors, which arise because of clients' previous relationships. For example, if a client has experienced authoritarian parenting which has resulted in their being passive and lacking in assertiveness, they will relate to the counsellor as if they are authoritarian, and will expect to be told what to do. (Colin Lago, Notes from a counselling course, Sheffield University)

T. Brown (ed.), The Psychology of Mathematics Education: A Psychoanalytic Displacement, 201–210.
© 2008 Sense Publishers. All rights reserved.

As an example of this phenomenon, reflect upon the common teaching pattern where a teacher responds to each student contribution. It echoes the pattern of one-to-one situations.

> The conventional model of the teaching-learning situation is based on the mother-infant relationship, a group of two, perpetuating the transference relationship. This is still the most highly prized educational relationship ... The relation between teacher and pupil is necessarily asymmetrical. The teacher is an authority in his academic subject, and the student is ignorant of it: the teacher is further invested with the authority of the institute, to which the student belongs only transiently. ... so the transference relationship hangs like a millstone round both their necks, mostly unquestioned and unchallenged. (Abercrombie, 1984, p. 125)

This mode of operating may encourage each student to feel that they are potentially in the presence of an authority to whom they must defer – as if the tutor has all the answers, positioned, like a Lacanian analyst, as the subject supposed to know (*le sujet supposé savoir*).

Žižek suggests that children ask their parents impossible questions ('Why is the sky blue, Daddy?') in order to catch the all-knowing parent in a state of not knowing. Is this what some students do in sessions like this? They seek for questions, which will expose the tutor's non-knowledge. (See Diaphony's account of her teacher in Baldino and Cabral's chapter in this volume.) They look for gaps, into which they can insert ourselves. As do school children in classrooms.

Therapeutic methods, and pedagogies, derived from the work of Rogers appear at first sight to offer no scope for resistance by the client or student in the manner that Žižek suggests ('Why is the sky blue, Daddy?' – 'Why do you think that it is blue?' replies the Rogerian therapist or teacher).

Althusser has pointed out that any ideology contains within it the potential for resistance to it. Examining Rogerian practices from the perspective of what might be its Master Signifier, which pins down the meaning of the signifiers of the Rogerian discourse is helpful in dealing with this apparent difficulty. At the focus of the Rogerian theory is the 'fully functioning autonomous subject' - and it is the presence of this fantasy which both reveals the ideological nature of Rogerian discourse, and allows us to identify ways of resisting. 'Why did you do that?' 'Dunno', 'She made me' are denials of this fantasy.

The remainder of this article consists of three incidents selected from my teaching last year and my personal reflections upon them. This is followed by some more general musings based upon my later reading of my accounts, some months later, as I put them together for this article.

A SHORT (NON)DIALOGUE

The students, who were sitting in an open circle, had been asked to look at a poster and had talked generally about it for a few minutes. I then asked them to invent some questions about the poster to be worked on later.

THE TRANSFERENCE RELATION IN TEACHING

Paul   I don't know what you mean Dave - what kind of question could I invent. I don't know any questions

Dave   (kneeling in front of Paul) ... silence ...

Paul   I said something earlier about the curve looking like a sine curve ... I suppose I could look at that ... I could find out if it was a sine curve ... I could draw it and find out

Dave   (... pause ...) OK

A speaker needs an audience. Compare this with the psychoanalytic position of the silent analyst whose mute, physical presence forces (enables?) the analysand to speak.

A speaker needs a voice. Gilligan (1982) has written about the difficulty that women experience in having a voice. French feminists, such as Irigaray and Cixous take a similar position. They suggest that a woman is always positioned as the Other in relation to language, the Big Other of the Symbolic, using the Lacanian terminology, and hence are forced take up a masculine position when engaging with language.

Working class men, students, are similarly positioned, albeit not as radically as women, in that there is a position, which is available for them, in theory if not in practice.

One of my stories about myself is that I get students to do something, to have an experience, and draw their attention to what they are doing or have done. Why did I remain silent and not draw Paul's attention to the fact that I had done nothing (or next to nothing, given my above comments)? I seemed to think that he would have realised this for himself and needed no more from me.

A difficulty shown by Beckett's 'Not I' is that of having a voice. In this work, the speaker denies the first person of the speaker. The speaker is female (though the stage directions may not specify this) – she monologues at length and at intervals says '...what?...who?...no!...she!...' as if negating the fact of herself speaking - note also that there is an auditor, who moves at each of these denials.

This points me at what may be an issue for many people; that of feeling that they can validly speak. I recall numerous occasions working with adolescents and adults on mathematics where they have denied the possibility of their having any knowledge, any insight into the situation, denied the possibility of having anything to say. An issue for me, for any teacher, is that of releasing them so that they can voice their thoughts, and to own them.

In the class or lecture room I take up, or more correctly, I am invested with, the position of the subject presumed to know (le sujet supposé savoir), to echo Lacan writing on the transference relation. My students presume that I have the knowledge, which they wish to acquire. From a psychoanalytic viewpoint, this is a misrecognition, which they have to work through. The 'transferential illusion is necessary'. Žižek, (1989) follows Lacan, in exploring the way in which it is a necessary part of the way in which language operates, in the way in which signifiers come to have more or less fixed meaning.

Did Paul have a voice, i.e. a position from which to speak, to (internally) hear and to respond to his own question? (And, note that Harold Pinter, another playwright who is highly sensitive to the way in which language works, emphasises silences and pauses – and there is a difference – one indicates that the thinking carries on – and an actor needs to know which is which, because they are acted differently).

The problem for me as a teacher is to find ways of working with my students so that, in the same way as analysands come to be free of their symptoms by working through the transferential relation, they come to their own understanding and control of the subject matter they are working upon.

Rogers denies that there is a problem with transference. Rogerian counselling as a method implies that the counsellor always rejects being positioned as the one who is in the know. Many educators have followed Rogers' (1969) own educational writings and attempted to devise analogous didactic methods (e.g. Brandes & Ginnis, 1986). As a teacher in secondary schools I developed my own practice along these lines – 'David manages, sets up the task, and counsels very gently' was an observation made on seeing a lesson conducted by me.

After reading Lacan, and noticing my tension with the interaction with Paul, I wish to reconsider my methodology. Rogerian practice fits comfortably with the notion of an autonomously functioning subject. Recent analysis from feminist, Marxist and ethnic perspectives question the ease of access to this position for those who are other than white, middle class and male.

PAULA

Paula was sitting at the extreme end of a row of computers. Immediately to her right was a wall. She sat turned slightly towards the wall, facing both the computer and the wall.

I noticed that I was reluctant to approach her. When I did go near her, she did not move, but remained facing away from me.

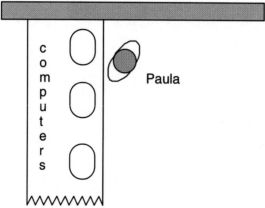

I imagined that she did not want me to interact with her.

THE TRANSFERENCE RELATION IN TEACHING

Others of the 25 students crammed into the room asked for my help, and seemed to welcome me when I wandered near to them.

I found it extremely difficult to even go near Paula. I noticed that I wanted to not go near her. When I deliberately chose to go and talk to her I found it hard to initiate a conversation with her. I felt afraid that she would reject any attempt I made to talk with her about her work.

As I looked at how she had positioned herself and oriented her body I imagined that she did not want to talk to me.

One day later I am still disturbed by this incident. The feelings that I had were my feelings. They were not hers. Because of my feelings I did not attempt to work with her in the way in which I tried to work with the other students.

I am now aware that I had projected my feelings, which I can encapsulate as a strong wish to not interact with her, onto her. In my writing an account of the incident I tried to signal that by deliberately using a language which, for me, evokes the technique from Gestalt therapy where one person involved in an interaction says to the other person 'I see you there sitting like that and I imagine that you are thinking, feeling ... , and I feel ... '.

Although this, for me, was an extreme incident I now wonder how often similar incidents occur, both in my teaching and in my personal life. I want to increase my sensitivity to such incidents so that I may notice them when they occur. I also want to work on ways of altering how I behave in such situations.

> Choosing in the moment to act in a certain way requires two things: noticing a possibility to choose, that is, recognising some typical situation about to unfold; having alternatives from which to choose, that is, being aware of alternative action or behaviour. (Mason, 1992)

I am working here with the conjectures from Mason that in order to change my behaviour I need to be able to choose. In order to choose I need to notice when I am about to do something, and to notice that I have a choice about what I do. These are not in themselves sufficient. I also need to rehearse alternative actions so that they are available to me in the moment.

An alternative way of behaving might be indicated by my noticing that the feelings were my feelings. This gives me some choices.

One choice is to recognise my feelings, but to act nevertheless as if they were not present. I might choose to approach the student and talk to them as I would any other. I would need to rehearse the usual kind of things I say when initiating an encounter with an already working student, and rehearse optional responses dependent upon the response.

Another possibility is to be open and honest about my feelings to the student. 'I'm sorry – I'm ignoring you because I imagine that you don't want me to talk to you.' This involves not just acknowledging my feelings to myself, but sharing these with students.

> in many cases (teachers) have been trained not to share with students what is going on in their minds or what they are feeling (Brandes & Ginnis, 1986, p. 46)

These are real choices to be made in the moment. For example, choosing the first course of action involves neglecting, in some sense, my feelings - there is a cost, which I will have to pay.

The second choice may not be helpful, because the self-disclosure involved might not be appropriate, or I might be dumping my feelings onto the student, as if I were attempting to make her responsible for my feelings.

If I wish to have the first choice psychologically available to me I need to prepare myself, not only to have the behaviour available (by rehearsing it and so on), I need to be sure that I can pay the psychological cost of putting aside my own feelings. I might, for example, practice the 'black box' technique which entails me imagining writing down my feelings, placing the paper inside the box, closing the lid and putting the box away, with the (to be fulfilled) promise that I return to the box and address my feelings at a later moment. (Sports psychologists have done a great deal of work on such techniques. See Hardy (1997) and Syer & Connolly (1998).)

Whilst rereading my writing, I notice that I am effectively using this method. By reflecting upon the interaction and upon my feelings, I am now addressing the emotions, which were stirred in the classroom.

This reminds me that emotions are always present in teaching and learning interactions. There is an ever-present affective component. Most writers on teaching stress the affective component, which applies to the pupils and students (under the heading 'motivation') – few discuss the affective dimension for the teacher.

ALISON

I was running a session on working in groups. There was a double agenda. The first was how we ourselves work. The second issue was the relevance of things, which we became aware of for our practice as teachers.

Half the group had discussed the advantages and disadvantages of working in groups for the learning of mathematics, while the other half had observed.

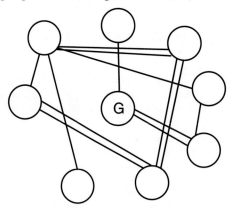

Group Interaction Analysis Diagram

Three observers had recorded an interaction analysis in the form of a diagram showing the participants, drawing lines to represent a speech act between the speaker and the person to whom it was addressed. If a statement was addressed to the group as a whole a line was drawn to a circle in the centre of the diagram representing the whole group. I had briefed them on this technique and told them to judge for themselves to whom statement were addressed.

We then got feedback from the discussion group and the observers. Two of the interaction analysis observers agreed that there were many statements addressed to the whole group. Alison disagreed. She had decided that if the speaker looked down at the table, or upwards in the air, or if the glanced around the table as if attempting to make eye contact with several group members, then it would be counted as an interaction with the whole group. On this basis, there were very few whole group interactions.

We listened to her observation.

I thanked her for her comments and added that I did not really want to get into issues to do with a proper definition of 'saying something to the whole group'.

Discussion moved on for the last minutes of the lesson.

The next day Alison approached me at the end of a lecture:

I wanted to talk to you about yesterday. I felt dismissed by what you said. I am interested in how we make judgments about things because that's one of the things we do as teachers. I just wanted to say that. I realise it was near the end of the session.

I apologised for my insensitivity and said that it might have been because although I also think that how we make judgments is important I was trying to avoid the discussion being distracted by what might turn into an argument about definitions.

Reflecting upon this I feel that I was attempting to parent the students in, at least, two ways. Firstly, I had conjectured that they would merely turn the discussion into a sterile definitional argument, thus avoiding the substantive issues. And clearly, I had not actually listened to Alison but responded as if I knew what she had intended by her words. Secondly, I was looking after the interests of the discussion group who I thought might feel threatened by Alison's observation. I want to be able to notice when I (am about to) act in a parental manner. 'Habits can be helpful; unquestioned habits can be unhelpful'. (Mason, 1992)

SOME (IN)CONCLUSIONS

Mellin-Olsen (1986, pp. 185-186) has written of Brousseau's notion of the 'didactic contract',

In its simple form the contract means that the teacher is obliged to teach and the pupil is obliged to learn. For the persons involved, the contract cannot be negotiated. Teacher and pupil are thus all the time busy inventing ever new forms of behaviour and interaction, which they hope can be in accordance with the contract, which are either interpretations of it or tolerable evasions.

Such a contract is a double-bind, as pupil and teacher are locked in an expectation of growth which can be established by circumstances outside their control. The brilliance of Brousseau's structure is, however, that in order for genuine learning to happen, the contract must be broken. In that case teacher and pupil manage to crash the double-bind:

To be obeyed, the contract must be broken, because knowledge cannot be transmitted ready-made and hence nobody - neither the teacher nor the pupil - can be really in command, can really control the contract. (ibid)

Brousseau is articulating what is, in psychoanalytic terms, an aspect of the transferential relationship inherent in the teaching learning interaction. This requires a certain amount of unpacking however.

For much of the psychoanalytic tradition the transference relationship is contrasted with the real relationship between counsellor and client (or teacher and pupil, for our purpose). Colin Lago has said that:

The transference relationship describes distorted perceptions of counsellors, which arise because of clients' previous relationships. For example, if a client has experienced authoritarian parenting which has resulted in their being passive and lacking in assertiveness, they will relate to the counsellor as if they are authoritarian, and will expect to be told what to do.

From this perspective, the real teacher pupil relationship is one where learning takes place by the pupil, where the didactic contract is broken. The transference relationship is the didactic contract, where the teacher is perceived by the pupil to be the one who has knowledge and can pass it across to the pupils. (And of course, the pupil positions the teacher in this role, and insofar as the teacher perceives this and accepts it, the teacher enters into counter-transference with the pupil). To make the parallel with Colin Lago's example more explicit, it is based upon a (mis)recognition. Both the pupils and the teacher are playing out 'the mother-infant relationship, a group of two, perpetuating the transference relationship'. (Abercrombie, 1984)

At first sight it seems easy for the teacher to avoid getting caught up in this. A methodology adapted from Rogerian practices: not explicitly telling pupils the answers and the techniques; forcing them by, for example questions, to take their attention to how they construct the knowledge for themselves, appears to allow teachers and pupils to evade the double-bind.

From a post-Lacanian psychoanalytic perspective however, it is not that easy. There are other forces operating than purely individual ones. Lacan draws our attention to the pre-existing Symbolic and to the feature he terms 'jouissance' (that might be understood as the enjoyment or emotions activated by regulative apparatus, such as a particular linguistic structure (Ed.)). Žižek has written of

> The necessary structural illusion which drives people to believe that truth can be found in laws describes precisely the mechanism of transference: transference is this supposition of a Truth, of a Meaning behind the stupid, traumatic, inconsistent fact of the Law. In other words, 'transference' names the vicious circle of belief: the reasons why we should believe are persuasive only to those who already believe. (Žižek, 1989, p. 38)

From the perspective of the pupil, they are trapped in this illusion; the illusion that knowledge is elsewhere, radically exterior to themselves, held within what Lacan terms the big Other of the Symbolic. And of course, so is the teacher. The paradox not addressed by person-centred counselling and student-centred learning, is that the illusion is a necessary one:

> Transference is, then, an illusion, but the point is that we cannot bypass it and reach directly for the Truth: the Truth itself is constituted through the illusion proper to the transference - 'the Truth arises from misrecognition'. (Lacan, quoted by Žižek, 1989, p. 57)

The point at issue here is that, at least within the cultural framework of European rationalism, it is a necessary presupposition that knowledge is independent of ourselves: that it has always been there. This is the point made by Lacan in the seminars where he reflects upon the Platonic dialogue in 'The Meno';

> When something comes to light, something which we are forced to consider as new, when another structural order emerges, well then, it creates its own perspective within the past, and we say - This can never not have been there, this has existed from the beginning. Besides, isn't that a property which our own experience demonstrates? (Lacan, 1991)

For the pupil, even though, from the viewpoint of radical constructivism, (for the client, from the viewpoint of non-directive counselling) they construct some new knowledge for themselves, it will appear as though it is precisely that knowledge which was already present, before the fact, and held by the teacher.

Paul needed the brute presence of a teacher in order, whilst constructing his own questions for and by himself, to maintain the fantasy that the questions pre-existed his articulation of them (and notice that fantasy is at the heart of all ideologies). In this reading, I was positioned by him as the sujet-presumé-savoir, who knew the questions to ask.

Abercrombie (1984) has described her teaching experiments with students in Higher Education who were learning to make scientific judgements. She describes the relative failure of traditional lecture models, where students were reinforced in their belief in the objective nature of scientific experimental facts. She then describes the difficulties of using non-directive methods, which gave rise to considerable frustration in the students. She then goes on to suggest the use of a

DAVE WILSON

group analytic based method, in which the transference relation is held within the student group, rather than being assumed by the tutor.

Salecl (1994, p. 55) has critiqued certain aspects of communist education using the notion of 'a state that is essentially a by-product'. (a notion developed by Jon Elster)

We cannot make states such as love, or respect, a direct goal: 'the real effect can only be achieved if we pursue some external goal'. An example within our currently predominating liberal model might be 'understanding'.

From a Lacanian perspective, we can never achieve the object of our desire.

The issue then arises as to what can be the legitimate goals of mathematics education, given that understanding cannot be a direct goal. And what strategies can a teacher most usefully adopt.

Gattegno (1987, p. vii) asserts that 'only awareness is educable'. I interpret this as his attempt to identify what can be a direct goal of education.

These last few paragraphs are markers to myself for further work as I continue to reflect upon my own practice.

REFERENCES

Abercrombie, M. L. J. (1984). Group analysis and higher education. In T. Lear (Ed.), *Spheres of group analysis* (pp. 119–137). London: Institute of Group Analysis.

Brandes, D., & Ginnis, P. (1986). *A guide to student-centred learning*. Cheltenham: Nelson Thornes.

Gattegno, C. (1987). *The science of education. Part one: Theoretical considerations*. New York: Educational Solutions.

Gilligan, C. (1982). *In a different voice*. Cambridge, USA: Harvard University Press.

Hardy, L. (1997). Psychological skills in climbing. In A. Fyffe & I. Peter (Eds.), *The handbook of climbing*. UK: Pelham.

Lacan, J. (1991). *The seminar of Jacques Lacan. Book II*. New York: Norton.

Mason, J. (1992). *Noticing*. Milton Keynes, UK: Centre for Mathematics Education, Open University.

Mellin-Olsen, S. (1986). *The politics of mathematics education*. Dordrecht: Kluwer.

Rogers, C. (1969). *Freedom to learn*. New York: Merrill.

Salecl, R. (1994). *The spoils of freedom: Psychoanalysis and feminism after the fall of socialism*. London: Routledge.

Syer, J., & Connolly, J. (1998). *Sporting body and sporting mind*. London: Simon & Schuster Ltd.

Žižek, S. (1989) *The sublime object of ideology*. London: Verso.

Dave Wilson
Manchester

DICK TAHTA

10. EVER PRESENT AFFECTIVITY

I enjoyed reading Dave Wilson's stimulating account of the transference relation in teaching. There are lots of useful observations in the educational literature about learners learning but not so many about teachers teaching. This must be partly because it is so difficult to give an honest account of what it is actually like to teach –most attempts to do this slide into idealised intention or pious hope. In reflecting on some incidents in his own classroom, Dave exposed himself. I appreciated his courage in revealing his feelings and the sensitivity with which he discussed the various interpretations open to him. But I also felt that the very delicacy of his self–awareness had left the other participants and their effects on the situation somewhat ignored. I would like to re–open the reflective possibility with a few remarks on his thoughts about the lesson with Paula. I emphasise that I will not of course be discussing the actual incident: I will be discussing my reading of his written account of it.

What we know about Paula:

- she was sitting 'turned slightly away to the wall';
- when Dave approached 'she did not move, but remained facing away from (him)';
- her name – fictitious or otherwise – echoes that of the student in another reported incident;
- she is otherwise absent from the account;

What we might speculate about Paula:

- how precisely does her absence punctuate Dave's discourse;
- is she the M(other) whose silence forces him to speak whereas Pa(ul) is the Father with whom he is mute;
- is the feminising ending of her name indeed a Lacanian 'petit a', indicating the lower case autre, the object of desire;
- what might her feelings have been during this incident?

What we know (from the article) about Dave:

- he 'imagined that she did not want to talk to (him)';
- he noticed that he 'wanted not to go near her', and that he 'found it hard to initiate a conversation with her';
- on reflection he found that the feelings he had were his alone: 'they were not hers', he insists, and emphasises this later by two bold–face references to '*my* feelings';

T. Brown (ed.), The Psychology of Mathematics Education: A Psychoanalytic Displacement, 211–218.
© 2008 Sense Publishers. All rights reserved.

- he believes in and is sensitive to 'an ever present affective component' in teaching and learning interactions.

What we might ask after reading Dave's account:
- does he protest too much that his feelings were only his own;
- why has he not offered any further explanation that would help him and his readers make some sense of the incident (for example, whether he had similar experiences on other occasions, or some hint of what the issues are that he is claiming are purely personal to him);
- how did he reject the reasonable hypothesis that must have occurred to him at some stage that Paula's emotions (part of that 'ever present affective component') might have been part of the situation;
- what sort of mechanism is he involving when he refers to his having 'projected' his feelings onto her?

It might help further reflection about some of these issues to add a few remarks about the psychoanalytic notions invoked in Dave's account. Inevitably a notion like transference will be not be easily pinned down but common to most usages is the imposition of an actual or imagined previous relationship onto a present one: for example, the student may see the teacher as a parent, or the teacher may see the student as a lover. The classical view is that transference is an internal mental event that does not necessarily affect the other, who may indeed not be present at the time. But where the other is present it is now more usual to assume that there will be some interactional consequence.

The possibility of a transference in the situation between Dave and Paula seems to lie in the suggestion that he has made her – in his mind – someone who does not want to interact with him. But he also supposes that his feelings have been projected onto her, and this can be quite a different matter, for in psychoanalytic usage this invokes the notion that feelings have been disowned, expelled and located elsewhere. In the one case – of transference – I make the other into someone I already know of from my past, whose feelings may be understood and shared; in the other case, I get rid of certain feelings by placing them – in my mind – with the other, whom I will now experience as quite different from me.

Dave reports that he felt Paula didn't want to speak to him, and this is consistent with a transference – he could have made her in his mind into someone who keeps him at a distance, someone who wouldn't be interested in him. But he also feels that he didn't want to speak with her, and this is consistent with a projection – he may have disowned the unapproachable parts of himself and placed them in her so that she has become in his mind someone to keep away from. It is difficult to interpret any further in the absence of any information from (or indeed about) Paula. But if we assume – as we surely should – that her feelings are also relevant, we would then have to invoke further possibilities. For instance, it could be possible that there has been a transference from her – for example he has been seen as a mistrusted authority figure. His own feelings are then a form of counter–transference, reflecting through his own sensitivity how she is treating him, but

EVER PRESENT AFFECTIVITY

also possibly involving some personal components – for example, he may (like most of us) have problems about being an authority figure.

On the other hand, it may be that Paula has enacted a complicated defence mechanism known as projective identification. There are different ways in which this can be understood. But one fairly straightforward interpretation in this case is that she may have disowned an unsociable angry part of herself, and projected this onto him. There are then various things that can happen: one of them is that Dave may become the sort of person she has constructed ('It is by means of a series of identifications that the personality is constituted and specified.') and may find himself not wanting to interact with her. His sensitivity picks up her feelings and he allows himself to become the non–interacting person whom she can perhaps now deplore – and whom he would probably usually be very concerned not to be.

These are but idle speculations; and in any case, failing further information, we could make many more – for example, that Paula was bored, stoned, an hallucination, or even someone who had crept into the class by mistake. My main point is that if psychodynamic notions are to be invoked in classroom accounts then standard reflective procedures common to most therapists and counsellors might also have to be considered. People who wish to 'address the emotions which (are) stirred in classrooms' need to have the courage to expose their own feelings, but they will also need to be able to sift through various interpretations of them and produce specific reasons why they come to the conclusions they do. An apparently unproblematic claim that what I feel in the classroom is entirely my own doing might in fact be true, but colleagues would need more than my mere assertions: they would want to confirm my interpretation by ascertaining clearly on what grounds I had rejected other possibilities.

A DISCUSSION BETWEEN DICK TAHTA AND DAVE WILSON

During the course of this discussion Dick wrote the draft of his own chapter 'Ever present affectivity' included above.

Dave:
I have been enjoying reading your thoughtful (and beautifully written) piece in Chreods. I wanted to write briefly about Paula. Her presence (in fact I mean absence) haunts your account of the episode. You emphasise a few times that on later reflection you had come to feel that you had projected your feelings onto her. You seem to be offering an example of your own transference – but without any further explanation of why you would have needed to do this at the time.

You are reminded that 'emotions are always present in teaching and learning interactions'. So – where is Paula in this account? What sort of feelings might she have been having? What might you suppose was her participation in the episode? The nearest you get to saying anything about this in your subsequent reflection is your strenuous denial that your feelings 'were not hers'. How do you know this so certainly?

DICK TAHTA

The very sensitivity with which you are concerned that some of your own personal baggage may have been brought into the situation makes it possible to ask you to take your own initial intuitions more seriously. The appropriate mechanism with which to discuss this episode may be 'projective identification'. May it not be possible that to some extent you have been expressing Paula's disowned feelings? Therapists do expect to be able to distinguish feelings that are aroused in them from those that are picked up from their clients. You seem very concerned in your account to show how it may be that you imposed your feelings on her. But you don't give any reason why you might have wanted to do this – and it is this sort of evidence that enables therapists to judge what's going on. Meanwhile – without any further evidence about that 'strong wish not to interact with her' – it must remain just as plausible that Paula has imposed feelings onto you.

Does this muddy the water too much? I would be interested to know more about Paula, about your relationship with her, and something about what it was that prompted you to choose the particular interpretation you gave.

Dick

Dick:
Thanks for probing me about my writing, and thanks for the nice comments.

I find it difficult to review this interaction with Paula. I was aware at the time of strong emotions within myself and of my inability, in the lesson, to deal with them, and with Paula. And I will find it difficult to work on.

My conjecture that I was projecting is based upon my noticing that 'I felt afraid that she would reject any attempt I made to talk with her'. Given my very real fears to do with rejection, especially focused around attractive women, I find this plausible. I see a woman, wish to talk with her, because I am attracted to her, but don't, because I am unsure of her response. And then in this kind of relationship where I am formally empowered, blame her.

My transference is based upon my distorted perception of our relationship. Although I am in a teaching relationship with her, Paula's posture, mannerisms evoke, without my knowing it explicitly, different relationships.

I know that I do not explicitly go into this in my published writing. Quite deliberately!

However – projective identification. I am not familiar with the term, so I might be way off-beam here.

Yes, this is certainly possible. It is only in the last few months that I have become aware of this possible interpretation. A friend has been working on a research project on adolescent drug overdoses, so she interviews young people shortly after discharge from hospital. After one interview early in the project she felt extremely depressed, and one of the supervising psychiatrists suggested that she might be taking into herself the strong emotions projected by the interviewee. This sounds like what you are describing.

At this moment, I am more drawn to the interpretation, which you are offering than to my original one. I am basing this on my recognition that I do tend to (over)insist upon being responsible for everything to do with myself – 'my feelings, not her feelings' – whilst knowing that this is not always appropriate (dammit, I have been badly treated in at least some instances!).

Distinguishing between interpretations, as you suggest therapists do, I need help with – supervision. At MMU, the senior counsellor has a few of us in group supervision. The original purpose of this has been to help with pastoral related tutorials with students. After a few meetings, it could be the case that enough trust has developed within the group for us to begin to explore teaching related issues. I hope so, and would certainly find it helpful.

Apologies for not replying earlier. I can list lots of reasons, but being full of self-doubt, suggest that they are merely excuses.

Thanks again for your comments.

Dave.

Dave:

Thanks for writing. I hope we can continue to interchange a little about the issues you raise – in the first place because I think it was really stimulating to read your article – a rare piece about what it is like to be a teacher teaching (rare I say because it is so much more common and so much easier to write about learners learning) – and secondly because I am very much involved in trying to distinguish the various directions in which feelings can flow in my current work with Relate. I think one has to put a lot of work into trying to sort out whose emotions are being experienced in counselling rooms, classrooms, marriages and so on. There are obviously untold possibilities of self-deception here, which is why it is useful to discuss these matters with colleagues. In the event your judgement about where the emotion lies is the decisive one and I have no doubt that you would have carefully considered this. I was most intrigued, however, by the positiveness with which you asserted that they were 'MY feelings'.

I am drafting a short piece for submission to a future issues of Chreods. I am finding this useful in the sense that I am having to try and say something straightforward about transference, counter transference, projection and proactive identification. There are some differences of opinion about these terms – which is quite useful because one can then use them in one's own way if they are found to be useful. I wouldn't want to argue with anyone who wanted to say that ALL the emotion I feel in any situation is mine. But it does seem to be helpful to think otherwise in couples counselling. And I think it would help in certain critical incidents in classrooms. Anyway unless you would prefer not I shall send you a draft soon. I wouldn't mind you hacking it around – perhaps thinking of a joint piece – whatever.

Dick.

DICK TAHTA

Dick:

I found your writing (*'Ever present affectivity'*) very helpful, and I shall return to its usefulness shortly.

First, however, I agree entirely with the point you make in it that 'if psychodynamic notions are to be invoked in classroom accounts then standard reflective procedures common to most therapists might also have to be considered' and that in order to address the emotions which are stirred in me, when teaching, I need to 'be able to sift through various interpretations of them'.

The major difficulty that I have with this, is how to do it. With whom do I talk? A practitioner engaged in counselling has a supervisor and, I assume, that issues such as these which arise for the counsellor are worked upon. A friend of mine who is involved in a research project, which entails her interviewing adolescents is able to use one of the research principals, a Winnicot Centre psychiatrist, in this way.

In my teaching experience I have never noticed that I have been in a position to do this. Now perhaps that is more to do with me than the structures within which I have worked, but perhaps not. Your response to my writing is a very new experience for me.

A more usual experience when talking to colleagues about working with a particular class or individual, is that discussion centres either around the problems which the student has (he/she is an attention seeker, is having a difficult time at home, is finding the subject matter too difficult, ...), or around practical suggestions about dealing with the class or individual (give her/him some easier work, ignore her/him, deal with her/him more firmly,...).

This can be both helpful and supportive, but has not helped me to deal with the particular emotions engendered in me. Because of this it may not be in practice that helpful, as I may be emotionally unable to try out some of the suggestions (I cannot be firmer with X because I am attempting to be a caring parent to X and I have some emotional investment in this).

One response from a colleague on reading what you wrote, and realising that it might be published publicly, was to ask me if it was OK, because 'Dick seems to be suggesting that you fancy Paula'. This seems both a reasonable reaction and to be missing the point. Insofar as it is a reasonable reason, it is going to be difficult to discuss my feelings towards my students with other teachers because we may all be backing off raising some real issues.

This is where I find the dialogue with you useful. Your writing clearly offered to me various interpretations. Projective identification had certainly not occurred to me - it is a notion that I had only recently come across, and was certainly not aware enough to apply it to my interaction with Paula. Some possible interpretations I am likely to not offer to myself, precisely because they are too uncomfortable for me to entertain, and it helps when someone else suggests them so that I can examine them (the idea that what I feel if affected by others is uncomfortable for me).

As you say, all of your offerings are 'but idle speculations' – but when I receive them and work with them, checking them out for the emotions which they evoke in me (and the last notion in my previous paragraph hit home!), they offer me an

216

opportunity to develop some insight into myself, which will help my action in future.

Dave.

Dave:

Thanks for writing – especially at a time when I imagine you must be quite busy. Your letter reminded me how much I miss being able to wander down a corridor and talk with someone about something of current concern. E-mail isn't always a satisfactory substitute – partly because most people are still in those corridors.

What you seem to have done so well in your writing is to open up the issue of how one shares with colleagues some intimate issues about teaching (as opposed to the more usual discussions about learning), This of course requires enormous trust and a readiness to share. I can imagine that one could benefit professionally by having some expert 'supervision', but the more appropriate model for most of us is I think the case-discussion-group (with or without the help of a 'consultant'). Unfortunately I haven't offered you a share of something from my recent teaching experience. The most important recently for me has been my three weeks' work with a mathematics education project in Cape Town (with Chris Breen). And I would certainly be glad to share some of that experience with you sometime, but the more telling examples of things like projective identification would come in fact from my bits of couples counselling and those are a bit removed from the issues about teaching that we might want to tease out.

I don't think of my draft as being yet ready for publication. I would like to think of it as a working document that we might be exploring alongside your article. For instance, it would be quite inappropriate to leave anyone with the idea that I might be suggesting that you fancy Paula. This might be – in your phrase – a reasonable reaction, but as you also say it missed the point. For a start, it does again leave Paula out of the equation. It also ignores the fact that in these encounters there are for all parties the ghosts of other encounters. I think there is a sense in which every student ('fancies' – supply the verb) his/her teacher. And every teacher (ditto) his/her student. Normally these are unconscious feelings. Often they become conscious in some vague way and have to be described in whatever language of desire is available. My feeling is that it is possible to share fantasies when one knows they are likely to remain fantasies. I think I would not share my feelings if I 'really' fancied a student, i.e. intended to do something about it. In the first place I wouldn't want my colleagues to know, in the second I wouldn't want to give him/her the burden of knowing. (As you can imagine this sort of thing is discussed almost *ad nauseam* in counselling circles: I upset my supervisor the other day by saying that in the event of my intending to sleep with a client I would hardly be telling the supervisor or my colleagues – I would be more concerned with getting on with it.)

So it ought to be possible to discuss the quite strong feelings around in your account of the lesson with Paula in terms of possible fancyings. But who fancies

DICK TAHTA

who and in what way must surely be far too complicatedly speculative. And there is the problem that will be of concern to you that people could slip into discussion of Paula as an inanimate object whereas she is for you a person. I think I wanted to emphasise her absence in your account. It is not that I wanted her brought in, however.

I hope we can continue to mull round these issues a little.

Dick.

CHRIS BREEN

11. TUGGING AT PSYCHOLOGICAL THREADS IN MATHEMATICS EDUCATION

In 2000 I presented two conference plenary papers in which I started thinking about the issue of fear of mathematics that I was encountering in my student classes (Breen 2000a, 2000b). In reviewing the current literature for these papers, I found a dearth of material exploring such psychological issues. My main source of inspiration came from what I believed to be the significant writing and interchange between David Wilson and Dick Tahta that first appeared in *Chreods* and which has been re-published in the earlier chapters of this section. In this chapter, I revisit those papers and attempt to highlight the main features that caught my eye at the time.

EXPERIENCING FEAR OF MATHEMATICS

I was in the middle of the third session with the primary group and they had seemingly mastered the basics of developing a formula for the nth term of an arithmetic progression of an apparatus-based problem using their own visualisation methods. I had to make a strategic decision whether or not to continue the lesson by giving them a similar example that would allow them to re-confirm their growing mastery or to give them something where they could use their newfound knowledge to move forward. I decided on the latter, and said, 'I think I'd like to give you a challenge now'. Their response was immediate. They immediately called out that the mere fact of my saying it was a challenge and it had raised their tension quotients off the scale! Although the first part of the new problem was extremely straightforward and was the same as the work they had already done (the challenge I had spoken of was to come in the second stage!), the class struggled enormously. Diana, in particular, became noticeably agitated and flustered, talking more loudly and suddenly burst into tears. Although she stayed in the room, she was unable to talk about the incident until the following day when she explained that the word 'challenge' had caused the turmoil and made her feel all her old insecurities.

Diana was a member of a class of 11 students who had enrolled for the Higher Diploma in Education (Primary) and were consequently participating in my twice-weekly two period class on the Method and Content of Primary School mathematics. The incident quoted above turned out to be only one of at least three occasions where one of the students burst into tears while doing mathematics in this class.

T. Brown (ed.), The Psychology of Mathematics Education: A Psychoanalytic Displacement, 219–229.
© *2008 Sense Publishers. All rights reserved.*

CHRIS BREEN

When I started teaching this difficult course almost 17 years ago, I discovered that students generally had a wide range of previous mathematics achievements levels ranging from a few students with one or two years of university mathematics to a few with almost no mathematics that had been passed after the first two years of High School. A recurring theme amongst the majority of the class was an almost total reliance on previously learnt-without-understanding algorithms, and a need to tell pupils how to do the sums. Each year there were a few students who became paralysed when faced with mathematics problems, and they were impossible to deal with in the large class. It became increasingly clear over the years that these students could do no other than pass on their fear of mathematics to future pupils in their classes, and I started an action research project to attempt to design a course that might begin to meet their needs. The results of this project and the important paradigm shifts in creating a different classroom environment were later described elsewhere (Breen 2001). However it became strikingly clear that the problem of Fear of Mathematics was not restricted to a few students with poor mathematical backgrounds. Even outwardly successful graduates with good school mathematics backgrounds showed extreme distress in mathematics at various times.

Subsequent to the development of the new method for teaching this class, I decided to offer a Summer School course called Second Chance Mathematics to run over five two-hour sessions for adults whose previous experience of mathematics had lead them to believe they were failures, but who have become dissatisfied with that label. Since first running this course three years ago, I have come across many successful adults who carry scars from their school encounters with mathematics. Part of the curriculum which resulted from the action research project encourages students to describe their thoughts and feelings about mathematics in journals and the following two extracts from people with higher postgraduate degrees bear testimony, I think, to the problem of fear of mathematics in society at large.

Extract One. Session Three dawned with new feelings of anxiety, and the additional fear of feeling foolish in front of everyone else who (I assumed) certainly would fare better than I in this lesson. And certainly in a peculiarly common manner the self-fulfilling prophecy manifested in a lot of careless, basic mistakes, made while actually trying to cope with feelings of inadequacy. The maths almost becomes secondary. The responses triggered by merely being in this environment are astounding... What is strikingly evident is the role of personalities within this context. I think the maths teacher has a profound responsibility to his/her pupils. He/she is in fact a major player in the development of self-concept – and look how most of us look! Fearful, nail-chewing, shivering idiots – which carries over into all areas of life until it becomes so internalised that it becomes an integral and accepted part of our own self-image. How amazing to think that maths has such power. In fact, not even maths itself, but the very thought of it. It is true to say that maths brings out every insecurity and vulnerability that we experience in our lives as a whole. We drag everything into maths – our whole life is laid bare and our defencelessness is exposed when we are forced to attempt to grapple with concepts that are beyond us. This learning maths is a painful process. It is not only about not grasping what is perceived as difficult but it is also about myself, my very being, all that I am and all that I can offer. There is not more. When all is said and done, that is it. That is me. So subsequently I is reduced to someone almost unacceptable. I say almost, because it cannot be that this subject holds such power, yet for some, it is sadly true that they become victims – slaves of a foolish, inconsequential form of logic. And their lives are destroyed by it.

Extract Two: But what was/is it about maths that so flaws me and floors me, that leaves me feeling so numb, so absent (as if I am aware of not being here), so fearful, so incapable, so incompetent, so childlike, so unable to function like an adult, so unable to remember things (formulae, procedures), so unable to be the person who I am for myself and for others in the rest of my world, so unable to construct internally coherent analyses that help myself and others to understand the complex relationships between (theories of) literature, (theories of) society and (theories of) psychoanalysis, so unable to think? All of these experiences and self-images came back to me when we worked on the second puzzle – with the matchsticks. I could not work out how to work out the problem – my mind just seized up. It went blank. I could not concentrate, something inside me was saying this is meaningless you don't understand this you can't understand this run away. When I could not concentrate I became even more anxious, blindly/irrationally grasping at the formulae, unable to understand them, copying them down incorrectly, becoming trapped in a vortex of ignorance. (I know this seems like a purple passage, but I want to communicate a sense of being caught in a downward spiral).

REVIEWING THE LITERATURE

These student writings convey an overwhelming sense of fear and anxiety engendered by their encounters with mathematics. They are also both very clear that it is the subject of mathematics that brings them to this position of fear. For me, their language of experience resonates with others who have been in differing traumatic situations. Faizel's story highlights this trauma.

It is the first session with the Secondary Maths students and we have been talking about personal school experiences of mathematics. There is a pause in the conversation and then Faizel puts his hand up to speak. He tells of his primary school teacher who used to humiliate him by putting a hosepipe down his trousers and turning the water on if he got a sum wrong so that the class would laugh at his wet pants.

In the face of these strong emotions, it seems that any attempt to try to teach them mathematics has to start by acknowledging and addressing this past experience that has allowed this fear to develop. While the structure of the courses in question have changed sufficiently to allow this fear to surface, questions remain as to what

CHRIS BREEN

appropriate strategies and techniques to use in remediation now that this fear has been expressed. It seemed inconceivable that this should be a new question, so inevitably the first step now was to consult the literature to determine what research had already been conducted into this problem of fear.

The earlier reference to the psychological support given to traumatised victims suggested that the annual conference proceedings of the Psychology of Mathematics Education (PME) organisation should be a promising starting point for such research. It quickly becomes apparent, however, that the use of the word Psychology in PME is, in practice, almost exclusively restricted to cognitive-oriented educational theory rather than to any psychoanalytic or -therapeutic theory. The links between psychoanalysis and mathematics education seem to have largely been silent themes at PME with only a few discernible exceptions between 1992 and 2000 (Pimm, 1994, and Baldino & Cabral 1998), and neither of these directly address the encountered dominance of fear in the mathematics classroom. The only PME paper that promised to relate to the strong feelings of the students towards mathematics was one by Vinner (1996) entitled 'Some psychological aspects of the professional lives of secondary mathematics teachers - the humiliation, the frustration, the hope'. Here, the author brought together a group of teachers to discuss answers that they had given to a short questionnaire about difficult topics that they teach and he asked them how they coped with these difficulties. He later commented on the similarity of these sessions with group therapy but did not take the matter further.

The journal, *For the Learning of Mathematics*, provided a more useful starting point. Tahta edited a special edition of the journal in 1993 focusing on the psychodynamics of mathematics education and contained several interesting articles, which gave a broad framework for a significant future research agenda. The most useful reference to fear of mathematics, however, was found in an earlier edition of the same journal. Early (1992) invited his mathematics students to think of a recent mathematics problem, which challenged them and then to find and write about fantasy images which capture the same feelings that they had experienced with regard to this problem. He was surprised at the strength of the images (which included frightening life-and-death situations) and subsequently analysed the submitted material using a theoretical framework based on the metaphors of alchemy (as used in Jungian psychodynamic theory) to capture the process of taking ignorance and turning it into gold. In the article, he describes how the various student images and stages of grappling with their mathematical difficulties parallel alchemic processes such as the burning off of impurities/emotional conflicts (calcinatio); the ascending process and liberation of the spirit (sublimatio); the reductive loosening of structure (solutio); and the darkness involved in the shattering of rigidity (mortificatio). Examples of different student images are given for each of the processes and the point is made that in Jungian theory there is no set order in which these various stages should take place, but each has to be honoured and respected. Early stresses that his aim is not to produce better mathematics students but rather to assist them in developing a deeper, more imaginative perspective from which to view their mathematical experience and

222

TUGGING AT THE PSYCHOLOGICAL THREADS IN MATHEMATICAL EDUCATION

perhaps their lives. A first reading of this paper suggests that some of the moves made in the approach, which has been described in Breen (2001), parallel stages of the alchemic process described by Early and attention to the inclusion of some of the missing stages could well further enrich the programme. It is clear, however, that the topic of fear of mathematics and how to deal with it is a neglected area in the literature of mathematics education. The already noted similarity between those fearing mathematics and panicking or freezing when confronted with mathematical problems, and those who have suffered traumas in their life suggests that the literature of psychotherapy would be the most fruitful starting point for a new literature search.

EVER PRESENT AFFECTIVITY 1: A TEACHER TEACHING

At the start of Dick's opening comment in his response to Dave that there are very few pieces of writing where teachers report on their teaching, he says:

> There are lots of useful observations in the educational literature about learners learning but not so many about teachers teaching. This must be partly because it is so difficult to give an honest account of what it is actually like to teach – most attempts to do this slide into idealised intention or pious hope. (Tahta, this volume)

At the start of a workshop on Teachers as Researchers (Breen, 1997), I offered participants the following section of writing from a teacher's journal.

> Attending to questions and answers is a demanding process. I get a sense that I become very focused. A contribution is made – I listen, respond, challenge, push, prod, tease, play and throw the response out to a different part of the room trying to involve as many people as possible. I know I try to ensure that one or two students don't dominate this part of the session and my aim is to be provocative. I'm all over the place – my eyes are everywhere and dodging into each and every part of the room. No wonder I feel tired afterwards! Shifting to activities is generally governed by time and group energy. It feels as if I am aware of a moment when the group's energy fades and where the gains become less and less the longer they stay with the topic. The move to activities heightens the energy again. Desks are cleared. People stand around wondering what's going to happen next. I become aware of space and connections and try to secure the environment by showing my ease with the room and with them. There's a forced slowness to my actions as well as a resoluteness.

Workshop participants were asked to comment on the status of the writer in terms of gender, qualifications and teaching experience. The overwhelming response was that this was beginner teacher who was insecure about her practice as she was not properly qualified and was new to teaching. In fact this was an extract from my own journal after 15 years of teaching. Participants commented that they expected more certainty from someone who had been teaching for such a long period. How

CHRIS BREEN

does one offer classroom material in a way, which does not give that certainty and at the same time makes a teacher's vulnerability open to the reader? Here is another classroom example.

> At the start of a lesson I noticed that Paul was talking to his friend and openly showing me that he was not paying attention. I walked across and showed them what to do in the problem that had been set. Paul responded that they were talking about something else, much more important than mathematics. There was a defiant challenge here and I was put on the spot to choose an appropriate course of action. In the end, I said, 'Fine, but outside is probably a more appropriate place to go and talk about non-maths things'. Paul glared at me and clenched his fists. I said, 'I know you want to hit me but it's my class and I'm afraid we have to do maths here'. Paul and his mate started to get up to go when Paul said, 'I've given up on maths and I don't want to talk about it because you are part of the problem!' His friend Pedro at the next table said, 'I agree'.

This is a situation of conflict in the classroom and the teacher is being called on to make a decision in the moment as to how to handle the disruption. What choices are open to the teacher? Has he already made some mistakes? It seems as if Paul is struggling with his mathematics and it is not clear whether fear is at issue here, but certainly a confrontation has arisen and the teacher is being asked to handle it. This conflict with the teacher seems to happen more frequently in classes where there is a high degree of fear or dislike of mathematics. In the example above, it seems clear that the teacher has fallen back into teacher mode and has invoked the authority of the expert in order to attempt to get Paul to co-operate. There is little chance for collaboration and the most that can be expected is some sort of co-operative venture. This is in fact, the way that I took the issue forward.

> I decided to leave Paul and went across to Pedro who was tight and tense. I talked gently to him and tried to make a plan. He told me that he was struggling with the basic maths and yet I was expecting him to work on the methodology. He was lost and had no chance of coping. I told him that I would change the structure of the sessions and treat the method section as an opportunity to do basic content if he'd prefer that. He agreed and undertook to ask me for help when he struggled. I then went back to Paul and told him of the plan I had made with Pedro. I offered to do the same with him, but he'd have to decide if that was what he wanted. To my surprise tears came to his eyes and we adjourned to my office where we were both able to tell our stories about an incident which had happened the previous week and had led to his dissatisfaction with my teaching.

The hermeneutic task of the teacher is to ask questions and challenge the student in a way that forces the student to become aware. The double bind involved in this approach, is that while the method is based on a crucial shift away from the 'getting an education' paradigm, the course itself is offered in the very institution which has been set up to practice this paradigm—the university. This site then

TUGGING AT THE PSYCHOLOGICAL THREADS IN MATHEMATICAL EDUCATION

determines certain 'non-negotiables' such as the awarding of marks and the setting of the curriculum by the lecturer. In order to have a chance of creating a different environment, the lecturer needs to be clear as to what s/he believes is achievable and act thereafter with integrity in sticking to this environment even when it becomes uncomfortable. The teacher is inviting the class to place their faces in the open and to work with them. This requires an enormous amount of mutual trust which the teacher, in particular, will have shown s/he deserves. It would be a major act of betrayal if the teacher proved to be unworthy of this trust.

A further incident occurred in the last session of work with the Second Chance Mathematics class and, while it continues the theme of fear in that the students self- select themselves as having had bad previous experiences with mathematics, the focus changes from the student attitude to the teaching contract.

> I had given the class some homework to explore the patterns involved in the 11 times table. I asked for feedback as to what people had found out overnight and was pleased to note that some new voices were keen to report. One student, Nothemba, gave the first part of an answer and waited for me to ask for more before continuing. I commented on the fact that this was a helpful way to answer in that it gave me the possibility of asking others to report their findings, and compared it to the norm where students usually were so excited with their own findings that they want to blurt it all out and, in so doing, spoil it for the others. One of the students, Tessa had been very excited with her explorations on the 9 times table the previous night and initially had her hand up at the start of this lesson indicating that she wanted to contribute but then withdrew it and sat in her chair with her hands folded looking away from the chalkboard. When I approached her to ask what was happening, she replied, 'It's OK, I've got your message loud and clear'. On two other occasions during the lesson I tried to engage with her to find out what had gone wrong, but she responded each time that she was fine and continued to remain uninvolved with her arms folded until the end of the session, when she joined the rest of the students in thanking me for the course.

The immediate question that comes to mind is what did I do wrong? How can I undo the damage? Tessa had changed in front of my eyes from an enthusiastic and excited participant to a rebellious and defeated student. The reflections in the earlier first student extract which commented on the profound responsibility of the teacher come back to haunt. In the absence of further information the teacher is left to construct different narratives, which may account for the student's response. Various hypotheses come to mind. For example, the teacher might have been irritated at the way that Tessa had been showing off in the class and had looked meaningfully at her when praising Nothemba's behaviour in order to put her in her place; or perhaps the teacher had led Tessa to feel that she was special in the class and so she was hurt when she was not called upon to show the results of her homework off to the class.

One result of the shared communication between Tahta and Wilson is that Wilson comments how unusual it is in teaching for a teacher to be able to examine

CHRIS BREEN

such things and Tahta responds by recommending a case study group with or without a leader. Tahta makes the further point that therapists and counsellors are trained to try to sort out what's in them and what's in the client. If psychodynamic notions are to be invoked in classroom accounts then standard reflective procedures common to most therapists and counsellors should also be considered. People who wish to address the emotions which are stirred in classrooms need to have the courage to expose their own feelings, but they will also need to be able to sift through various interpretations of them and produce specific reasons why they come to the conclusions they do.

Clarke (1988) contrasts her training as a teacher with that of her preparation as a gestalt therapist. She comments on the many similarities of the tasks and skills expected of both teacher and therapist especially in their dealings with those who are not coping. She highlights the lack of a focus on process in the preparation of teachers especially with regard to work on self. She notes that both teacher and therapist should ideally be intimately and easily familiar with their subject and therefore free to pay attention to their clients or pupils. She claims that it is the processes by which this subject matter becomes troublesome or intolerable that is the domain of the teacher and therapist. She describes the best teacher as being one who has fully integrated her own learning about the processes, which are the stuff of mathematics. Equally important as a person, she is sufficiently free of worries about herself not to be prey to comments that her pupils might make or concerns about not knowing or making mistakes. With these conditions prevailing her attention can be free to see and understand what is actually going on in and between her pupils. She goes on to make some interesting comparisons between her training as a therapist and her training as a teacher.

> One of the features of my own training in Gestalt, which I have valued enormously is that we started with self-experience; we then went on to do work with one another and were supervised and finally we learned the theory. This means that priority was given to awareness of the self, including self in relation to others, of course, and to unlearning, unpicking, discovering and letting go of, where appropriate, precisely those behaviours we will expect to meet in clients. So that in my dealings with a client I am relatively free and clear of self-absorption and I can attend to the other without putting clutter in his or my way. So what they are asserting, I believe rightly, is that the prerequisite is personal self-awareness, the next step is understanding the processes further, and that theoretical content is last and additional but necessary.... My own experience of teaching was the reverse. Three years of content, one year afterwards of more content and a little self-awareness and more attention to process. This reversal seems akin to the norms – I expect people to 'fail' for as long as they need to – you expect them to 'succeed' rapidly. (Clarke, 1988, p. 142)

A resonance with this theme can be found in Blanchard-Laville (1991), who conducted some research focusing on the role of the unconscious in decisions made by the teacher. She believed that in the teaching situation there is a subject (in the psychoanalytic sense of subject of the unconscious) present. When making decisions in the teaching situation, the teacher is subjected to internal pressures acting upon him from the unconscious without his knowledge. This leads to a process whereby the teacher repeats former experiences without recalling the prototype and with the very real impression that on the contrary this is something completely motivated by the present moment. Based on her findings, Blanchard-Laville developed a system for training mathematics teachers inspired by the work of the Balint group, in which they do psychological work linked to their professional practice. The group of teachers meets for 2 hours every 2 weeks and focus on the psychological implications of their own accounts of incidents with a view to gaining access to their unconscious. Her work led her to believe that it is possible for a teacher to develop beyond the reach of what can be achieved through pedagogical guidance or the teacher's own will to change. Teachers have developed a capacity to identify what is at stake for them in classroom episodes and hence become less 'split' inside themselves and more flexible and alive in their exchanges with pupils.

These musings need to refer back to the incident described. There is a block in the student's progress that can either be confronted or ignored. Different interpretations will lead to different possibilities for action. Choosing in the moment to act in a certain way requires two things: noticing a possibility to choose, that is recognising some typical situation about to unfold; having alternatives from which to choose, that is, being aware of alternative action or behaviour. The difficulty is that a great deal of the information is inaccessible. In addition, Early's identification of different stages suggests that the rejection of the teacher and his/her authority (mortificatio) might form a necessary part of the search for coagulate (the highest form where the solution is reached) the death of the teacher and his/her authority.

EVER PRESENT AFFECTIVITY 2: LOOKING FOR MORE INTERPRETATIONS

In his original analysis of a classroom situation, Wilson had been drawn to the concept of transference (the imposition of an actual or imagined previous relationship onto a present one) in trying to understand his actions, but the response from Tahta draws attention to other possible interpretations which might draw on concepts such as counter-transference (picking up and being influenced by what another is transferring), projection (disowning the unapproachable parts of oneself and placing them on another) and projective identification (being influenced and reacting according to another's projection).

This interaction between Dick and Dave as it seemed that here was a model that began to address the issues raised by Clarke in a way, which did not diminish the integrity of the observations of the teacher. It also linked to Varela's plea (Depraz, Varela & Vermersch, 2003) for serious attention to be paid to what he called

CHRIS BREEN

Second Person research – an exchange between situated individuals focusing on a specific experiential content developed from a first-person position.

Elsewhere (Breen, 2007), I have reported on a similar situation where I offered some of my data about Monique, a student teacher who really struggled with her fear of mathematics, to Dick for his thoughts. In a similar conversation to that reported in this book between David and Dick, Dick started asking me questions about various aspects of the text to which he was drawn. This was in keeping with Varela's Second Person approach. I was presenting data from my own first-person experiential position. Dick was offering subjective comments, which were embedded and situated within his own lived experience. While these comments could not be considered objective statements of reality, they did provide me with a wealth of alternate perspectives on the experience, whose realisation adds to my possibilities for future action.

Although long neglected, I am drawn to the comments of Davis (1992) when he says that:

> People don't understand what it (teacher development) is like. I tell people that this is a lot more like psychoanalysis than it is about telling somebody a new recipe.

The publication of this book marks an important step in the exploration of this difficult but important field.

REFERENCES

Baldino, R., & Cabral, T. (1998). Lacan and the school's credit system. In *PME 22*. Stellenbosch, South Africa.

Blanchard-Laville, C. (1992). Applications of psychoanalysis to the inservice training of mathematics teachers. *For the Learning of Mathematics*, *12*(3), 45–51.

Breen, C. (1997). Teachers as researchers? In V. Zack, J. Mousley, & C. Breen (Eds.), *Developing practice: Teachers' inquiry and educational change*. Geelong: Deakin University Press.

Breen, C. (2000a). Fear of mathematics: Why aren't we learning from the 'shrinks'? In E. Fernandes & J. P. Matos (Eds.), *Proceedings of XI - SIEM*. Funchal, Madeira, November 6–7.

Breen, C. (2000b). Becoming more aware: Psychoanalytic insights concerning fear and relationship in the mathematics classroom. In *PME 24*. Hiroshima, Japan.

Breen, C. (2001, April). Coping with fear of mathematics in a group of preservice primary school teachers. *Pythagoras*, *54*, 42–50.

Breen, C. (2007). Sending out a crow in search of new mud: an email from Dick. *For the Learning of Mathematics*, *27*, 3–7.

Clarke, R. (1988). Gestalt therapy, educational processes and personal development. In D. Pimm (Ed.), *Mathematics, teachers and children*. London: Hodder and Stoughton.

Davis, R. (1992). Teachers: The key to success. *ETS FOCUS*, *27*, 18–20.

Depraz, N., Varela, F., & Vermersch, P. (2003). *On becoming aware: A pragmatics of experiencing*. Amsterdam: John Betjamins.

Early, R. (1992). The alchemy of mathematical experience. *For the Learning of Mathematics*, *12*(1), 15–20.

TUGGING AT THE PSYCHOLOGICAL THREADS IN MATHEMATICAL EDUCATION

Pimm, D. (1994). Attending to unconscious elements. In *PME 18*. Lisbon, Portugal.

Vinner, S. (1996). Some psychological aspects of the professional lives of secondary mathematics teachers - The humiliation, the frustration, the hope. In *PME 20*. Valencia, Spain.

Chris Breen
Graduate School of Business
University of Cape Town

ABOUT THE AUTHORS

Tamara Bibby, Institute of Education, London.
Tamara works in the Faculty of Culture and Pedagogy of the Institute of Education, London, where she is a lecturer in learning and teaching. Her current research focus relates to the development of psychosocial understandings of experiences of pedagogy. In this she draws on her background in primary education and her particular interest in the learning and teaching of primary mathematics. She has just completed an ESRC funded research project 'Children's learner identities in mathematics' (RES-000-22-1272) upon which this chapter is based. Her publications include:
Shame: an emotional response to doing mathematics as an adult and a teacher. *British Educational Research Journal,* 2002, *28*(5), 705-722.
Creativity and logic in primary school mathematics: a view from the classroom. *For the Learning of Mathematics,* 2002, *22*(3), 10-13.

Chris Breen, University of Cape Town
Chris is currently an Associate Professor in the School of Education as well as a visiting lecturer at the Graduate School of Business at the University of Cape Town. Chris has recently ended his three-year term of office as President of the International Group for the Psychology of Mathematics Education. His current work on understanding dimensions of complexity and diversity in working within both the education and corporate worlds has been strongly influenced by his experience of living through a time of extreme change in South Africa. Reference to recent articles and student work can be found at www.chrisbreen.net.

Tony Brown, Manchester Metropolitan University
Tony, the editor of this present volume, is Professor of Mathematics Education at Manchester Metropolitan University where he heads the research student programme. He recently spent two years away from Manchester to become the first Professor of Mathematics Education in New Zealand, based at the University of Waikato. He has research interests in mathematics education and language, practitioner research in education and teacher education. His books include: *Mathematics Education and Language: interpreting hermeneutics and post-structuralism, Action Research and Postmodernism* (with Liz Jones), *New Teacher Identity and Regulative Government* (with Olwen McNamara), and *Regulative Discourses in Education: A Lacanian perspective* (with Dennis Atkinson and Janice England).

Tony Brown, Escalate, University of Bristol
Tony is Director of ESCalate, the Higher Education Academy subject Centre, based at Bristol University. This follows previous jobs at St Mark and St John

ABOUT THE AUTHORS

College, Plymouth and University of Hull, working in the areas of mathematics education, and teacher development. Tony has been a counsellor for Relate and has also taught in secondary and primary schools. Recent publications include:

Negotiating psychological disturbance in pre-service teacher education, *Teaching and Teacher Education*, 2006, *22*, 675-689.

Shifting psychological perspectives on the learning and teaching of mathematics. *For the Learning of Mathematics*, *25*(1) 2005

Tânia Cabral and Roberto Baldino, State University of Rio Grande do Sul, Brazil

Tânia graduated from the mathematics teacher's program of the Federal University of Rio de Janeiro (UFRJ) took a doctor's degree in Mathematics Education from State University of São Paulo (USP). She is a member of the Brazilian School of Psychoanalysis-SP. Roberto has an engineering degree from the State University of Rio Grande do Sul (UFRGS) and a doctor's degree in mathematics from the Pure and Applied Mathematics Institute (IMPA) in Rio de Janeiro. They both teach in an engineering program at the new State University of Rio Grande do Sul. They have published several papers in the area of Mathematics Education and Psychoanalysis:

Inclusion and diversity from Hegel and Lacan point of view: do we desire our desire for change? *International Journal of Science and Mathematics Education* 2006, *4*, 19-43.

Affect and cognition in pedagogical transference: a Lacanian perspective, (2004). In M. Walshaw (Ed.) *Mathematics education within the postmodern*, 141-158.

Tony Cotton

Tony is Associate Dean of Education at Leeds Metropolitan University. His most recent book, Improving Primary Schools, Improving Communities, published by Trentham Books explored the ways in which Primary schools can focus on fairness and justice and still ensure learners succeed academically. Tony is a founder member of the group 'Mathematics Education and Society', a group that has now held five major international conferences. Recent publications include:

Critical Communication in and through Mathematics classrooms. In A. Chronaki & I. M. Christiansen (Eds.*)* (2004) *Challenging Perspectives on Mathematics Classroom Communication.* Greenwich CT: Information Age.

Problematising culture and discourse for mathematics education research: defining the issues – tools for research' (with Hardy). In P. Valero & R. Zeven-bergen (Eds.). *Researching the socio-political dimensions of mathematics education.* Dordrecht: Kluwer.

What can I say, and what can I do?: Archaeology, narrative and mathematics education research. In Walshaw, M. (Ed.) (2005) *Mathematics education within the postmodern.* Greenwich CT: Information Age.

Elizabeth de Freitas, Adelphi University, New York

Liz is an Associate Professor at the Department of Curriculum and Instruction,

School of Education, Adelphi University, New York. Her interests include narrative inquiry, life history, biographical re-storying strategies for teacher development, critical theory and post-structural critiques of normative discursive practices within educational institutions, equity issues within mathematics education, history of mathematics, trans-discipline curriculum, arts-informed research and experimental epistemology, fiction-as-research. Her publications include:

Plotting intersections along the political axis: The interior voice of dissenting mathematics teachers. *Educational Studies in Mathematics*, 2004, 55(1-3), 259-274.

Opening the research text: Critical insights and in(ter)ventions into mathematics education (2008 co-edited with K. Nolan).

Kathleen Nolan, University of Regina, Regina, Canada.

Kathleen is Associate Professor in the Faculty of Education, where she teaches undergraduate and graduate courses in mathematics and science curriculum. Her research interests include mathematics post-structural and socio-cultural intersections and narrative research methodologies. Her publications include:

How should I know? Pre-service teachers' images of knowing (by heart) in mathematics and science. Rotterdam, The Netherlands: Sense Publishers.

Opening the research text: Critical insights and in(ter)ventions into mathematics education. (2008 co-edited with E. de Freitas).

Dick Tahta

Dick was a second-generation Armenian immigrant for whom mathematics was the only thing that made sense in his first confusing experience of an English primary school. He eventually became a mathematics teacher and then a lecturer in education at Exeter University. Sadly he died in 2007 before completing an additional chapter for this book. He has co-authored *Starting Points* and various books for teachers including *Images of Infinity* (Leapfrogs, 1983). He guest edited a special groundbreaking issue of the journal *For the Learning of Mathematics* here mathematics education and psychoanalysis appeared together for possibly the first time.

Margaret Walshaw, Massey University, New Zealand

Margaret is a Senior Lecturer at Massey University, New Zealand. She teaches courses in mathematics education and in education research methods. She has recently published a book entitled: *Working with Foucault in Education* (Sense Publishers) and co-authored *Effective pedagogy in Mathematics/ Pangarau: Best Evidence Synthesis Iteration (BES).* She is editor of the book *Mathematics education within the postmodern.*

David Wilson, Manchester Metropolitan University

Dave has recently retired as a Senior Lecturer at Manchester Metropolitan University where he was a teacher educator. He is presently convening a seminar series: History, Philosophy and Culture of Mathematics and its Teaching.

NEW DIRECTIONS IN MATHEMATICS AND SCIENCE EDUCATION

Volume 1
Learning Science:
A Singular Plural Perspective
W.-M. Roth, *University of Victoria, Canada*
Paperback ISBN 90-77874-25-9 Hardback
ISBN 90-77874-26-7

Volume 2
Theorems in School:
From History, Epistemology and Cognition to
Classroom Practice
P. Boero, *Universita di Genova, Italy* (Ed.)
Paperback ISBN 90-77874-21-6 Hardback
ISBN 90-77874-22-4

Volume 3
The Culture of Science:
Historical and Biographical Perspectives
K. Tobin, *The Graduate Center, City University
of New York*, USA & W.-M. Roth, *University of
Victoria, Canada* (Eds.)
Paperback ISBN 90-77874-33-X Hardback
ISBN 90-77874-35-6

Volume 4
Teaching to Learn
A View from the Field
K. Tobin, *The Graduate Center, City University
of New York*, USA & W.-M. Roth, *University of
Victoria, Canada* (Eds.)
Paperback ISBN 90-77874-81-x Hardback
ISBN 90-77874-91-7

Volume 5
**Understanding Teacher Expertise in Primary
Science:**
A Sociocultural Approach
A. Traianou, *Goldsmiths College, University of
London, UK*
Paperback ISBN 90-77874-88-7 Hardback
ISBN 90-77874-89-5

Volume 6
On The Outskirts of Engineering
Learning Identity, Gender, and Power via
Engineering Practice
Karen L. Tonso, *Wayne State University, USA*
Paperback ISBN 978-90-77874-94-3 Hardback
ISBN 978-90-77874-96-7

Volume 7
Science Learning, Identity
Sociocultural and Cultural-Historical
Perspectives
Wolff-Michael Roth, *University of Victoria,*
Canada and Kenneth Tobin, *City University of
New York*
Paperback ISBN 978-90-8790-080-9 Hardback
ISBN 978-90-8790-090-8

Volume 8
How Should I Know
Preservice Teachers' Images of Knowing (by
Heart) in Mathematics and Science
Karen T. Nolan, *Regina University*
Paperback ISBN 978-90-8790-212-4 Hardback
ISBN 978-90-8790-213-1

Volume 9
Great Ideas in Science Education
Case Studies of Noted Living Science
Educators
Xiufeng Liu, *University of Buffalo, SUNY, USA*
Paperback ISBN 978-90-8790-226-1 Hardback
ISBN 978-90-8790-227-8

Volume 10
**Science Education at the Nexus of Theory
and Practice**
Yew Jin Lee and Aik Ling Tan, *National
Institute of Education, Singapore*
Paperback ISBN 978-90-8790-420-3 Hardback
ISBN 978-90-8790-421-0

Volume 11
The Multiple Faces of Agency
Innovative Strategies for Effecting Change in
Urban School Contexts
Alberto J. Rodriguez, *San Diego, State
University*
Paperback ISBN 978-90-8790-436-4 Hardback
ISBN 978-90-8790-435-7

Volume 12
**Research in Mathematics Education in
Australasia 2004-2007**
Helen Forgasz, Anastasios Barkatsas, Alan
Bishop, Barbara Clarke, Stephen Keast, Wee
Tiong Seah and Peter Sulivan, *Monash
University, Australia*
Paperback ISBN 978-90-8790-499-9 Hardback
ISBN 978-90-8790-500-2

Volume 13
The Psychology of Mathematics Education:
A Psychoanalytic Displacement
Tony Brown, *Manchester Metropolitan
University*
Paperback ISBN 978-90-8790-556-9
Hardback ISBN 978-90-8790-557-6